Green Finance and Investment

Sustainable Infrastructure for Low-carbon Development in the EU Eastern Partnership

HOTSPOT ANALYSIS AND NEEDS ASSESSMENT

OECD

BETTER POLICIES FOR BETTER LIVES

Please cite this publication as:
OECD (2021), *Sustainable Infrastructure for Low-carbon Development in the EU Eastern Partnership: Hotspot Analysis and Needs Assessment*, Green Finance and Investment, OECD Publishing, Paris, *https://doi.org/10.1787/c1b2b68d-en*.

ISBN 978-92-64-53204-5 (print)
ISBN 978-92-64-66738-9 (pdf)

Green Finance and Investment
ISSN 2409-0336 (print)
ISSN 2409-0344 (online)

Photo credits: Cover © mika48/Shutterstock.com.

Corrigenda to publications may be found on line at: *www.oecd.org/about/publishing/corrigenda.htm*.

Foreword

This project is part of the International Climate Initiative (IKI). The Federal Ministry for the Environment, Nature Conservation and Nuclear Safety (BMU) supports this initiative on the basis of a decision adopted by the German Bundestag.

This report has been compiled within the GIZ program "Capacity Development for climate policy in the countries of South East, Eastern Europe, the South Caucasus and Central Asia, Phase III".

As a service provider with worldwide operations in the fields of international cooperation for sustainable development and international education work, GIZ works together with its partners to develop effective solutions that offer people better prospects and sustainably improve their living conditions. GIZ is a public-benefit federal enterprise and supports the German Government and a host of public and private sector clients in a wide variety of areas, including economic development and employment promotion, energy and the environment, and peace and security.

This report was prepared by Douglas Herrick under the supervision of Kumi Kitamori, Jean-François Lengellé and Virginie Marchal as part of the work of the GREEN Action Task Force hosted at the OECD. Aday Nygmanov compiled the database following methodology developed by Alin Horj.

The authors gratefully acknowledge the comments and contributions from colleagues across the OECD, partner organisations and government agencies. This report benefited from comments from the following OECD experts: Francesco Alonso, Ksenia Lytvynenko, Alexandre Martoussevich, Gabriela Miranda, Daniel Quadbeck, Antti Rauhala and Geoff Upton. The authors are indebted to the following external experts, whose comments greatly improved the draft report: Michael Begak (GIZ external consultant), Sarah Duhr (GIZ), Julia Gerlach (GIZ), Sergiu Gradinaru (GIZ), Julia Grishchenkova (GIZ), Andrei Isac (Regional Environmental Centre Moldova), Tatsiana Kananchuk (Ministry of Natural Resources and Environmental Protection, Republic of Belarus), Jari Kauppila (ITF), Mikheil Khuchua (GIZ), Irina Korolenko (GIZ), Stephan Kroel (GIZ), Lara Lukina (Ministry of Natural Resources and Environmental Protection, Republic of Belarus), Dejan Makovsek (ITF), Steffi Mallinger (GIZ), Pavlo Masiukov (GIZ), Anna Petrus (IEA), Darya Sotnikova (Ministry of Economy, Republic of Belarus), Ilka Starrost (GIZ), Olena Symonenko (GIZ), Ketevan Vardosanidze (GIZ), Talya Vatman (IEA), Aya Wietzorrek (GIZ) and Oscar Zarzo Fuertes (GIZ) as well as the Energy Community Secretariat.

The report was prepared for publication by Lupita Johanson.

Table of contents

Tables

Figures

Reader's guide

This report presents key findings from an analysis of the strengths and weaknesses of existing institutional frameworks for strategic planning of sustainable infrastructure in the six countries of the European Union's Eastern Partnership in Eastern Europe and the Caucasus: Armenia, Azerbaijan, Belarus, Georgia, Moldova and Ukraine. It follows the methodology and format developed for a similar study published in 2019, *Sustainable Infrastructure for Low-carbon Development in Central Asia and the Caucasus*, which covered eight countries: Azerbaijan, Georgia, Kazakhstan, Kyrgyzstan, Mongolia, Tajikistan, Turkmenistan and Uzbekistan. Two chapters from the present report – Azerbaijan and Georgia – are updated versions of the chapters published in the aforementioned 2019 study.

It also provides an inventory of infrastructure projects, both planned and under construction, in the region, with the objective of assessing the extent to which infrastructure plans are consistent with long-term development, climate and environmental objectives.

The Overview provides a brief outline of the trends observed in the regions.

Chapters 1 to 6 present country profiles that consist of three components:

1. **a rapid assessment** of the challenges and opportunities related to investment, climate and infrastructure;
2. **an analysis** of hotspot infrastructure projects, which are defined as infrastructure projects (planned and under construction) with potentially high environmental, social and economic impacts;
3. **an overview** of strengths and shortcomings in the existing framework for strategic infrastructure planning.

Due to limited data availability, the data points for the six countries included in the present study are not always comparable. The authors have included the most recent data points available and, as much as possible, have used the same sources for each sector. When possible, other data points were included from national statistics offices from the most recent year available.

Methodology: building the database of infrastructure projects

The analysis draws on a database of infrastructure projects compiled by the OECD. The database covers six countries (Armenia, Azerbaijan, Belarus, Georgia, Moldova and Ukraine) and five sectors:

- **Transport** (including airports, roads, railways, multimodal transportation hubs, transportation and logistics centres).
- **Energy** (including projects related to electricity generation, electric power transmission and distribution, upstream oil and gas, oil and gas pipelines).
- **Industry** (including manufacturing projects related to iron and steel production, cement plants, petrochemical plants, fabricated metal products, coke and refined petroleum).
- **Mining and quarrying** (including of metal ores such as gold, chrome, copper, zinc, iron, tin, uranium).

- **Water** (including water supply, water facilities, irrigation and drainage projects, rehabilitation).

The database covers infrastructure projects planned and under construction in the period 2000 to 2020, and draws on the following sources of information:

- **International financial institutions and national development banks web sites**: Asian Development Bank (ADB); Asian Infrastructure Investment Bank (AIIB); European Bank for Reconstruction and Development (EBRD); Eurasian Development Bank; European Investment Bank (EIB); Black Sea Trade and Development Bank (BSTDB); China Export-Import Bank; International Monetary Fund (IMF); OPEC Fund for International Development (OFID); World Bank; Kreditanstalt für Wiederaufbau (KfW).
- **Investment promotion agencies**: Azpromo, Invest in Belarus, Invest in Georgia, Invest Moldova Agency, Ukraine Invest.
- **Commercial databases**: Bloomberg New Energy Finance, Dealogic, IJGlobal, Thomson ONE.
- **Public Datasets**: Centre for Strategic and International Studies – Reconnecting Asia; EaP Transport Database; AidData.
- **Other sources**: Sourcewatch; Institute for Energy Economics and Financial Analysis (IEEFA); Emerging Markets Forum; DAC/OECD Credit Reporting Database; Georgia Co-Investment Fund; International Tax and Investment Center (ITIC).

Note that the infrastructure estimates based on this database are uncertain, as there is no official tracking or collection of infrastructure investments at the national nor subnational level. There is no systematic tracking of comprehensive and comparable country-level data on infrastructure investments. While commercial databases and websites provide interesting insights on current projects and investments, the analysis is not comprehensive and can bring some inaccuracies. Data should be interpreted as indicating general trends rather than exact investment volumes. Main sources of uncertainties come from the following methodological challenges:

- **Comparability of data** between different sources of information: there are no harmonised definitions of sectors or project status (planned, under construction, on-hold) across databases.
- **Double counting projects and their values**: individual infrastructure projects can have several entries in a given database, both due to multiple phases of construction and the fact that single cross-border project`s components were assigned to two or more countries' inventories. The database was reviewed several times to eliminate multiple entries for individual infrastructure projects from different data sources, but some double counting may still persist.
- **Underestimate of some infrastructure projects (small scale, private sector led)**: the quantitative analysis in the present study is based on projects that represent more than USD 10 million. There could also be a significant data gap on the financing volume of infrastructure projects that are not backed by multilateral development banks, as data related to private investments tend to be confidential or only available through commercial databases;
- **Accuracy of project status**: Certain projects may be miscategorised due to limited information available at the project level, particularly on their status. Databases are not updated in real time and infrastructure projects' statuses regularly change. Projects were re-categorised when inaccuracies became apparent through comments from country representatives or press articles. The project status categories represent the status reported in the database as of June 2020.

Methodology: Selection of "hotspot" projects

Hotspot projects refer to infrastructure projects with potentially high impact in terms of economic, environmental and social outcomes. Those projects were selected against four criteria:

- **Scale**: The volume of dollars invested in an infrastructure project provides a proxy for potential economic and social benefits – or risks – associated with a given project (job creation, FDI). The database only contains large-scale infrastructure projects, with a minimum value of USD 10 million.
- **Environmental impact**: This criterion captures the extent to which infrastructure investment contributes to environmental objectives of the country. Projects with a potential high environmental impact include:
  (a) projects that have a negative environmental impact and are incompatible with a low-carbon future (e.g. coal-fired power plants);
  (b) projects that have a positive environmental impact and help countries engage on a low-emission future (e.g. renewable energy);
  (c) projects that could potentially have a very high impact on the environment given their scale and their impact on landscapes (e.g. large hydro projects, trains lines, roads).
- **Connectivity impact**: The region has considerable room for improvement on connectivity with the rest of the world. The extent to which a project contributes to improving regional and domestic connectivity and integration is a proxy for its potential economic benefits.
- **Project status**: Project status categories in the database are 'planned', 'under construction', 'completed' or 'cancelled'. This criterion assigns more value to projects where the government still has an opportunity to influence or mitigate negative impacts of projects on future development through cancellations, careful assessments or redesigns. These categories are 'planned' and 'under construction'. Based on the information available from different databases and development partners, the project status has been clustered into different categories.

Executive Summary

Prior to the COVID-19 pandemic, the countries of the European Union's Eastern Partnership (EaP)[1] had experienced rapid growth and, in many cases, begun undertaking sweeping market reforms. As EaP countries turn their attention to the economic recovery, the planning and delivery of sustainable infrastructure that provides high-quality essential services (e.g. electricity, mobility) could allow governments to stimulate the economy while laying the groundwork for more sustainable development patterns aligned with long-term climate and development goals. EaP countries continue to diversify their economies and energy supplies and chart diverging courses towards alignment of legislation and policy with regional integration initiative (i.e. the Eurasian Economic Union in the cases of Armenia and Belarus; the European Union in the cases of Georgia, Moldova and Ukraine). At the same time, their infrastructure systems require increased investment to support inclusive economic development and facilitate integration into global value chains.

In the transport sector, EaP countries need to scale up investment to take advantage of their strategic position along emerging transport corridor initiatives including the EU's Transport Corridor Europe-Caucasus-Asia (TRACECA) initiative and China's Belt and Road Initiative (BRI). At present, poor quality transport networks, including ageing road and rail systems, as well as numerous regulatory and policy barriers to cross-border flows constrain economic growth and trade. In many EaP countries, marked service disparities between urban and rural districts act as a barrier to economic opportunities for rural residents.

In the energy sector, most EaP countries' primary concern is energy security through diversification of supply. In terms of power generation, renewable energy sources and, in the cases of Armenia and Belarus, nuclear energy are important components of countries' diversification strategies. However, existing capacity of electricity generation from renewable sources remains small in most EaP countries, and current investment trends do not demonstrate a major shift in energy mixes across the region, which still depends heavily on fossil fuel-fired power plants (particularly natural gas and, in the case of Ukraine, coal). There is considerable scope for improving the efficiency of transmission and distribution systems to reduce losses as well as for improving the energy efficiency of heating systems and building stock.

The current infrastructure gap in EaP countries combined with the economic downturn resulting from COVID-19 represent a major challenge in the region, but also an opportunity to promote infrastructure projects that will boost investment and employment while contributing to progress towards long-term objectives of the Paris Agreement and the Sustainable Development Goals (SDGs).

Many of the infrastructure projects planned and under construction in the region do not yet fully support countries' long-term development and climate objectives. Some large-scale energy projects for improving energy efficiency and integrating renewables into the energy supply have emerged, but in most cases the current slate of projects does not amount to the transformative scale needed, and continues to perpetuate

[1] The EU Eastern Partnership (EaP) is a joint initiative for strengthening the relationships between the European Union, its member states and six countries (hereafter the Eastern Partnership countries): Armenia, Azerbaijan, Belarus, Georgia, Moldova and Ukraine.

the regional dependency on fossil fuels. Many transport projects aim to refurbish existing road infrastructure assets and improve domestic connectivity. However, rail systems in many EaP countries are falling into disrepair as the modal share of cargo and passenger turnover as well as investment priorities shift in favour of road transport.

Mainstreaming climate and development considerations in infrastructure investment decisions and strategies is needed and requires action on multiple fronts; from upstream sustainable infrastructure planning to project prioritisation, financing and delivery. The following improvements in existing institutions and strategies could help countries improve consistency between their long-term development goals and current investment plans:

- Developing, adopting and implementing long-term economic development plans with clear priorities and targets supplemented by a cascading system of shorter-term and sector-specific strategies, development programmes and action plans;
- Developing, adopting and implementing mid-century low-emission development strategies, as encouraged by the Paris Agreement, to evaluate current projects and mid-term strategies against long-term visions and goals;
- Improving coordination between ministries and agencies to develop integrated and cross-sectoral infrastructure strategies that account for the trade-offs and synergies between different SDGs;
- Integrating environmental and social impacts in infrastructure project evaluation and prioritisation, through the systematic use of Environmental Impact Assessment, and the adoption and implementation of international standards for sustainable infrastructure;
- Strengthening capacities related to the planning, screening, construction and operation of sustainable infrastructure projects, at all levels of governments.

Overview

This report presents the regional situation of infrastructure investments in the countries of the EU Eastern Partnership, including the gap between growing infrastructure needs and sluggish investment flows, and the resulting challenges for trade integration and regional connectivity. It describes regional infrastructure development initiatives, including TRACECA and the Belt and Road Initiative, and their potential role in improving connectivity. It also presents the makeup of current infrastructure investments in the six countries of the Eastern Partnership (Armenia, Azerbaijan, Belarus, Georgia, Moldova, Ukraine), focusing on the transport and energy sectors.

The infrastructure gap

Relatively poor quality infrastructure has hampered regional integration, connectivity and economic development

The countries of the European Union's Eastern Partnership (EaP)[1] are increasingly setting development objectives to take advantage of their strategic location between the markets of Europe and Asia, but the relatively low quality of infrastructure impedes further development of trade and local economies. Despite increased levels of domestic investment in recent years and increasing interest from foreign investors as EaP countries improve their investment climates, investment needs to be scaled up to facilitate economic development, provide high-quality, reliable and sustainable infrastructure services (e.g. electricity, mobility, drinking water and sanitation) and integrate into global value chains.

The increased trans-Eurasian overland transit could be an important turning point for Eastern Europe, the Caucasus and Central Asian (EECCA) countries towards greater trade integration. Given that in recent years China has established itself as a more central player in global value chains, and trade between China and Europe is currently averaging over USD 1 billion a day, opportunities exist for EECCA countries in sectors such as industrial and consumer goods, textiles, and machinery and equipment (Kunzel et al., 2019[1]).

Overall, the connectivity of EaP countries depends on how well they are positioned in global logistics networks, infrastructure and services. Across the region, there is considerable scope to improve connectivity with the rest of the world. According to one measure of connectivity (defined in terms of access to global GDP as compared to Germany, one of the best global performers), the connectivity gap of Eastern European EaP countries (Belarus, Moldova and Ukraine) is larger than in the South Caucasus (Armenia, Azerbaijan and Georgia). While the Eastern European EaP countries enjoy access to global GDP of around 30 to 40 percentage points below that of Germany, while in the South Caucasus (Armenia, Azerbaijan, Georgia) the gap stands at about 20 to 30 percentage points (Figure 0.1). In this regard, EaP countries are better positioned than the countries of Central Asia, which were the subject of a previous OECD review of infrastructure plans (OECD, 2019[2]), but remain at a disadvantage compared to other emerging economies in the region, notably in Southeast Europe and North Africa.

International trade is relatively important to EaP countries, but their trade and logistics systems underperform compared to those of similarly trade-reliant countries across the globe (Figure 0.2). At present, the cost of shipping a container from Chengdu, China to Europe via the Trans-Caucasus Transit

Corridor is about USD 3 500 – 4 500 per forty-foot equivalent unit (FEU), while the Northern Corridor via Russia costs USD 2 800 – 3 200 per TEU and the maritime transportation costs only USD 1 500 – 2 000 per FEU. Despite this cost disadvantage, land connections via the Trans-Caucasus Transit Corridor and the Northern Corridor offer a valuable opportunity to increase the capacity and resilience of routes fsor containerised freight between Asia and Europe while stimulating market competition between routes. The Non-EaP countries, such as Kazakhstan and Turkmenistan, also stand to benefit from further development of the Trans-Caucasus Transit Corridor in particular, since it would facilitate trade access for these countries to Europe (World Bank, 2020[3]).

Figure 0.1. Global connectivity

Access to Global GDP (%)

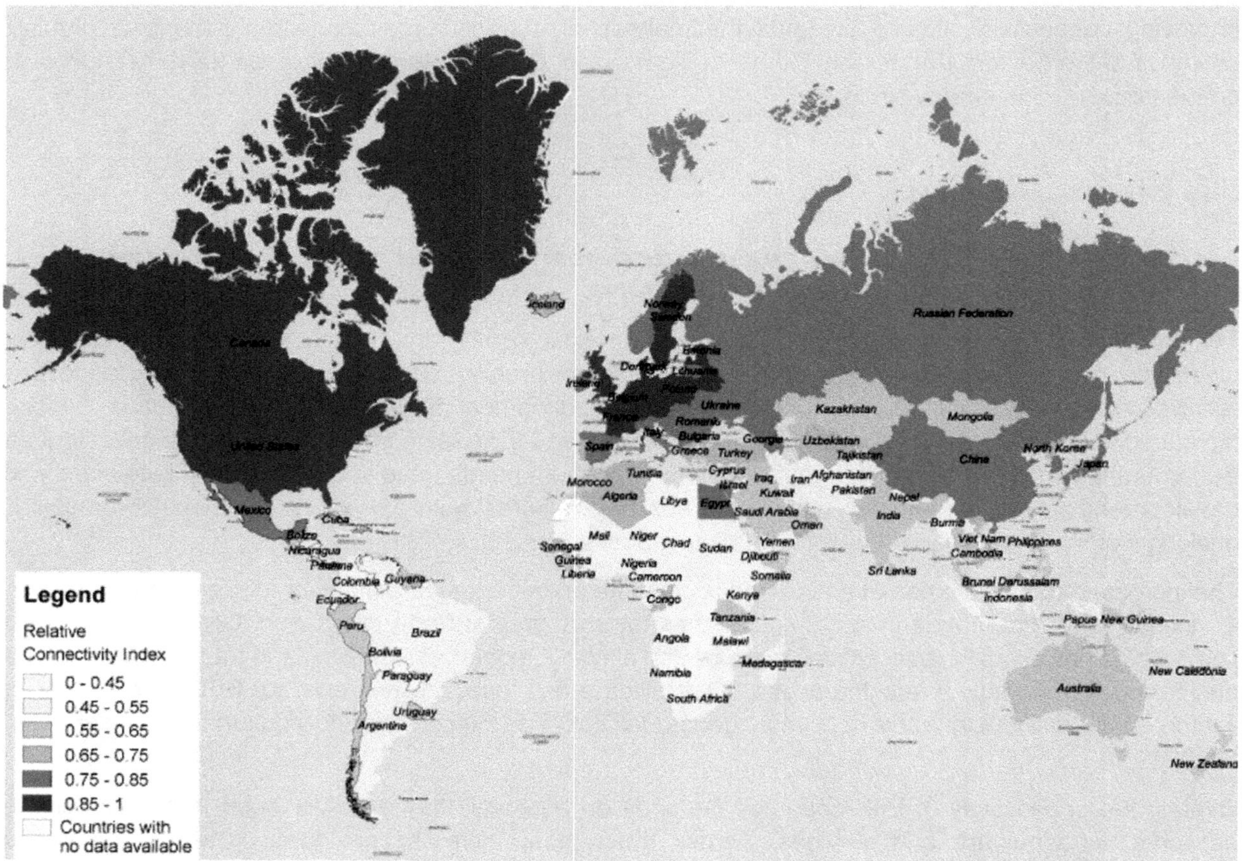

Source: ITF (2019[4]), "Enhancing Connectivity and Freight in Central Asia", International Transport Forum Policy Papers, No. 71, OECD Publishing, Paris.

Figure 0.2. Logistics costs and trade openness

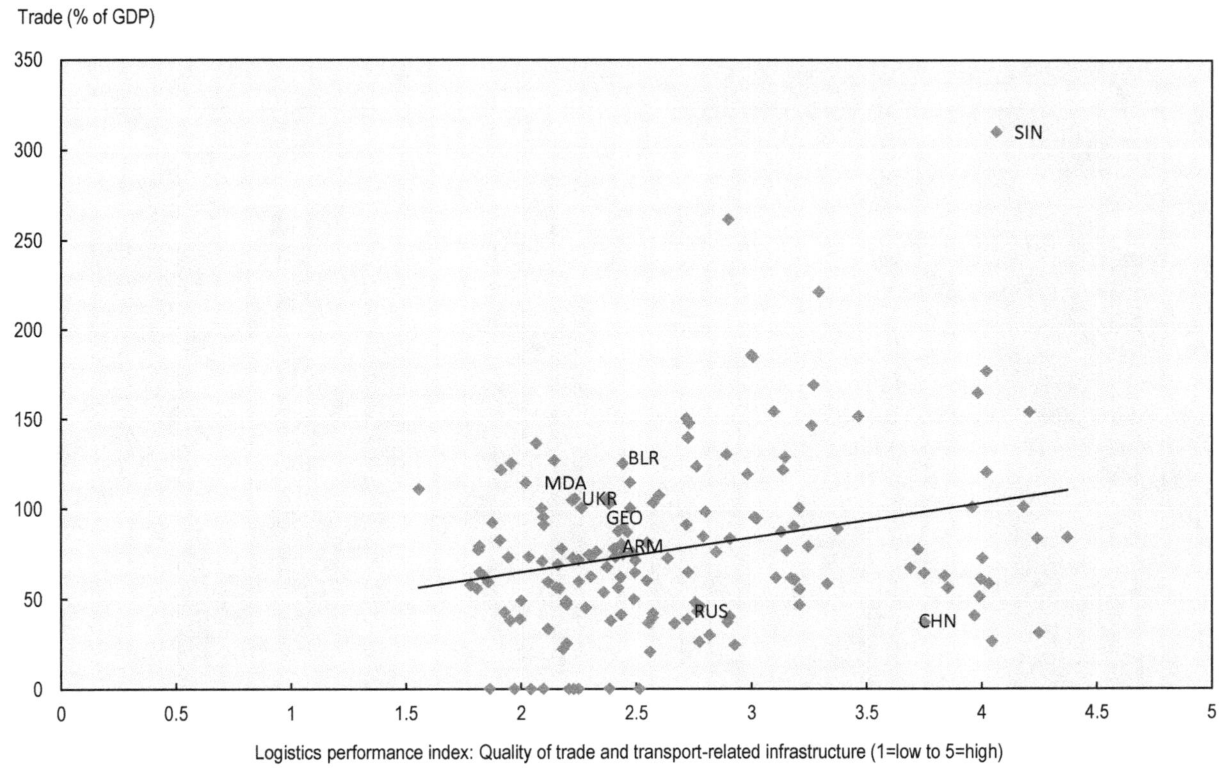

Source: World Bank (2021[5]), *Logistics Performance Index* (database), https://lpi.worldbank.org/international/aggregated-ranking; World Bank (2021[6]), *World Development Indicators (database)*, World Bank, https://data.worldbank.org/

The performance of logistics infrastructure in EaP countries, as measured by the World Bank's Logistic Performance Index (LPI) infrastructure indicator, has not demonstrated a clear upwards trend over the past decade and, in some cases, appears to be in decline (Figure 0.3). While EaP countries in the South Caucasus have remained at the same level or shown slight improvement, the countries of Eastern Europe have, as a rule, performed worse on this metric in recent years than in the early 2010s. In general, low-quality infrastructure leads to high costs of transportation, which hampers competitiveness. With few exceptions such as Azerbaijan, economies of the region still face challenges linked to underperforming transport infrastructure and services as reflected in a number of infrastructure indicators and perception assessments (Table 0.1).

Figure 0.3. The World Bank's Logistic Performance Index, Infrastructure Indicator

Score from 1 to 5 (best)

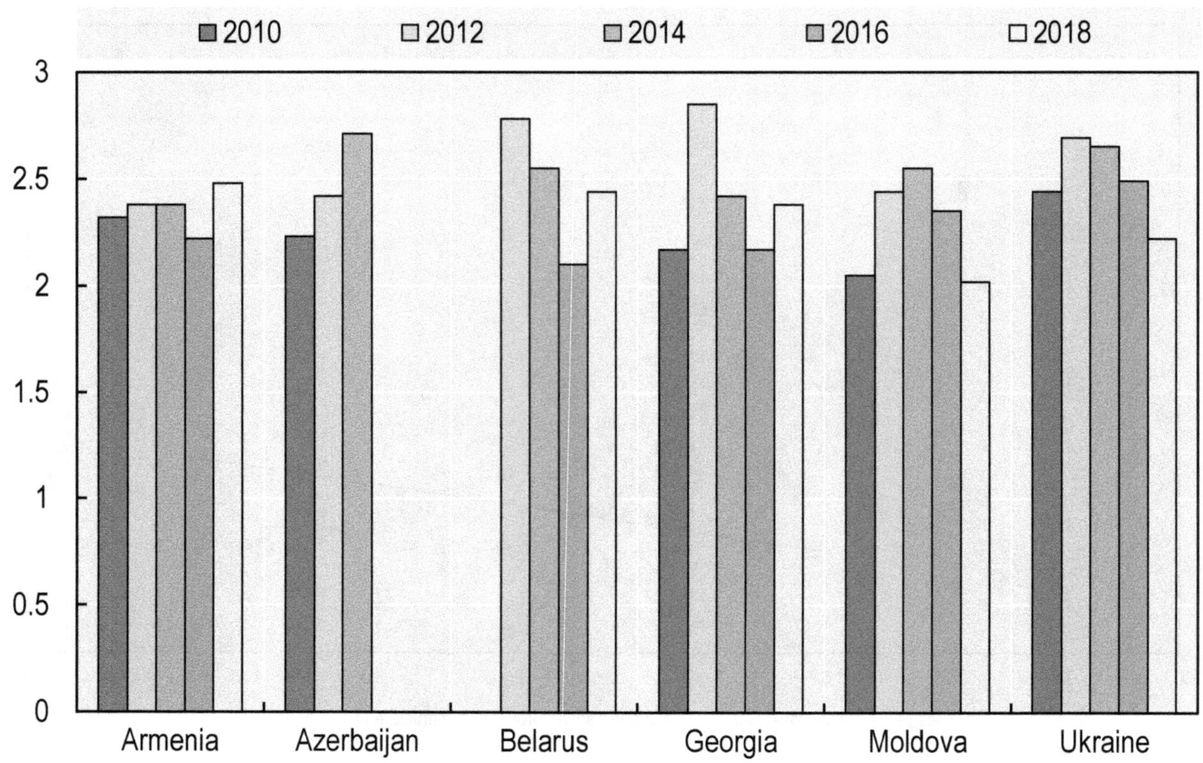

Source: World Bank (2021[5]), *Logistics Performance Index* (database), https://lpi.worldbank.org/international/aggregated-ranking

With regards to the energy sector, all countries have achieved universal access to electricity. However, energy infrastructure assets, notably transmission and distribution lines, are generally of poor quality due to underinvestment in maintenance and replacement of existing facilities in the past decade: losses along the electric grid are high, and power outages frequent. Coal is a major source of energy only in Ukraine, but natural gas and other fossil fuels remain crucial components of EaP countries' energy mixes. Reliance on fossil fuels extends even to countries like Georgia, where hydroelectricity is by far the largest source of electricity but, due to seasonal variation, needs to be supplemented by imported natural gas. Continued investment in fossil fuel-fired power generation risks locking certain EaP countries into unsustainable development pathways.

Table 0.1. Selected infrastructure indicators in the EU Eastern Partnership

	Armenia	Azerbaijan	Belarus	Georgia	Moldova	Ukraine
Energy						
Electricity production from coal sources (% of total) 2019	0	0	<0.1	0.1	0	30.8
Electric power transmission and distribution losses (% of output) 2019	11.1	9.8		6.8	18.8	10.3
Transport						
Quality of roads, 1 (worst) – 7 (best), WEF 2019	3.6	5.2		3.8	2.6	3.0
Quality of train services, 1 (worst) – 7 (best), WEF 2019	3.1	5.2		3.9	3.0	4.2
Quality of seaport services, 1 (worst) – 7 (best), WEF 2019	2.4	5.1		3.8	2.3	3.9
Quality of air transport infrastructure, 1 (worst) – 7 (best), WEF 2019	4.6	5.8		4.4	4.4	4.0
Water and sanitation						
People using safely managed drinking water services (% of population with access) 2017	86.5	73.6	94.5	80.0	72.9	92.0
People using safely managed sanitation services (% of population with access) 2017	48.2		80.5	27.2		68.5

Source: World Bank (2021[6]), World Economic Forum (2019[7])

Energy, including fuel combustion from transport, accounts for more than half of all greenhouse gas emissions in EaP countries, ranging from 62% in Belarus and Georgia to 75% in Azerbaijan. Due in part to ageing, inefficient infrastructure and insufficiently insulated buildings, there is considerable scope for energy efficiency improvements and, consequently, greenhouse gas emissions reductions. The largest greenhouse gas emitter in absolute terms among EaP countries is Ukraine, by far the most populous country in the region, with emissions that are nearly twice those of the other five EaP countries combined. Ukraine's emissions have declined since independence and currently amount to less than half of their pre-independence levels (Figure 0.4). In per capita terms, Belarus is the largest emitter, closely followed by Ukraine.

Figure 0.4. GHG emmissions by country, 1990-2015

In ktCO2e

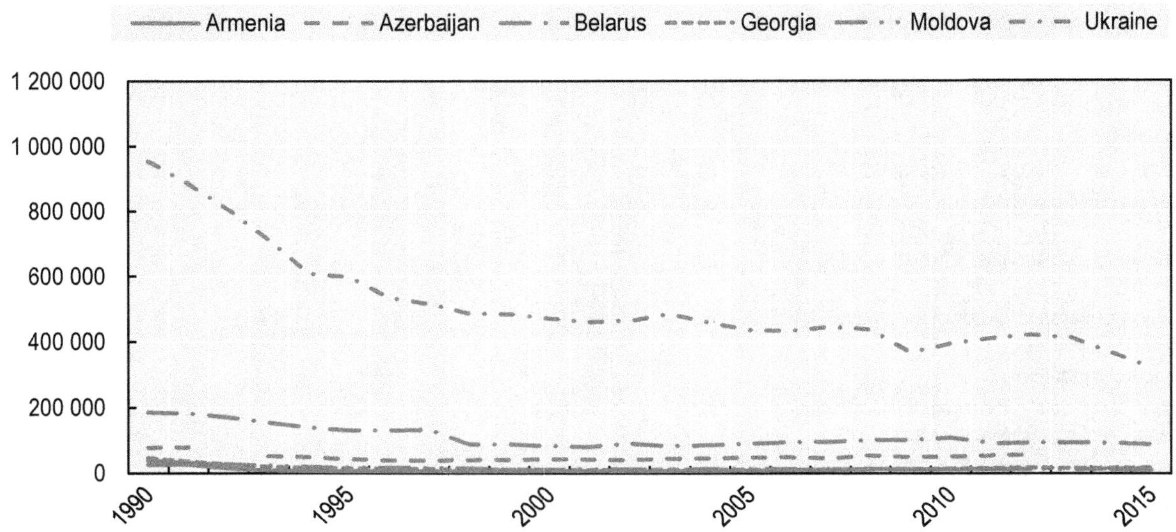

Source: World Bank (2021[6]), *World Development Indicators (database)*, World Bank, https://data.worldbank.org/indicator/EN.ATM.GHGT.ZG

Regional initiatives are an opportunity to close the infrastructure gap

The EaP countries' economic development strategies recognise the need to address infrastructure bottlenecks and to enhance connectivity. A number of sub-regional projects, programmes and strategies focus on transport infrastructure and are intended to increase connectivity, improve infrastructure service delivery and spur competitiveness (Table 0.2). This includes the European Union's Transport Corridor Europe-Caucasus-Asia (TRACECA), which focuses on the development of trade and transport connections as well as broader economic relations between the European Union and twelve countries, including five of the six EaP countries. Such regional programmes aim to provide sufficient infrastructure to ensure a high level of transport connectivity and integration into different modes of transport (OECD, 2018[8]).

Table 0.2. Regional transport corridor initiatives in Eastern Europe, the Caucasus and Central Asia, including the EaP countries

Project name	Amount of investment (in USD billion)	Countries or continents covered
Belt and Road Initiative (BRI)	900-8000	**Europe**, Asia, Africa
The Central Asia Regional Economic Cooperation (CAREC) Program	31.5	Afghanistan, **Azerbaijan**, People's Republic of China, Georgia, Kazakhstan, the Kyrgyz Republic, Mongolia, Pakistan, Tajikistan, Turkmenistan, Uzbekistan
Transport Corridor Europe Caucasus Asia (TRACECA)	0.16	**Armenia**, **Azerbaijan**, Bulgaria, **Georgia**, Kazakhstan, Kyrgyzstan, Iran, Moldova, Romania, Turkey, **Ukraine**, Uzbekistan, Tajikistan, Turkmenistan, plus the member states of the European Union.
Trans-Asian Railway (TAR)	75.6	Afghanistan, **Armenia**, **Azerbaijan**, Bangladesh, **Belarus**, Bhutan, Brunei, Cambodia, China, India, Indonesia, Iran, Kazakhstan, Laos, Mongolia, Nepal, Pakistan, South Korea, Russia, Sri Lanka, Tajikistan, Thailand, Turkey, Turkmenistan, Uzbekistan, Vietnam.

Source: ITF (2019[4]), "Enhancing Connectivity and Freight in Central Asia", International Transport Forum Policy Papers, No. 71, OECD Publishing, Paris.

Another significant global infrastructure initiative with significant implications for Eastern Europe and the Caucasus is China's Belt and Road Initiative (BRI). Proposed in 2013, the BRI aims to improve global connectivity and co-operation. While the scope of the BRI is not clearly defined, there are two main components involving investments in infrastructure, namely the Silk Road Economic Belt (the overland "Belt") and the New Maritime Silk Road (the sea routes constituting the "Road") (Freund and Ruta, 2018[9]). The Belt will link China to Central and South Asia and onward to Europe, while the Road will better connect China with Southeast Asia, the countries of the Persian Gulf, East and North Africa and to Europe. The BRI could significantly improve trade, investment and living conditions for citizens in the region. However, this will only occur if China and the individual recipient countries implement deeper policy reforms aimed at improving transparency, expanding trade, improving debt sustainability, while mitigating environmental, social and governance risks (World Bank, 2019[10]). As part of the BRI, there are six proposed overland economic corridors, two of which pass through the EaP countries: the New Eurasian Land Bridge (which connects China to Europe via Kazakhstan, Russia and the Eastern European EaP countries) and the China-Central Asia-West Asia Economic Corridor (which passes through the South Caucasus).

In recent years, certain EaP economies have become large recipients of Chinese investments, with over USD 20.6 billion of investments between 2005 and 2020 (Figure 0.5). The China Global Investment Tracker, a database that tracks investment projects by China worldwide, demonstrate that most of these investments in the EaP region focus on the energy sector, accounting for almost half (48% or USD 9.9 billion) of total investments. The transport sector received the second most investment (24.5% or USD 5 billion), followed by real estate (8%) and metals (8%). The largest recipient of Chinese investments in the region is Ukraine (USD 10.5 billion, mostly in energy and transport), followed by Belarus (USD 5.4 billion, spread across energy, transport, agriculture and real estate), Azerbaijan (USD 2.2 billion, mostly in metals and real estate) and Georgia (USD 2.1 billion, mostly in transport).

Figure 0.5. Chinese investment across EaP countries, by sector

In USD million

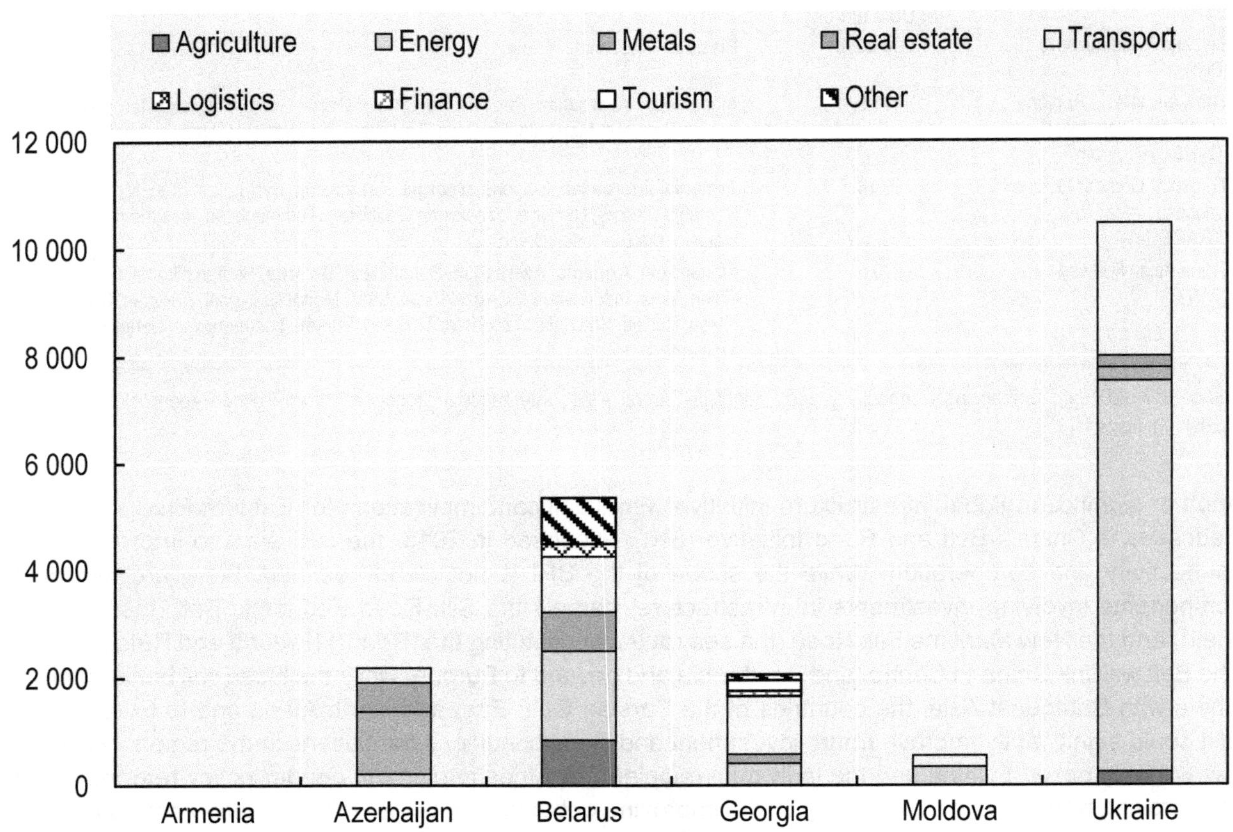

Source: American Enterprise Institute (2021[11]), "China Global Investment Tracker", http://www.aei.org/china-global-investment-tracker/

The investment environment

The investment climate is improving in the EaP region but private sector participation needs to be scaled up

In recent years, EaP countries have implemented reforms that have made them more attractive destinations for investment. Their improving investment climates are reflected in selected indicators in Table 0.3. According to the World Bank Doing Business indicators, the region has made progress in the areas of fiscal, regulatory and political reforms. Increased electricity access, coupled with strengthened rule of law and better corporate tax regulations have further improved the confidence of investors to invest in individual countries in the region. For instance, Georgia has become one of the most open economies in the world in terms of ease of doing business, ranking 7th worldwide in 2020. Azerbaijan also performed relatively better than its regional peers in 2020, ranking 34th. In most countries, deeper reforms are needed to further leverage domestic and international private investment. An endemic problem in several EaP countries is corruption, which not only discourages investment but also impacts public service delivery and infrastructure development due to misuse of funds. Corruption is perceived to be a particularly pervasive problem in Azerbaijan, Moldova and Ukraine.

Table 0.3. Selected investment climate indicators in EaP countries

	Armenia	Azerbaijan	Belarus	Georgia	Moldova	Ukraine
GDP per capita (USD, constant 2010 dollars, 2019)	4 732	5 880	6 679	4 978	3 720	3 225
FDI, net inflows (as % of GDP, 2019)	1.9%	3.1%	2.0%	7.3%	5.0%	3.8
Number of procedures [and number of days] to start a business, 2020	3 [4]	3 [3.5]	4 [8.5]	1 [1]	4 [4]	6 [6.5]
Number of procedures to get electricity, 2020	2	7	3	3	6	5
Number of tax payments per year, 2020	15	9	7	5	10	5
Hours required to file taxes per year, 2020	264	159	170	216	183	328
Ability to trade across borders (0 to 100 best performance), 2020	91.7	77	96.5	90.1	92.3	80.1
Corruption Perceptions Index (rank out of 180 countries, 2020)	60	129	63	45	115	117

Source: World Bank (2021[6]), Transparency International (2020[12]).

Overview of current infrastructure projects, planned and under construction

The OECD's database on large-scale infrastructure investment projects in the transport, energy, industry and water sectors (see Reader's guide for information on methodology and scope) tracks around USD 120 billion of planned and under construction infrastructure projects in the six EaP countries – Armenia, Azerbaijan, Belarus, Georgia, Moldova and Ukraine. Energy projects account for just under half (46% or USD 55 billion), followed by transport (35% or USD 42 billion) and industry and mining projects (16% or USD 19 billion) (Figure 0.6). Finally, water projects, primarily water supply and sanitation projects, account for 2.5% (USD 494 million) of total investments tracked by the database.

Within energy projects, electricity generation projects account for over half of investments by value (63% or USD 40 billion) followed by oil and gas pipelines (13% or USD 8.5 billion) and upstream oil and gas (11% or USD 7.1 billion). Capital-intensive nuclear energy projects in Armenia and Belarus make up just over half of all power generation investments in EaP countries, while hydroelectric projects, particularly in Georgia, account for 29.8% of power generation investments. Non-hydro renewable projects, predominantly wind, collectively account for a further 15.7%. Many EaP countries have prioritised energy security and diversifying their energy mixes away from natural gas. Armenia and Belarus have adopted strategies based on nuclear energy development, while other EaP countries have begun turning to renewables as a means of diversifying power supply.

In the transport sector, road projects represent two thirds of investments by value (66% or USD 27.8 billion), while rail accounts for 16% of transport investments (USD 6.6 billion). In certain EaP countries, investment projects focus on improving and expanding existing road networks, due to concerns about domestic transport connectivity and providing access to quality roads to facilitate economic mobility.

Country-by-country analyses of trends in infrastructure investment in the six EaP countries are presented in Chapters 1-6 of the present report.

Figure 0.6. Investment projects in the Eastern Partnership, by country and sector

In USD million

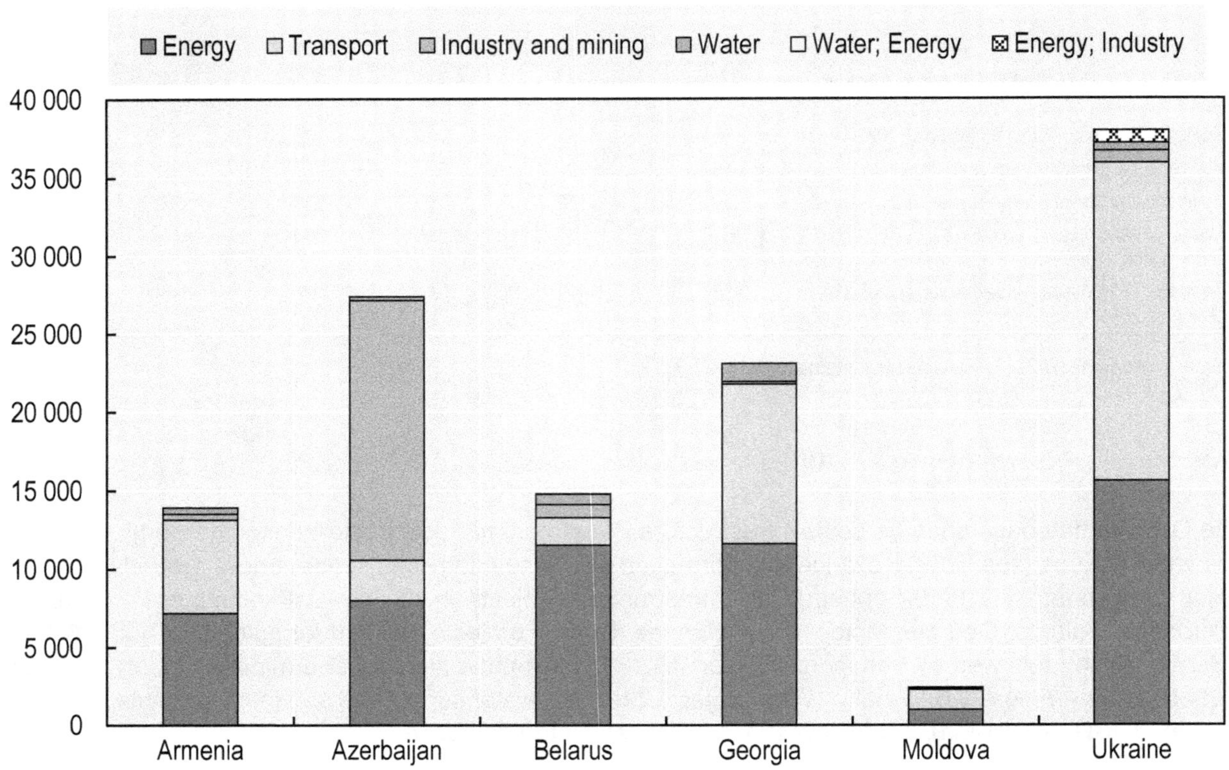

Source: OECD analysis based on accessed databases as of June 2020.

References

American Enterprise Institute (2021), *China Global Investment Tracker*, http://www.aei.org/china-global-investment-tracker/ (accessed on 1 August 2019). [11]

Freund, C. and M. Ruta (2018), *Overview: BRI at a Glance*, World Bank, https://www.worldbank.org/en/topic/regional-integration/brief/belt-and-road-initiative (accessed on 1 August 2019). [9]

ITF (2019), *Enhancing Connectivity and Freight in Central Asia*, International Transport Forum, Paris, http://www.itf-oecd.org. [4]

Kunzel, P. et al. (2019), "Opening Up in the Caucasus and Central Asia: Policy Frameworks to Support Regional and Global Integration", *18*, No. 7, International Monetary Fund, Washington, D.C., https://www.imf.org/en/Publications/Departmental-Papers-Policy-Papers/Issues/2018/06/19/Opening-Up-in-the-Caucasus-and-Central-Asia-Policy-Frameworks-to-Support-Regional-and-Global-45910 (accessed on 1 August 2019). [1]

OECD (2019), *Sustainable Infrastructure for Low-Carbon Development in Central Asia and the Caucasus: Hotspot Analysis and Needs Assessment*, Green Finance and Investment, OECD Publishing, Paris, https://dx.doi.org/10.1787/d1aa6ae9-en. [2]

OECD (2018), *Enhancing Connectivity through Transport Infrastructure: The Role of Official Development Finance and Private Investment*, The Development Dimension, OECD Publishing, Paris, https://dx.doi.org/10.1787/9789264304505-en. [8]

Transparency International (2020), *Corruption Perceptions Index 2020*, https://www.transparency.org/en/cpi/2020/index/nzl (accessed on 28 February 2021). [12]

World Bank (2021), *Logistics Performance Index*, https://lpi.worldbank.org/international/aggregated-ranking. [5]

World Bank (2021), *World Development Indicators (database)*, https://datacatalog.worldbank.org/dataset/world-development-indicators. [6]

World Bank (2020), *Improving Freight Transit and Logistics Performance of the Trans-Caucasus Transit Corridor: Strategy and Action Plan*, World Bank Group, Washington, D.C., https://openknowledge.worldbank.org/bitstream/handle/10986/33554/Improving-Freight-Transit-and-Logistics-Performance-of-the-Trans-Caucasus-Transit-Corridor-Strategy-and-Action-Plan.pdf?sequence=1&isAllowed=y (accessed on 13 February 2021). [3]

World Bank (2019), *Belt and Road Economics: Opportunities and Risks of Transport Corridors*, World Bank Group, Washington, D.C., http://documents.worldbank.org/curated/en/715511560787699851/Main-Report (accessed on 1 August 2019). [10]

World Economic Forum (2019), *The Global Competitiveness Report 2019*, World Economic Forum, Geneva, http://www3.weforum.org/docs/WEF_TheGlobalCompetitivenessReport2019.pdf. [7]

Notes

[1] The EU Eastern Partnership (EaP) is a joint initiative for strengthening the relationships between the European Union, its member states and six countries (hereafter the EaP countries): Armenia, Azerbaijan, Belarus, Georgia, Moldova and Ukraine.

1. Investment in sustainable infrastructure in Armenia

This chapter describes sustainable infrastructure planning in Armenia and presents current trends in investment in large-scale infrastructure projects. It compares Armenia's infrastructure plans in the energy, transport, industry and water sectors against its international commitments under the Paris Agreement on climate change and the Sustainable Development Goals (SDGs). The chapter also explores Armenia's strategic documents for long-term economic development, sectoral development and the environment, including those related to climate change mitigation and adaptation. It identifies misalignments between stated goals and observed investment flows and provides recommendations to improve strategic planning for sustainable infrastructure.

State of play: economy, investment and climate change in Armenia

Economy and trade

Table 1.1. Key indicators on Armenia's economy

Population (2019)	2 957 731
Urbanisation rate (2018)	63.1%
Annual population growth (2018)	0.2%
Surface area	29 740 km2
GDP (USD, current price, 2019)	13 673 million
GDP per capita (USD, current price, 2019)	4 732
Real GDP growth (year-on-year change, 2019)	4.8%, -4.5%
Inflation (average consumer price, y-o-y change, 2017)	1.4%
Exports of goods and services (% of GDP, 2018)	37.8%
Imports of goods and services (% of GDP, 2018)	53.5%
FDI, net inflows (% of GDP, 2018)	2.0%
General government net lending/borrowing (% of GDP, 2019, 2020)	-1%, -5.1%
Unemployment (% of total labour force, 2019)	17.7%

Source: World Bank (2021[1]), *World Development Indicators (database)*, World Bank, https://datacatalog.worldbank.org/dataset/world-development-indicators; IMF (2020[2]), *World Economic Outlook: October 2020*, International Monetary Fund https://www.imf.org/external/datamapper/GGXCNL_NGDP@WEO/OEMDC/ADVEC/WEOWORLD

Economy and demographics

Armenia is an upper-middle income country in the Caucasus. It is the least populous country in the South Caucasus, with a population of around 3 million. Its population fell by 18% from a peak of 3.5 million in 1990 prior to independence until its low point in 2010 (2.87 million), but has since experienced modest growth.

Armenia's GDP followed a similar but more dramatic downward trend, shrinking to less than half of its pre-independence size of USD 6.4 billion in constant 2010 dollars to USD 2.9 billion in 1993. Since then the country's economy has enjoyed a period of near-uninterrupted economic growth, reaching more than double its previous pre-independence peak (USD 13.7 billion by 2019).

Armenia's diaspora has played an influential role in Armenia's economic development following independence in 1991. For instance, between 1994 and 2004, 69% of Armenia's foreign investors had ties to the diaspora (World Bank, 2017[3]). Although it is difficult to establish the exact size of the Armenian diaspora, government estimates put the number at about twice that of the national population, with between 1.2 and 2 million in Russia alone (Gevorkyan, 2017[4]).

Remittances sent by Armenian migrant workers in Russia have historically been an important source of capital but their volume fluctuates depending on the economic situation in Russia. Between 2010 and 2014 remittances were equal to between 17% and 20% of GDP, but following the contraction of the Russian economy in 2015 remittances have dropped considerably (13.3% of GDP in 2017, 11.2% in 2019 and are currently in line with other countries of the Eastern Partnership (EaP)[1] (Georgia, 11.6%; Ukraine, 11.2%) (World Bank, 2021[1]).

In 2019, services accounted for 54.2% of Armenia's GDP, making the country more service sector-oriented than neighbouring Azerbaijan (37.4%) but less so than Georgia (60.5%). Armenia's economy is the most reliant on manufacturing in the South Caucasus region, with the sector accounting for 11.8% of GDP (compared to 8.8% in Georgia and 5.0% in Azerbaijan) (World Bank, 2021[1]).

COVID-19 pandemic's impact on Armenia has been substantial and far-reaching. As of February 2021, Armenia had the second most confirmed COVID-19 cases per capita among EaP countries after Georgia. Since the beginning of the pandemic, Armenia has diagnosed about 56.6 cases per thousand inhabitants compared to 22.8 in Azerbaijan, 27 in Belarus, 65.4 in Georgia, 40.5 in Moldova and 29.3 in Ukraine. Armenia's death rate is the highest in the region: 1 049 deaths per million inhabitants compared to 311 in Azerbaijan, 187 in Belarus, 817 in Georgia, 921 in Moldova and 562 in Ukraine (Roser et al., 2020[5]).[2]

Armenia imposed strict measures to contain the spread of the coronavirus, closing schools and non-essential businesses and restricting travel and public gatherings (OECD, 2020[6]). Armenia's GDP contracted by 3% in 2020, a smaller drop than in many EaP countries, but a significant deviation from its pre-crisis growth rates (7.5% in 2017, 5.2% in 2018). The government's economic stimulus plans (e.g. USD 305 million economic support package) are modest in size, equal to about 2.2% of GDP, compared to 8-10% in developed countries. Some targeted measures could have a positive environmental impact, such as reforestation programmes to create seasonal employment opportunities, but post-crisis development strategies closely resemble the pre-crisis status quo (i.e. focus on metallurgy and manufacturing) (OECD, 2021[7]).

The International Monetary Fund (IMF) approved a 3-year Stand-By Arrangement (SBA) in 2019, prior to the onset of the COVID-19 pandemic. The USD 248 million SBA was augmented in 2020 to USD 443 million. The SBA, which the government initially indicated would be treated as precautionary, aimed to support Armenia's efforts to improve economic fundamentals, aid in the implementation of structural reforms and provide space for spending on infrastructure development and a cushion against shocks. Twin shocks struck Armenia's economy in 2020 in the form of the COVID-19 pandemic and an armed conflict with Azerbaijan, which severely impacted Armenia's economy. As of December 2020, the IMF judged Armenia's performance under the SBA to be satisfactory despite the sizeable challenges it faces (IMF, 2019[8]; IMF, 2020[9]).

Trade

Armenia has been a member of the World Trade Organisation since 2003. Unique among the countries of the South Caucasus, Armenia is a member of the Eurasian Economic Union along with Belarus, Kazakhstan, Kyrgyzstan and the Russian Federation. Unlike the other members, Armenia does not share a border with any members of the bloc. It joined the Customs Union in 2013 and the Eurasian Economic Union's single market in 2015. Similar to the European Union, the Eurasian Economic Union guarantees the 'four freedoms': free movement of goods, services, capital and persons.

Armenia had previously begun negotiations with the European Union on an Association Agreement, like those in force in Georgia (since 2016), Moldova (since 2016) and Ukraine (since 2017), but these were suspended following Armenia's accession to the Eurasian Economic Union in 2015. Armenia and the European Union signed a Comprehensive and Enhanced Partnership Agreement in 2017 that takes into account Armenia's commitments as a member of the Eurasian Economic Union. When it enters into force, the agreement will replace the Partnership and Cooperation Agreement (in force since 1999); it has been provisionally applied since 2018.

The European Union's Eastern Partnership (EaP) is a key initiative for continued cooperation between the EU, its member states, Armenia and the give other EaP countries. It aims to strengthen ties and encourage reform on a number of policy areas, including on governance, connectivity, economic development and environmental protection.

Armenia has been an Observer of the European Union's Energy Community since 2011. Armenia joined the Eurasian Economic Union in 2015, therefore choosing a policy orientation that does not completely comply with the *acquis communautaires* of the European Union. However, there is broad agreement that energy policy reform following the basic principles of the legal framework upon which the European Union and the Energy Community Contracting Parties have successfully reformed their energy sectors would be beneficial also for Armenia. Although its Observer status does not entail any rights or obligations, the Energy Community's Secretariat provides policy guidance on reforming Armenia's energy sector.

Armenia's geographic situation complicates the country's integration into regional trade and transport networks. Unlike neighbouring Georgia and Azerbaijan, Armenia is landlocked and exposed to significant trade routes limitations. These are linked to the border restrictions to the west with Turkey and to the east with Azerbaijan due to the unresolved dispute over the Artsakh/Nagorno-Karabakh region as well as from international sanctions on the Russian Federation (its main trading partner) and Iran (its neighbour to the South). Armenia has no formal diplomatic relations with Azerbaijan or Turkey, and all border crossings are closed.

Georgia and Iran provide Armenia's only land borders to external markets, and both come with their own challenges. Armenia's border with Georgia is of particular importance, since international sanctions limit trade opportunities with Iran and Armenia's trade with Russia, its main trading partner, transits through Georgia. Seasonal weather conditions impede overland transport through the Verkhniy Lars border crossing between Georgia and Russia, while unreliable ferry services from Georgia's Black Sea ports hinder the access of Armenian goods to external markets (UNCTAD, 2019[10]).

Despite Armenia's membership in the Eurasian Economic Union, it has been allowed to maintain its 1995 free trade agreement with Georgia. The Eurasian Economic Union's founding treaty permits bilateral trade agreements signed before 2015 and, since all Eurasian Economic Union members had pre-existing free trade agreements with Georgia prior to joining, trade flows to and from Georgia have been largely unhindered by Armenia's membership. As Georgia establishes deeper ties with the European Union (notably via its Deep and Comprehensive Free Trade Agreement and Association Agreement) and Armenia continues to transpose legislation in accordance with the Eurasian Economic Union, there is a risk that barriers to trade between the two countries will emerge (GET Georgia, 2016[11]).

Armenia's most important trade partner is Russia, which accounts for 23% of Armenia's exports and 27% of imports (Figure 1.1 (a) and (b)). Armenia's trade relationships with other members of the Eurasian Economic Union, however, are much less consequential; Belarus, Armenia's second most important trade partner in the Eurasian Economic Union, accounts for less than 1% of exports and imports. The European Union, on the other hand, is a very important trade partner, especially for exports. Since joining the Eurasian Economic Union, however, exports to other Eurasian Economic Union countries have doubled, while the European Union's share of Armenia's exports is in decline. About 29% of Armenia's exports go to the European Union, with the most important export markets being Bulgaria (7%), Germany (7%) and the Netherlands (5%). 21% of Armenia's imports come from the EU; Germany (4.5%), Italy (3%) and France (2%) were the main import origins. Beyond the two trading blocs, China (10% of imports), Georgia (6% of imports), Iran (5% of imports) and Switzerland (18% of exports) are major partners.

Armenia's mining industry is responsible for the majority of its exports. Mineral products (26% - mostly copper ore, 24% of exports), precious metals (17% - mostly gold, 12% of exports) and metals (14%) account for over half of the country's exports, with the remainder coming from Armenia's textiles and foodstuffs industries. The country's main exports in the latter category are rolled tobacco (9% of exports) and hard liquor (7%). Armenia's imports are less concentrated in particular industries; machines (20%) and mineral products (13% - particularly petroleum gas, 7%, and refined petroleum, 5%) are the largest categories.

Figure 1.1. Trade of Armenia

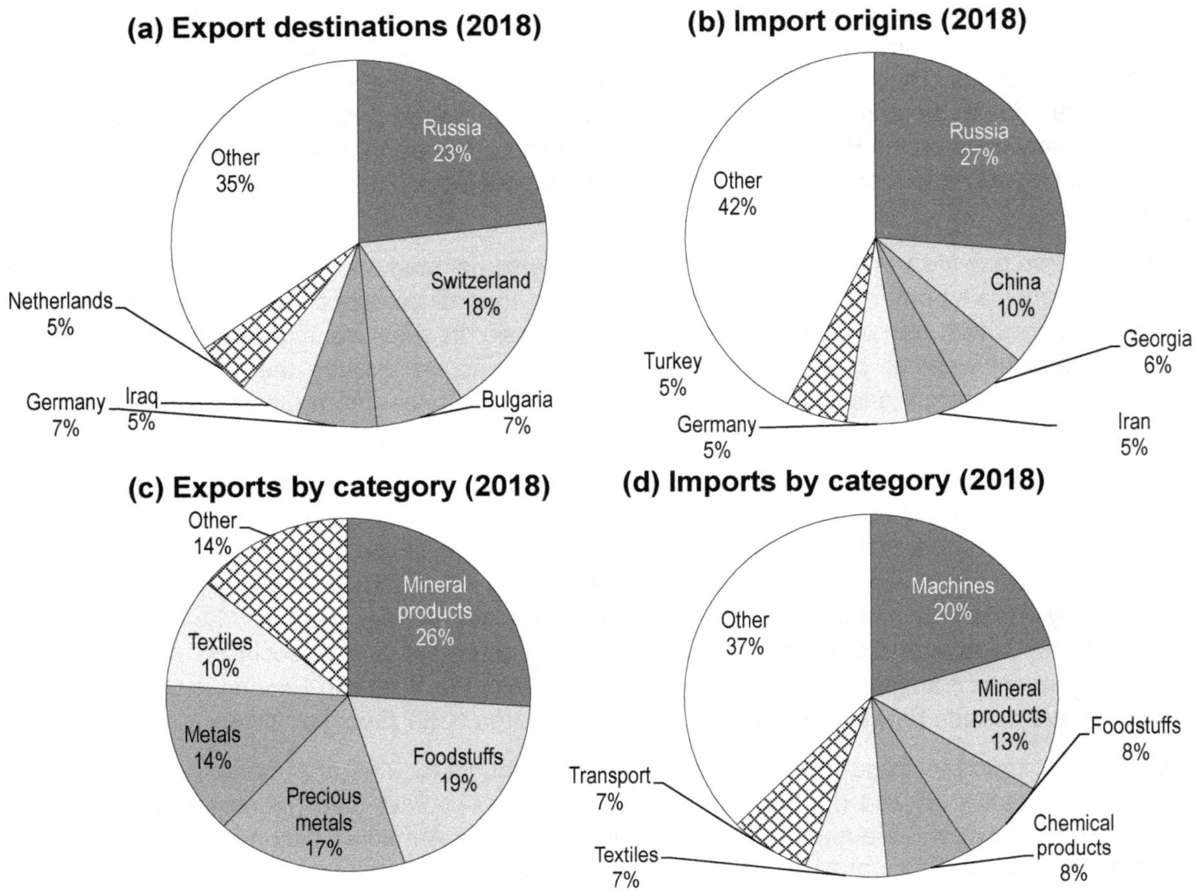

Source: Observatory of Economic Complexity (2020[12]), *Armenia: Exports, Imports and Trade Partners*, Observatory of Economic Complexity, https://oec.world/en/profile/country/arm

Investment climate

Since independence, Armenia has carried out numerous regulatory reforms that have improved its overall investment and business climate. Although Armenia is home to over 140 state-owned enterprises, liberal foreign investment legislation and a series of privatisations following independence have fostered a large private sector accounting for about three-quarters of the country's national activity (UNCTAD, 2019[10]). Investors have expressed concerns about weak competition policies, high levels of operational business risk, cronyism and vested interests (World Bank, 2017[3]), and the government that came to power following the 2018 Armenian Revolution, also known as the Velvet Revolution, has consequently made eliminating corruption a priority. Corruption, however, remains a significant problem (Mejlumyan, 2020[13]).

The Armenia Development Strategy for 2014-2025 sets the objective for Armenia to become one of the top twenty countries in the World Bank's annual Doing Business rankings by 2017 and reach the top fifteen by 2025. Armenia did not achieve its goal in 2017; it ranked 38th, lower than Georgia (16th) but higher than Azerbaijan (65th) (World Bank, 2017[14]). Armenia has made consistent progress on most of the Doing Business indicators, but due to faster reforms elsewhere, it has often slipped in the rankings. For instance, it reduced the time required to open a business (18 days in 2004 compared to 4 days in 2020) and the complexity of the tax system (54 payments requiring over 570 hours on average per year until 2012 compared to 15 payments requiring approximately 260 hours per year in 2020). However, despite some improvements on most metrics, Armenia still ranked 47th in the 2020 edition (World Bank, 2020[15]).

In the wake of the 2018 Armenian Revolution, the electorate voted out several parliamentarians with consequential business interests and influence, and the newly elected government began a sweeping anti-corruption campaign to eliminate systemic corruption (US Department of State, 2019[16]). According to Transparency International's Corruption Perceptions Index, perceptions of corruption in Armenia have already improved markedly. In 2018, Armenia ranked 105 out of 198 countries surveyed, but by 2019 it ranked 77th. However, conflicts of interest, a lack of transparency and accountability in public operations combined with low trust in the judiciary and law enforcement continue to hinder the government's anti-corruption efforts (Transparency International, 2019[17]). Armenia has a regional strategic advantage in the high-tech and information technology sectors thanks to its highly educated population, particularly in science, technology, engineering and mathematics. Given Armenia's unfettered access to the markets of the Eurasian Economic Union, international companies have set up branches and subsidiaries in the country. However, businesses face several challenges in Armenia due to its relatively small domestic market, its closed borders and the resulting poor access to export markets and weak observance of the rule of law (US Department of State, 2019[16]).

Despite certain distinct advantages, Armenia underperforms compared to regional competitors in attracting foreign direct investment (FDI). In Armenia, average per capita FDI inflows dropped from USD 193 between 2009 and 2013 to USD 98 between 2014 and 2018, whereas its neighbours experienced the opposite trend: Azerbaijan increased from USD 154 to USD 357 and Georgia increased from USD 225 to USD 414. Investor caution explains much of the decline in FDI since 2008, as investors hesitate to return to Armenia following recent political upheavals (UNCTAD, 2019[10]).

In an effort to streamline state institutions, the government disbanded Business Armenia (previously known as the Development Foundation of Armenia), the country's investment promotion agency (IPA), and transferred its responsibilities to the Ministry of Economy (Office of the President of the Republic of Armenia and UNCTAD, 2020[18]). In 2020, Armenia established the Investment Support Centre under the Ministry of Economy to act as the country's IPA (OECD, 2020[19]).

Between 2003 and 2017, Armenia attracted USD 7.3 billion of FDI to greenfield projects, mostly to the financial services sector (27%), communications (19%) and metals (16%) (Figure 1.2). Infrastructure-related investments, particularly in alternative/renewable energy sources (9%) and the transportation sector (4%), also attracted considerable FDI inflows.

Figure 1.2. Greenfield FDI in Armenia by economic activity, 2003-2017

Cumulated greenfield FDI capital between January 2003 and September 2017 in USD million

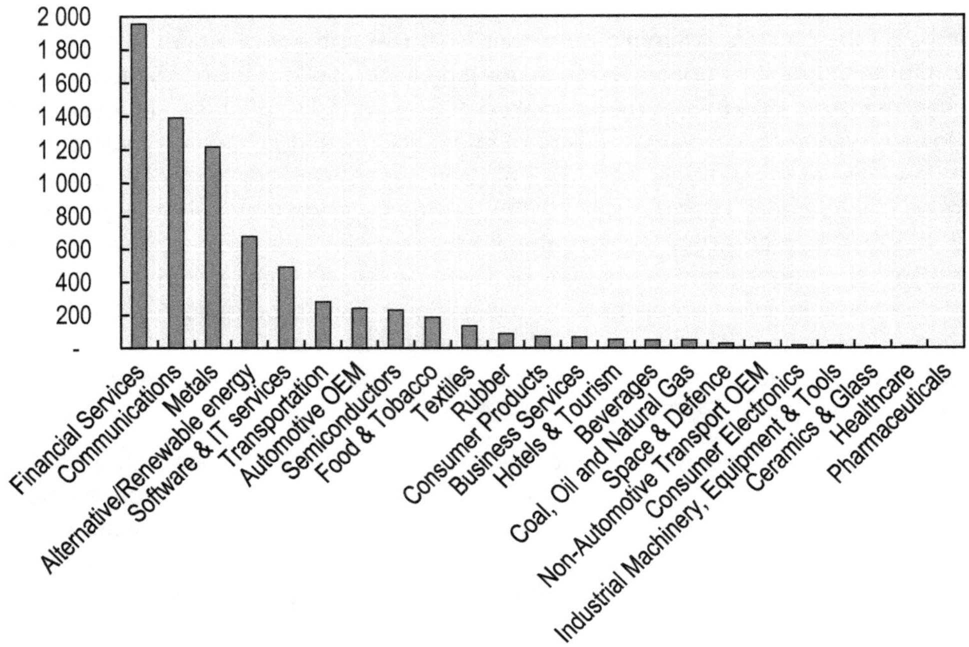

Source: OECD based on fDi Markets (2019[20]), fDi Markets: the in-depth crossborder investment monitor (database), fDi Markets, https://www.fdimarkets.com/

Russia, Armenia's most important trade partner, remains the largest foreign investor, accounting for 41% of the country's FDI stock in 2017 (Figure 1.3), down from almost 60% in 2008. Since then, Russian FDI has shifted towards gas and telecommunications from its earlier focus on real estate and mining. As a bloc, the European Union (21%) is Armenia's second largest investor with a relatively stable share over the past decade. France (5%), Germany (4%) and Cyprus (4%) are the EU member states that invest the most. France focuses on the beverage industry and water supply and sanitation services while Germany concentrates on manufacturing and the extraction of basic metals. The large share (9%) of FDI derived from Jersey can be explained by the registration of Lydian International Limited, a gold mining corporation that fully owns the large-scale Amulsar Gold Project in Armenia. Other major investors include Argentina (6%, wine and airports), the United States (4%, IT and electricity) and Lebanon (4%, telecommunications, food and waste disposal) (UNCTAD, 2019[10]).

A prominent Armenian diaspora is a common feature of many of Armenia's important FDI source countries, including Russia (41%), Argentina (6%), France (5%), Cyprus (4%), the United States (4%) and Lebanon (4%).[3] The diaspora has played an important role in Armenia's development through FDI, humanitarian aid and other transfers since its independence. Between 1994 and 2004, approximately 68% of companies benefiting from FDI were linked to the diaspora (World Bank, 2017[3]).

The majority (76% in 2018) of Armenia's public debt is denominated in foreign currencies, but this figure has been steadily declining. Armenia aims to reduce its relatively high ratio of public and publicly guaranteed debt to GDP (56% in 2018) and projections predict it will reach 50% by 2023. Although the government has improved fiscal and macroeconomic stability and begun to reduce the public debt, Armenia remains vulnerable to external shocks, particularly from global trade tensions and the economic situation in Russia (IMF, 2019[21]).

Figure 1.3. Armenia's FDI stock by country of origin, 2017

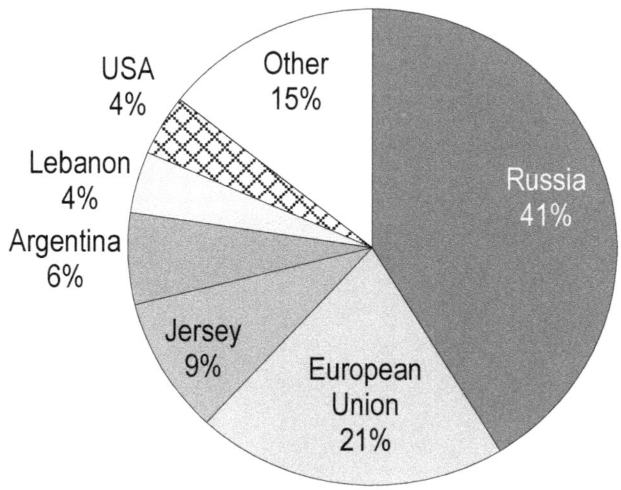

Note: Jersey is a Crown dependency of the United Kingdom
Source: UNCTAD (2019[10]), *Investment Policy Review: Armenia,* United Nations Conference for Trade and Development, Geneva, https://unctad.org/en/PublicationsLibrary/diaepcb2019d3_en.pdf

Climate change

Given the country's small size, Armenia's emissions account for only 0.02% of global greenhouse gas (GHG) emissions. Armenia's GHG emissions shrank dramatically in the early 1990s as the constituent republics of the Soviet Union achieved independence. After peaking at 26 $MtCO_2e$ in 1990, Armenia's GHG emissions reduced more than fourfold to 6 $MtCO_2e$ in 1996. Since then, Armenia's emissions have steadily increased, reaching between 12 $MtCO_2e$ in 2012 (according to World Bank data) or 10 $MtCO_2e$ in the mid-2010s (according to Armenia's 4th National Communication) (Figure 1.4). The post-independence drop in emissions reflects the contraction of Armenia's economy in the early 1990s; GDP halved between 1990 and 1993. Economic growth has since decoupled from GHG emissions resulting in decreased GHG intensity (0.89 $kgCO_2e$ per USD in 2016 compared to 4 $kgCO_2e$ per USD in 1990). Despite this improvement, Armenia's economy remains significantly more emissions-intensive than the OECD average (0.35 $kgCO_2e$ per USD in 2012). Armenia's per capita emissions have dropped from 7.3 tCO_2e in 1990 to 3.4 tCO_2e in 2016 (World Bank, 2021[1]).

Armenia's stated GHG emissions targets are among the most ambitious in the former Soviet Union. In its first Nationally Determined Contribution (NDC), Armenia committed to achieving ecosystem neutral GHG emissions by 2050, conditional on international support. Its per capita target is to achieve 2.07 tCO_2e (Government of Armenia, 2015[22]).

Figure 1.4. GHG emissions and GDP of Armenia, 1990-2019

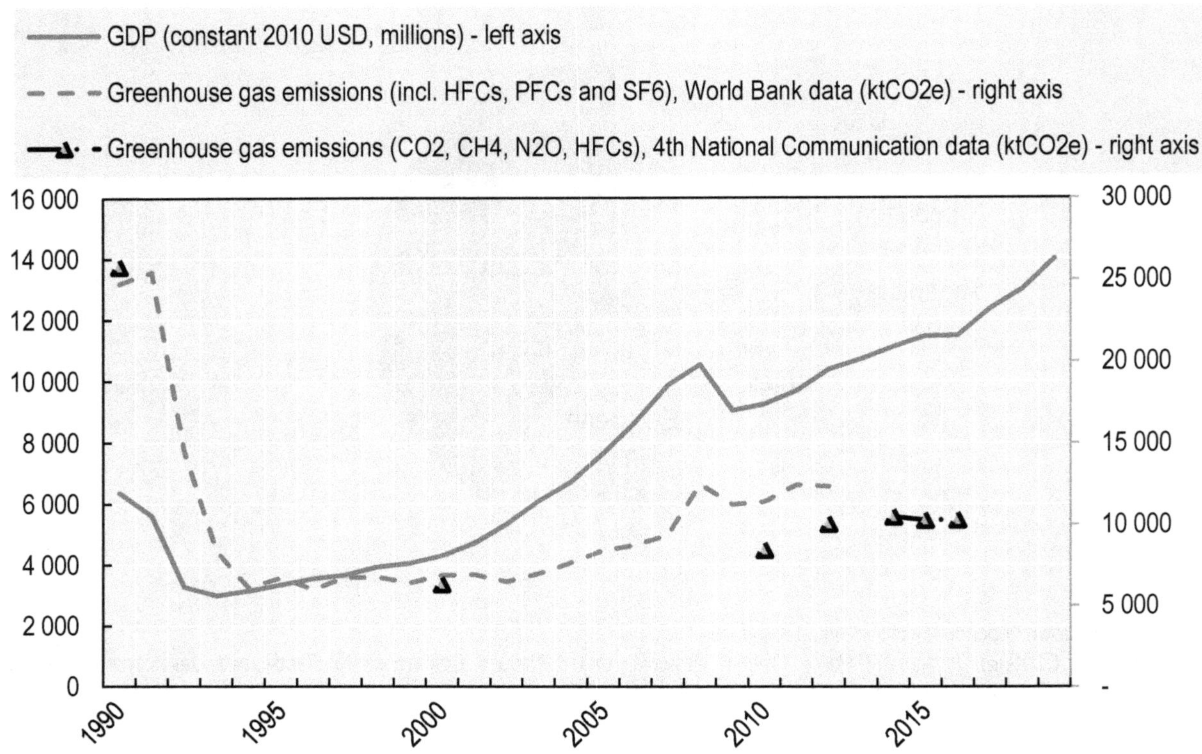

Source: World Bank (2021[1]), World Development Indicators (database), World Bank, https://data.worldbank.org/indicator/EN.ATM.GHGT.ZG; Ministry of Environment of the Republic of Armenia (2020[23]), *Armenia's Fourth National Communication on Climate Change under the United Nations Framework Convention on Climate Change*, https://unfccc.int/sites/default/files/resource/NC4_Armenia_.pdf

Energy (including fuel combustion from transport) has accounted for the majority of Armenia's GHG emissions since independence, but the share has decreased over time, from 88% in 1990 to 68% in 2000 and 64% in 2016. Conversely, agriculture's share of emissions has grown from 8% in 1990 to 21% in 2000 and 22% in 2016. Industrial processes and products use (2% in 1990, 8% in 2016) and waste (2% in 1990, 6% in 2016) make up the remainder of Armenia's GHG emissions. In absolute terms, energy-related emissions remain far below their pre-independence levels (22.7 $MtCO_2e$ in 1990 to 6.6 $MtCO_2e$ in 2016), but emissions from all other sources have grown (e.g. 2.0 $MtCO_2e$ of agriculture-related emissions in 1990 compared to 2.3 $MtCO_2e$ in 2016) (Ministry of Environment of the Republic of Armenia, 2020[23]).

Armenia has already begun to experience some of the effects of climate change. The annual mean temperature in Armenia increased by 1.23°C on average (1929-2016), average precipitation has decreased by 9% (1935-2016) and the frequency and intensity of natural disasters and floods have increased. These trends are expected to continue if global emission rates remain on their current course (Ministry of Environment of the Republic of Armenia, 2020[23]). Armenia's agricultural sector is particularly vulnerable as precipitation decreases and water stress intensifies. Extreme weather events led to AMD 72.71 billion (approximately USD 182 million) in damage to crops between 2009 and 2013 (World Bank, 2017[3]). In the future, climate scenarios predict declines in crop yields (8-14% by 2030), the productivity of irrigated land (24%) and overall pasture area and productivity (4-10% by 2030). Rising temperatures will also negatively impact Armenia's ecosystems; models predict that fragile mountain ecosystems will shift vertically by 250-300m, erosion and desertification will increase and aquatic ecosystems, including the Caucasus's largest freshwater body Lake Sevan, will suffer from eutrophication and decreased water quality (Ministry of Environment of the Republic of Armenia, 2020[23]).

Armenia's infrastructure needs and current plans

The overall quality of Armenia's infrastructure is relatively adequate, however its transport metrics are poor compared to its neighbours (Figure 1.5). Armenia faces infrastructure bottlenecks, some beyond its direct control, such as its few operating international border crossings. Its outdated transport infrastructure and, in particular, the low capacity of its border crossings with Iran and, crucially, the border crossing between Georgia and Russia that provides Armenia's only land access to the Russian market are major barriers to Armenia's competitiveness and integration into global value chains (World Bank, 2017[3]). Armenia ranked 92nd in the World Bank's Logistics Performance Index in 2018, up from 141st place in 2016 (World Bank, 2019[24]).

Figure 1.5. Quality of infrastructure in Armenia

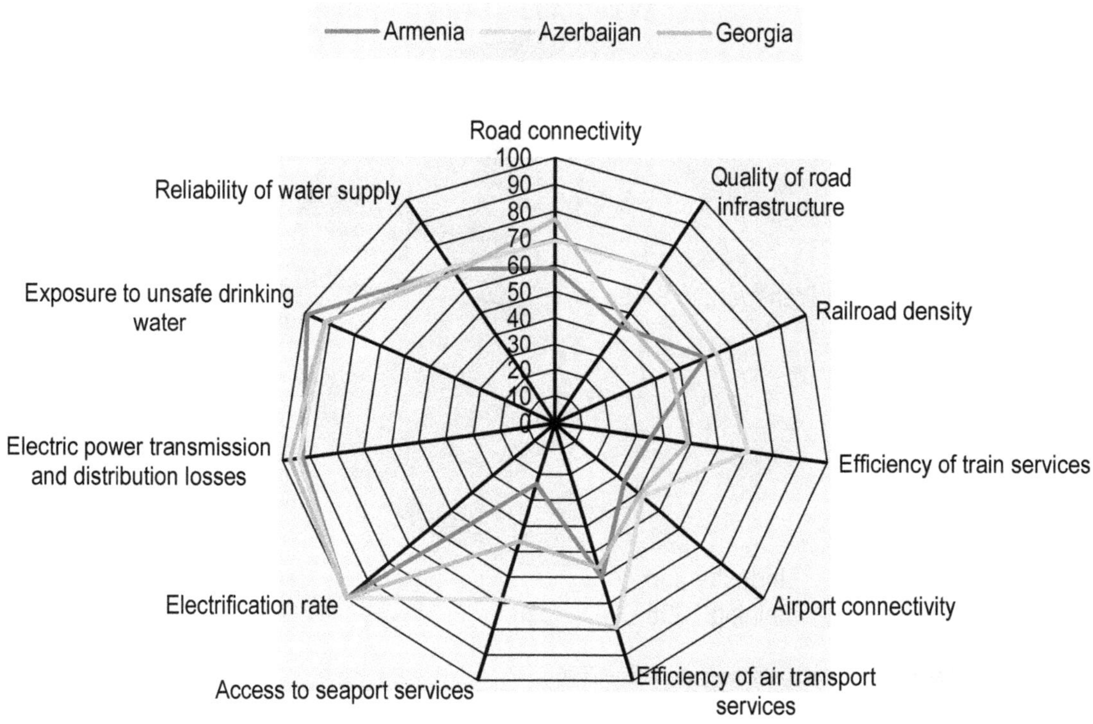

Source: World Economic Forum (2019[25]), *The Global Competitiveness Report 2019*, World Economic Forum, http://www3.weforum.org/docs/WEF_TheGlobalCompetitivenessReport2019.pdf

Armenia needs to invest USD 450-600 million annually into economic infrastructure, including energy, transportation, water supply and sanitation and telecommunications (World Bank, 2017[26]). In its *Strategic Programme of Prospective Development (2014-2025)*, the government set annual infrastructure investment targets by sector: 1.4-1.5% of GDP in transport (85% of which would be dedicated to the road network, and 15% to other projects), 0.3% of GDP in energy, 0.3% of GDP in irrigation and 0.4% of GDP in drinking water systems (Government of Armenia, 2014[27]). Jointly, these targets amount to about USD 340-350 million per year, below the estimated annual needs. Between 2014 and 2016, Armenia invested

EUR 88 million annually on transport infrastructure (ITF, 2020[28]), which amounts to less than 1% of the country's GDP, significantly below the government's set target.

The OECD's database tracks 34 major infrastructure projects planned and under construction in Armenia with a cumulative value of USD 13.9 billion. By value, energy projects account for the largest share (51%, USD 7.2 billion), closely followed by the transport sector (43%, USD 5.9 billion) (Figure 1.6). By comparison, industry and mining projects (USD 395 million) and water projects (USD 409 million) represent much smaller shares of total investment in Armenia's infrastructure (3% each).

Figure 1.6. Investment projects in Armenia, by sector

Planned and under construction, in USD million

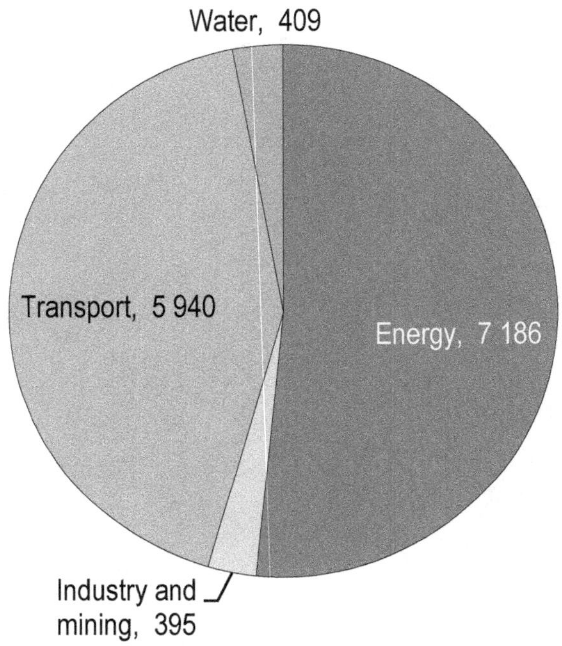

Source: OECD analysis based on accessed databases as of June 2020.

Transport

High trade costs caused in part by transport infrastructure and poor connectivity hinder the Armenia's continued development. Armenia could benefit from reforms in the areas of formalities, governance and impartiality, information availability, involvement of trade community, advance rulings and fees and charges (OECD, 2020[29]). Although the government has consistently maintained transport infrastructure as a priority the quality of its domestic transport network has deteriorated due to a lack of investment in maintenance. Only 500 km of the country's 1 329 km of railways are in working condition, and even the operational sections are in need of maintenance and modernisation. Armenia's road network is also in poor condition, contributing to a persistent problem with road safety (ADB, 2019[30]).

These shortcomings in quality and performance stem from underinvestment in transport infrastructure. Over the past decade, Armenia's per capita investments in infrastructure have fluctuated, never exceeding USD 50 per capita between 2008 and 2016 (Figure 1.7). In comparison, over the same period, per capita investments in transport infrastructure were about USD 126 on average annually in Azerbaijan and USD 101 on average annually in Georgia (ITF, 2019[31]). Armenia's investment in inland transport has focused on its road network rather than rail transport. In recent years, rail's share in total investments has decreased markedly.

Figure 1.7. Inland transport infrastructure investment in Armenia (2008-2016)

Modal share (%) of total inland infrastructure investment (left axis) and total inland transport infrastructure investment in current USD per capita (right axis)

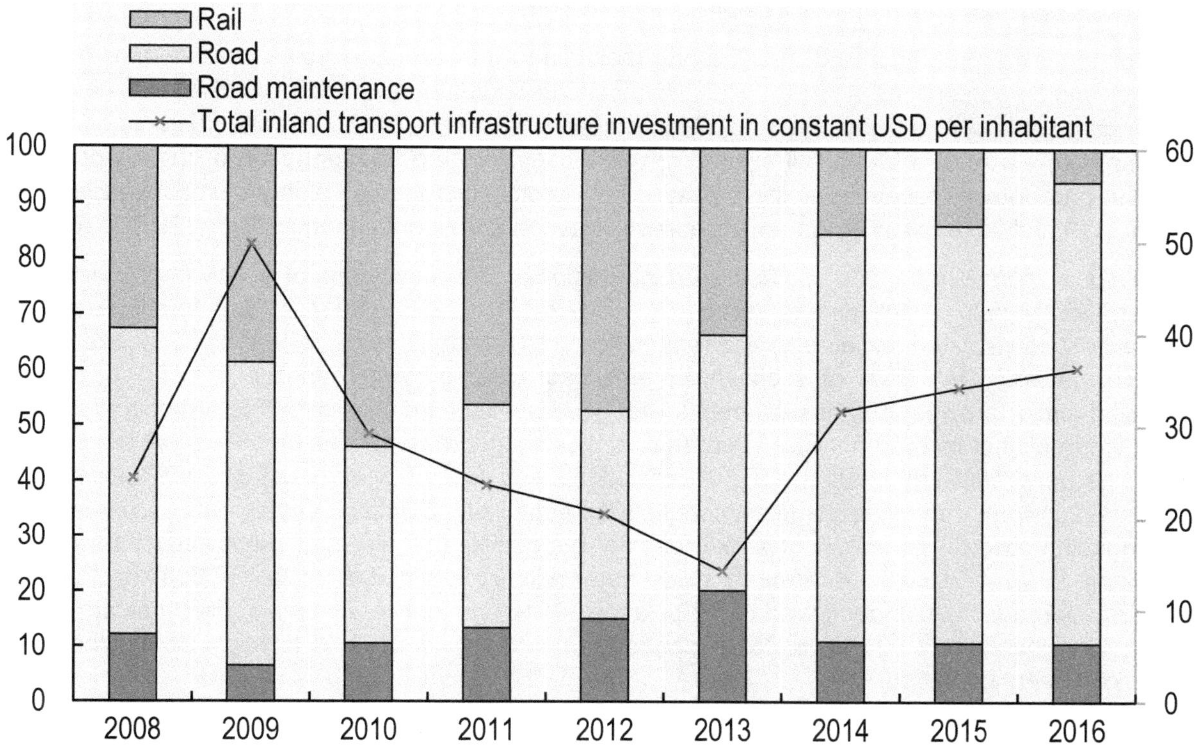

Source: ITF (2019[31]), *Transport performance indicators*, International Transport Forum, https://doi.org/10.1787/trsprt-data-en

Armenia's rail network does not extend to the south of the country, since the line that prior to the breakup of the Soviet Union connected Meghri (near the border with Iran) to the capital Yerevan ran through what is now the Autonomous Republic of Nakhchivan, an exclave of Azerbaijan. As such, Armenia has no rail connections with the Iranian rail network, and its pre-independence connections to Azerbaijan and Turkey are closed due to long-standing political conflicts. Armenia's only international rail connection is to Georgia but, due to the Georgian-Abkhazian conflict, Georgia lacks a direct rail connection to Russia, relying instead on its Black Sea ports of Batumi and Poti for shipments to the Russian port of Novorossiysk.

Although rail is among the most efficient and lowest emitting modes of transport, accounting for 8% of the world's passenger turnover and 7% of freight turnover while emitting only 2% of the transport sector's energy-related emissions (IEA, 2019[32]). However, the development of rail projects faces major constraints due to the Armenian rail system's lack of cross-border connectivity and the current condition of the network. Moreover, the government's limited fiscal space means the necessary spending is not forthcoming. For this reason, the government has opted for a greater focus on road infrastructure development, to which it plans to dedicate 85% of the state's transport-related investments (Government of Armenia, 2014[27]). These investment patterns will further lock Armenia's transport system into a high-emission development pathway that could run counter to the government's 2050 emissions reduction targets expressed in its

NDC, but the focus on secondary roads and domestic connectivity in the road network contributes to regional development and reduction of urban-rural disparities.

Unique among EaP countries, Armenia relies heavily on natural gas for its transport sector. Compressed natural gas (CNG) accounts for 70% of fuels in Armenia due to its lower price (2.5 times cheaper than gasoline) and its promotion as a cleaner fuel by the government, notably in public transport development. A heavy excise tax applied to diesel but it was exempt from VAT until 2018, when the VAT exemption was lifted but the excise tax was reduced. Natural gas remains exempt from excise tax. CNG also benefited from an excise tax exemption until its phase-out in 2016 (OECD, 2018[33]).

Due to connectivity problems and insufficiently maintained infrastructure, rail's modal share for both passenger and cargo services is limited. Rail only accounted for 0.2% of passenger trips in 2018, and its share for cargo is in decline (about 10% in 2018 compared to 24% in 2012). The vast majority of exports are transported via road, but the rail system remains useful for the transportation of mining products. Armenia's road network faces mounting pressure from rapidly increasing freight volumes, which tripled between 2015 and 2018 following Armenia's accession to the Eurasian Economic Union (EBRD, 2019[34]).

Armenia's government has made domestic and international connectivity one of its key priorities. One of the government's main objectives expressed in its Strategic Programme 2014-2025 is to ensure reliable road links between isolated settlements and regional centres (i.e. administrative centres of each region, or *marz* in Armenian). Only 30% of such settlements had suitable road connections in 2014, and the government aim to provide 90% of settlements with good-quality road links by 2025. Armenia also plans to boost the quality of its road network in general, achieving 'good' conditions on 65% of all roads in the country's network (100% of international, 60% of national and 45% of local roads) by 2025 (Government of Armenia, 2014[27]). Improving domestic connectivity, especially to smaller settlements, is an essential step in reducing poverty, since 70% of Armenia's poor live outside of the capital, particularly in rural areas (World Bank, 2017[3]). Since 2014, Armenia's road network has expanded marginally (7 568 km of general purpose motor roads in 2019 compared to 7 792 km in 2014), and local road development has accounted for most of the increase (3 895 km in 2019 compared to 3 801 km in 2014) (Statistical Committee of the Republic of Armenia, 2020[35]).

Another key objective for Armenia is to develop the north-south corridor linking the country's two open international borders with Georgia and Iran. This will include an extension to the national rail network, establishing international connections with Iranian rail lines and reconnecting Armenia's currently operating network with the country's southern districts (Government of Armenia, 2014[27]). Armenia and Iran have discussed establishing a rail link for over a decade, but the project has encountered difficulty attracting investors. Most recently, one of the project's backers opened an international lawsuit against the government of Armenia in 2018 and, as a result, the project's status is unclear (Gabrielian, 2018[36]). The Armenian government has also expressed interest in normalising relations with Turkey and, in the medium term, reopening border crossings between the two countries (Government of Armenia, 2017[37]). However, the 2020 Nagorno-Karabakh war with Azerbaijan, supported by Turkey, casts doubt on any speedy normalisation of relations.

Armenia's planned and current transport infrastructure projects account for around USD 5.9 billion, split between railways (50% or USD 3 billion) and road (48% or USD 2.8 billion) (Figure 1.8). Urban public transport projects (2% or USD 99 million) in Yerevan, make up the remainder. A single large-scale rail project, the Iran-Armenia Rail Link, accounts for the entirety of rail's share in Armenia's investments. Given the current state of Armenia's domestic rail network, the project, if completed, could face major obstacles to functioning at its full design capacity. Road investments tracked in the OECD database are more varied, focusing on improving the capacity and reliability of international roads and improving domestic connectivity for isolated settlements.

The hotspot projects identified in the OECD's database of infrastructure projects planned and under construction in Armenia echo the country's vision for developing the transport sector outlined in the

Strategic Programme 2014-2025 (Figure 1.8). Plans to improve the quality of roads and domestic connectivity feature prominently among the projects under construction. However, more ambitious and expensive projects, such as improvements to the country's rail network and primary trade corridor, remain stalled at the planning phase.

Figure 1.8. Transport projects in Armenia, by sub-sector

Planned and under construction in USD millions

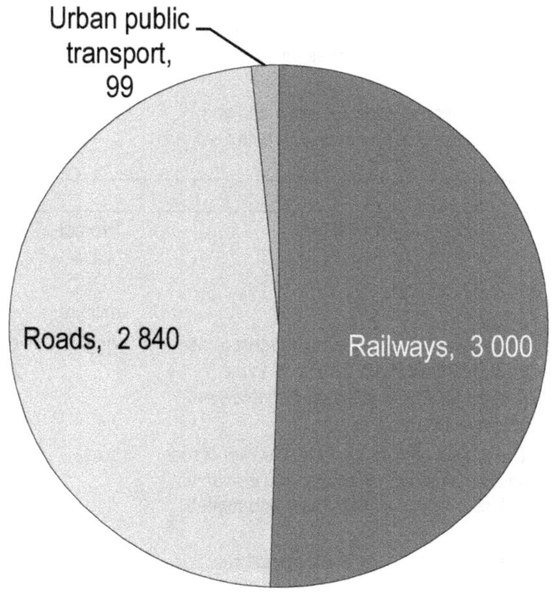

Source: OECD analysis based on accessed databases as of June 2020.

Table 1.2. Hotspot projects in the transport sector in Armenia

Name	Sub-sector	Description	Project value (USD million)	Source	Type of investment
(a) Under construction					
Armenia M6 Interstate Road	Road	The project will rehabilitate and modernise 90 km of road between Vanadzor (central Armenia) and Bagratashen (on the border with Georgia).	110	EIB	Brownfield
Lifeline Road Network Improvement Project	Road	The project will rehabilitate local roads and improve access to services for 60 000 people.	75	IBRD, Government of Armenia	Brownfield
Border Crossing and Infrastructure Improvements	Road	The project improves 7 km of roads and modernises 3 border crossings with Georgia.	67	EIB	Brownfield
(b) Planned					
Iran-Armenia Rail Link	Rail	The railway will provide the shortest route from Georgia's Black Sea ports to the Persian Gulf by connecting Armenia's rail network with Iran's.	3 000	Government of Armenia, Russian Railways	Greenfield
North-South Corridor Investment Programme	Road	The project aims to modernise 93 km of road between Agarak and Bavra via Yerevan as well as customs infrastructure and related facilities.	1 440	ADB, NIP, EIB, EDB, Government of Armenia	Brownfield
Sustainable Urban Development Investment Programme	Road	The project develops the transport sector in 12 major and secondary cities, including road improvements in Yerevan.	575	ADB, Government of Armenia	Brownfield

Note: Refer to the Reader's guide for the present report's definition of 'hotspot' and other information on how the projects above were selected and prioritised. ADB = Asian Development Bank; EDB = Eurasian Development Bank; EIB = European Investment Bank; IBRD = International Bank for Reconstruction and Development; NIP = Neighbourhood Investment Platform.
Source: OECD database as of June 2020.

Energy

Like other former Soviet Union countries, Armenia has achieved universal electricity access. While increased investment in the energy sector is important to support Armenia's continued development, the energy affordability for households must remain central to policy making. Households spend on average 12.4% of their budgets on energy and 6% on electricity alone. 11.2% of households are classified as 'electricity poor', while 52.5% are 'energy poor'.[4] As increased investments apply upward pressure on electricity tariffs, regulators face the challenge of tackling energy poverty for lower-income households (World Bank, 2017[3]). Following the collapse of the Soviet Union and the energy crisis in the early 1990s, the district heating system in Armenia completely broke down. There was minimal uptake of the roll-out of 'autonomous heating', in which small gas-fired boilers heat a building or group of buildings, and Armenians have instead turned to inefficient, individual wall-hung natural gas boilers (OECD, 2018[33]).

Armenia has abolished most subsidies related to the energy system inherited from the Soviet period, but subsidies remain in the form of targeted support for low-income households and foregone government revenue due to tax exemptions for diesel[5] and natural gas (exempt from excise taxes). As the government continues reforming energy subsidies, there is scope to redirect support to encourage the development of power generation from renewable sources and improve energy efficiency. Clear communication, awareness-raising and targeted support for low-income households are essential to ensure the social acceptability of subsidy and pricing reform measures (OECD, 2018[33]).

At present, Armenia's electricity infrastructure underperforms compared to the infrastructure in neighbouring countries. Armenia's electricity transmission and distribution systems lead to losses 11.1% of the electricity they transport, whereas the loss rates are lower in Azerbaijan (9.8%) and Georgia (6.8%) (World Economic Forum, 2019[25]). Armenia's power sector also suffers from reliability problems, with 34% of firms experiencing electricity outages, more than in Azerbaijan (16%) and less than in Georgia (54%) (World Bank, n.d.[38]). Age and lack of maintenance are major contributors to the underperformance of Armenia's electricity infrastructure. On average, electrical substations are about 35 years old, and most have not undergone any major upgrades or refurbishments after construction (World Bank, 2017[3]). Unlike Georgia, Moldova and Ukraine, Armenia is not a Contracting Party of the EU's Energy Community, but it has been an Observer since 2011 (Energy Community, 2019[39]). Although this status grants Armenia no legal rights or obligations, the Energy Community Secretariat regularly publishes recommendations to reform the country's energy sector. The Secretariat's most recent recommendations highlighted the benefits of energy market liberalisation, which would improve the sector's efficiency and help Armenia meet its obligations under the Eurasian Economic Union to establish a wholesale electricity market (Energy Community, 2017[40]).

Armenia is a net energy importer. In 2018, Armenia's domestic energy production covered just over a quarter (0.82 Mtoe) of its total primary energy supply, with the shortfall made up via imports (2.27 Mtoe). Armenia is, however, a net exporter of electricity, exporting electricity to Iran (140 ktoe) (IEA, 2019[41]). Armenia has no proven oil reserves and very limited local natural gas reserves which remain unexploited. As a result, Armenia fully relies on imports for natural gas, its primary energy source, and oil (IAEA, 2018[42]). The vast majority of Armenia's gas imports come from Russia (2 billion cubic metres per year, or about 80%) with a smaller share imported from Iran (500 million cubic metres annually, or 20%). Although Armenia and Iran have both expressed interest in ramping up cross-border gas trade, Armenia faces the challenge of balancing energy security concerns from diversifying its gas supply with the risk of contravening US-imposed sanctions on Iran (Harutyunyan, 2019[43]).

Armenia generates electricity almost exclusively from three sources. Natural gas accounts for 43% of Armenia's electricity generation, while nuclear (27%), which also relies on imported fuel, and hydroelectric power plants (30%) make up the remainder (Figure 1.9). Power generation from other renewables sources is extremely limited: 19 GWh from solar PV and 2 GWh from wind in 2018.

Figure 1.9. Electricity generation by source

GWh, 2018

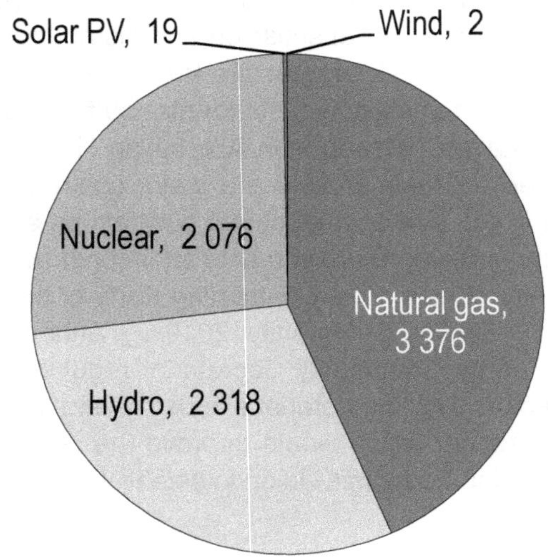

Source: IEA (2021[44]), *Electricity Information 2020*, International Energy Agency, https://www.iea.org/data-and-statistics

Armenia has made energy security one of its primary objectives in the energy sector. A major challenge that Armenia faces in this regard is its reliance on old power plants that have reached or surpassed their operational life. Most notably, the Metsamor nuclear power plant – the only nuclear power plant not only in Armenia but in all of the South Caucasus – was scheduled for decommissioning in 2016, but due to insufficient replacement capacity, its service life was extended to 2026 (OECD, 2018[33]). Therefore, Armenia's need to ramp up energy infrastructure investment stems not only from increasing energy demand but also a pressing need to replace outdated generation capacity.

One way in which Armenia plans to improve energy security is through the development of renewable energy. Armenia aims to derive 21% of its power generation from renewable energy sources by 2020 and 26% by 2025. These renewable targets included source-specific objectives: 377 MW of installed hydroelectric generation capacity by 2020, 397 MW by 2025; 50 MW of wind and geothermal respectively by 2020, 100 MW by 2025; and 40 MW of solar photovoltaic by 2020, 80 MW by 2025 (IEA, 2016[45]). Armenia introduced tax breaks for households that generate electricity from small-scale solar and wind facilities for their own consumption and distribution through the national grid (Bertelsmann Stiftung, 2020[46]).

To bolster its energy independence, Armenia has focused on further developing its hydroelectric potential and diversifying its power sector through the deployment of renewables, particularly solar and geothermal. Armenia enjoys considerable hydroelectric potential thanks to the large number of rivers that run through its territory, but the intensive development of hydroelectric stations that often neglect legal requirements and standards has depleted river flow (Bertelsmann Stiftung, 2020[46]).The most recent available statistics on power generation[6] indicate that non-hydro renewables account for a miniscule share of Armenia's electricity: 0.6%. Generation in the first half of 2020 indicate that Armenia will miss its 2020 renewable electricity generation targets by a wide margin. Armenia aimed to generate 117 GWh and 88 GWh of wind and solar energy respectively in 2020 but only produced 1.4 GWh of wind and 8.7 of solar in the first half of the year. Although Armenia had planned to generate 373 GWh of geothermal energy by 2020, there are still no geothermal power stations integrated into the Armenian electric network (Statistical Committee of the Republic of Armenia, 2020[47]).

Armenia's Strategic Programme 2014-2025 highlights several large-scale projects designed to meet the country's energy security and diversification goals. Armenia plans to improve its power network's connections to the Georgian and Iranian electricity systems through the construction of new transmission lines and substations as well as refurbishment of existing infrastructure. Armenia aims to dedicate 0.3.% of its annual budget to improving energy efficiency and the country's transmission and distribution system. In terms of generation, Armenia's Strategic Programme singles out the rehabilitation of the Vorotan hydroelectric power plant, preliminary work towards exploiting the country's geothermal potential (Government of Armenia, 2014[27]).

Despite how prominently geothermal and wind feature in Armenia's objectives for the development of renewables in the country's power generation system, there are no projects planned or under construction using either technology in the country's pipeline, which is largely dominated by nuclear and solar projects (Figure 1.10). The further development of nuclear energy, through the construction of a third unit of the Metsamor nuclear power plant, dwarfs the proposed power generation capacity from other sources. Increased nuclear electricity generation is a key component of Armenia's strategy to reduce reliance on natural gas imports and as a potential way to increase electricity exports to neighbouring countries. While there is a broad consensus that constructing replacement capacity for the existing Metsamor unit is necessary, the focus on a new nuclear unit as opposed to other alternatives (i.e. rapid scale-up of renewables) has received shakier support. Prominent cabinet ministers have proposed studying other alternatives more seriously (Schneider et al., 2018[48]). This nuclear project as well as electricity transmission refurbishments to improve cross-border connections with Georgia and Iran are among the hotspot energy infrastructure projects identified in the OECD's database (Table 1.3). Solar photovoltaic projects make up a quarter of new power generation.

Figure 1.10. New electricity generation capacity in Armenia, by energy source

In MW

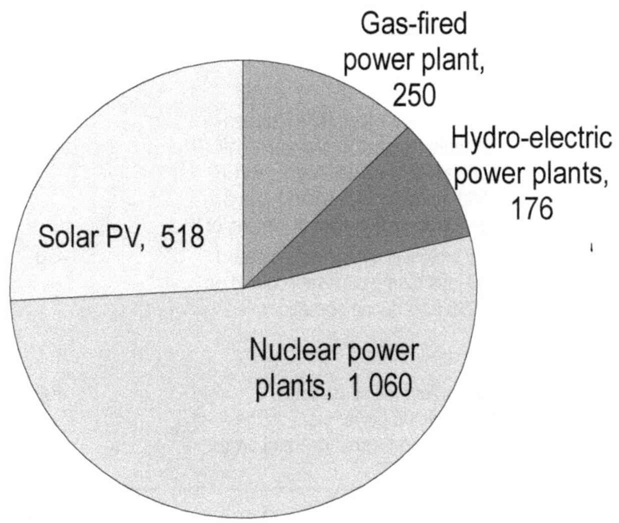

Source: OECD analysis based on accessed databases as of June 2020.

Table 1.3. Hotspot projects in the energy sector in Armenia

Name	Sub-sector	Description	Project value (USD million)	New capacity (MW)	Source	Type of investment
	a) Under construction					
Tatev, Shamb & Spandaryan Hydroelectric Portfolio Acquisition and Rehabilitation	Hydroelectricity plants	The project will install new turbines, generators, transformers and auxiliary electrical and mechanical equipment are planned to replace outdated components of the Tatev, Shamb and Spandaryan hydroelectric power plants. This refurbishment aims to extend the life cycle of the plants and improve reliability and safety of their operations.	195	N/A	IFC, FMO, DEG	Brownfield
Shnogh Hydroelectric Power Plant	Hydroelectricity plants	The project will construct a new power plant on the Debed river near Shnogh, a village 20 km south of the Georgian border.	150	76	Debed Hydro LLC, The Robbins Company, Government of Armenia, Investors Club of Armenia	Greenfield
Electricity Supply Reliability Project	Electricity transmission and distribution	This project will replace a 230 km section of transmission line between the Hrazdan thermal power plant and Shinuhayr substation as well as several 220kV transmission lines currently in poor condition.	102	N/A	IBRD, Government of Armenia	Brownfield
Tatev, Shamb & Spandaryan Hydroelectric Portfolio Acquisition and Rehabilitation	Hydroelectricity plants	The project will install new turbines, generators, transformers and auxiliary electrical and mechanical equipment are planned to replace outdated components of the Tatev, Shamb and Spandaryan hydroelectric power plants. This refurbishment aims to extend the life cycle of the plants and improve reliability and safety of their operations.	195	N/A	IFC, FMO, DEG	Brownfield
	b) Planned					
Armenian Nuclear Power Plant 3	Nuclear power plant	Metzamorenergoatom, a Russian-Armenian joint stock company, will build an AES-92 unit (with a VVER-1000 model V-392 reactor) with a service life of 60 years at Metsamor.	5 000	1 060	Government of Russia, Government of Armenia	Greenfield
Yerevan-2 Armpower Greenfield Combined-Cycle Power Plant	Gas-fired power plant	The project is expected to create 1 200 jobs during construction and up to 230 jobs during operations.	473	250	IFC, MIGA, World Bank, ADB	Greenfield
Meghri Hydroelectric Power Plant	Hydroelectric power plant	The project will construct a hydroelectric power plant on the Aras river near the Armenia–Iran border.	400	100	Government of Armenia, Government of Iran	Greenfield

Note: Refer to the Reader's guide for the present report's definition of 'hotspot' and other information on how the projects above were selected and prioritised. ADB = Asian Development Bank; DEG = German Investment Corporation (*Deutsche Investitions- und Entwicklungsgesellschaft*), a subsidiary of KfW; FMO = *Nederlandse Financierings-Maatschappij voor* Ontwikkelingslanden, a Dutch development bank; IBRD = International Bank for Reconstruction and Development; IFC = International Finance Corporation; MIGA = Multilateral Investment Guarantee Agency.
Source: OECD database as of June 2020.

Industry, mining and water

Following independence, the focus of Armenia's economy shifted from industry towards agriculture and trade. However, the mining sector continued to develop even as manufacturing and other industries remained stable or declined. Mining and quarrying account for approximately 2% of Armenia's GDP and the majority of the country's exports. The sector is also a top performer in attracting foreign investment and generates employment opportunities, particularly in rural areas (World Bank, 2016[49]). Despite these changes, Armenia's manufacturing sector remains large (76% of industrial output by value) and is concentrated primarily in the production of foodstuffs, beverages (including wine and spirits) and tobacco goods (Figure 1.11). Although mining and quarrying only accounted for 13% of industrial output in 2019, its year-on-year growth (24%) is considerably higher than the manufacturing sector's (4%) (Statistical Committee of the Republic of Armenia, 2020[47]).

Figure 1.11. Industrial output by NACE subsection

2019, in million AMD

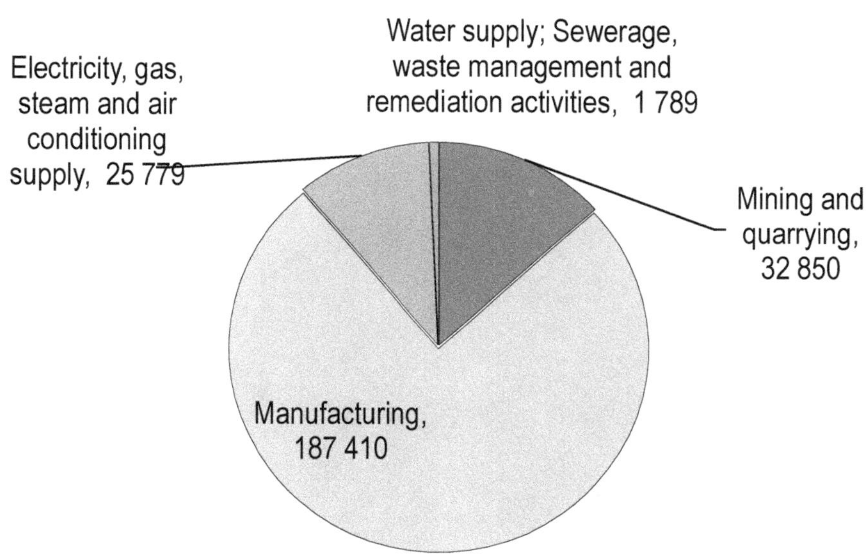

Note: AMD = Armenian dram; NACE = Nomenclature statistique des activités économiques dans la Communauté européenne [Statistical Classification of Economic Activities in the European Community]
Source: Statistical Committee of the Republic of Armenia (Statistical Committee of the Republic of Armenia, 2020[47]), "1.2. Производство (услуги) 1.2.1. Промышленность" [1.2. Production (services) 1.2.1. Industry], *Socioeconomic Situation of the Republic of Armenia, January-December 2019,* https://www.armstat.am/en/?nid=81&id=2236

The mining sector also plays an outsized role in environmental deterioration, particularly in the region of Eastern Europe, the Caucasus and Central Asia (EECCA) as highlighted by recent OECD analysis (OECD, 2019[50]). In Armenia, the enforcement of national legislation and international standards in the mining sector is weak, and the proposed expansion of existing mines and the establishment of new ones have triggered strong civil society responses calling for improved environmental stewardship (Bertelsmann Stiftung, 2020[46]). Poorly managed mines pollute both air and waterways during their operation and, following the closure of mining sites, they remain environmental liabilities that require careful planning and regulation to rehabilitate the land. Both the government and the mining industry are responsible for ensuring that mining companies minimise the impact of their activities on the environment (World Bank, 2016[49]). In 2017, Armenia joined the Extractive Industries Transparency Initiative. Most recently, alongside efforts to improve the overall investment climate, support to new mining development experience considerable public resistance.

In this context, the OECD's database of large-scale infrastructure projects tracks one major mining project in Armenia, the Amulsar Mine, owned by Lydian International, a multinational gold mining concern registered in the British Crown dependency of Jersey. The mining site will be the largest in Armenia, with an estimated 142 million tonnes of mineral resources, including 2.6 million tonnes of contained gold ounces (Benton, 2020[51]). Development of the mine halted in 2018 in response to environmental protests and blockades but is slated to restart shortly. Mining operations in Armenia have lacked sufficient oversight of tailing ponds, which has led to contamination of soil, groundwater and surface water with toxic chemicals (OECD, 2019[50]). Questions have been raised about irregularities in the studies conducted about the mine's impact on the environment, and the government has promoted legislation that would weaken Armenia's freedom of environmental information law, which environmentalists view as benefiting mining concerns over local communities (Mejlumyan, 2020[52]). Expansion of the mine without improvement of tailing pond management and transparent access to credible environmental information could translate into increased pollution and negative impacts on human health.

The database also tracks several smaller-scale water infrastructure projects, in irrigation and water supply and sanitation, but no industry projects (Figure 1.12).

Figure 1.12. Industry, mining and water infrastructure projects in Armenia, by sub-sector

Planned and under construction in million USD

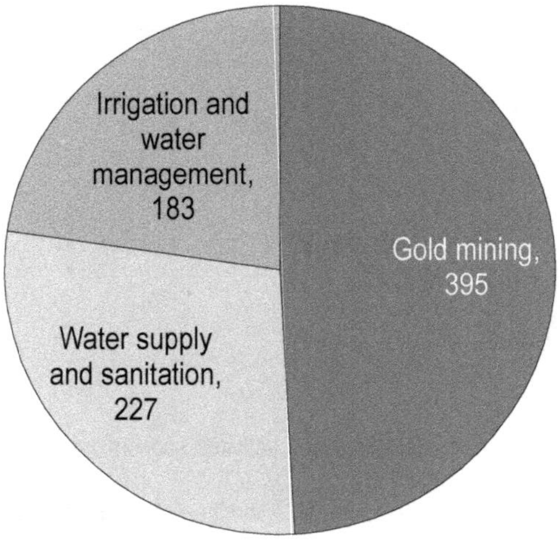

Source: OECD analysis based on accessed databases as of June 2020.

On certain metrics, Armenia's water supply and sanitation infrastructure performs better than in neighbouring countries. Only 3.1% of Armenia's population is exposed to unsafe drinking water, whereas in Azerbaijan and Georgia the figure is significantly higher (10.3% and 9.8% respectively) (World Economic Forum, 2019[25]). Armenia's sanitation services, however, are inadequate, particularly in rural areas where over half of the population rely on unimproved facilities. The continued use of such facilities has direct negative impacts on the environment and public health. Preliminary estimates indicate that the necessary investments in Armenian sanitation infrastructure are sizeable: approximately EUR 2.6 billion over 7-10 years (OECD, 2017[53]). In its Strategic Programme 2014-2025 Armenia plans to dedicate 0.4% of GDP to water supply and sanitation and 0.3% to irrigation. Its primary objective in water infrastructure development is to minimise territorial disparities in access to clean and safe water supply and sanitation (Government of Armenia, 2014[27]). Armenia's large-scale water investments in the OECD database align well with this objective as the vast majority focus on improving water supply and sanitation as well as irrigation in rural areas and secondary cities.

Strengths and weaknesses of existing institutional set-up for sustainable infrastructure planning

Strategic planning and links between long-term goals, infrastructure plans and environmental considerations

Armenia has developed an adequate legal framework for strategic planning, policy development and co-ordination, but it lacks comprehensive support from the centre of government (e.g. the Prime Minister's Office) in the form of guidelines and guidance. Since 2018, Armenia has implemented a number of reforms in its planning procedures, including a shift from annual towards multiyear government programmes. The updated system will enhance strategic planning, centralise the assessments of strategies' impacts and take better account of comments received during public consultations.

Armenia's strategic planning documents would however benefit from more clearly defined objectives and cost estimates as well as fewer, better focused outcome-level indicators as well as better alignment between them. The government does not publicly report on progress in the implementation of the strategic programme on a regular basis (OECD, 2019[54]). Vertical co-ordination between planning authorities and implementation-level bodies is often weak: In water management, for instance, the planning of irrigation, water supply, and hydropower investment programs, which are all managed at the central level, are insufficiently linked to existing river basin management plans (OECD, 2018[55]).

Before these reforms, Armenia adopted its *Strategic Programme for the Future Development of the Republic of Armenia 2014-2025*, but the country still lacks a clear, long-term development vision and lower-order strategic documents (e.g. short-term government programmes, sector-specific development programmes) do not align with the country's overarching strategic development programme. Armenia needs a clear long-term vision for its economic and infrastructural development accounting for the transition towards lower greenhouse gas emissions and improved resilience to the effects of climate change. Armenia should consider adopting a longer-term strategic vision to 2050 following the good practices of its peers (e.g. Kazakhstan 2050 Strategy, Ukraine's 2050 Low-Emission Development Strategy). A clear vision extending beyond relatively short business and political cycles will allow Armenia to begin planning now for the transformational changes necessary to meet long-term goals like those set out in the Paris Agreement. The government is in the process of developing a strategy to 2050, the Armenia Transformation Strategy 2050, which will and define 16 overarching goals mostly corresponding to the SDGs with dedicated targets, indicators, tasks and solutions.

Armenia has been a party to the UNECE Convention on Environmental Impact Assessment in a Transboundary Context since 1997 and the related Protocol on Strategic Environmental Assessment since 2011. Armenia's 2014 law 'On environmental impact assessment and expertise' covers both EIA and SEA requirements, but the SEA provisions in particular are not fully aligned with the Protocol. The EU-funded programme EaP GREEN and its successor programme EU4Environment, implemented jointly by the OECD, UNECE, UNEP, UNIDO and the World Bank, have been helping Armenia improve its environmental assessment processes.

Although Armenia has adopted a raft of climate-relevant environmental legislation, many of the country's existing climate-relevant laws and policies lack a focus on climate change. Responding to this problem, the government has opted to develop national action plans for all climate-sensitive sectors, and recent strategies (e.g. the 2017 National Strategy on Disaster Risk Management) have begun to integrate climate change concerns. Armenia is also in the process of updating its NDC with support from the EU-funded EU4Climate programme (EU4Climate, 2020[56]).

Institutional set-up and decision-making processes

Armenia restructured its government in 2019, reducing the number of ministries from 17 to 12. The Ministry of Economic Development and Investments combined with the Ministry of Agriculture to form the Ministry of Economy, while the Ministry of Energy Infrastructures and Natural Resources and the Ministry of Territorial Administration and Development merged to create the Ministry of Territorial Administration and Infrastructure. The latter also houses transport-related functions that the Ministry of High-Technology Industries formerly managed. The changes raised concerns from opposition politicians about overloaded mandates for the ministries and the risk of inefficient policy development and implementation (Avetisyan, 2019[57]). One advantage of the restructuring is the combination of energy-, transport- and territorial management-related functions into a single infrastructure ministry, which could encourage more integrated infrastructure planning across key, carbon-intensive sectors.

With the support of the Swiss Agency for Development and Co-operation, the International Bank for Reconstruction and Development, USAID and the Asian Development Bank, Armenia established the Armenian Territorial Development Fund to help implement the *Strategic Programme for the Future Development of the Republic of Armenia 2014-2025.* Its focus, similar to that of its predecessor the Armenian Social Investment Fund, is on rural development programmes.

Armenia performs better than its peers on several indicators of the quality of its policy development and co-ordination processes (Figure 1.13). The state's decision-making processes, for instance, are more transparent and open to public and inter-institutional consultation than in Georgia and Ukraine, but on most metrics there is still room for improvement to align with best practices.

Figure 1.13. Policy development and co-ordination indicators

Armenia (2019), Georgia (2018) and Ukraine (2018)

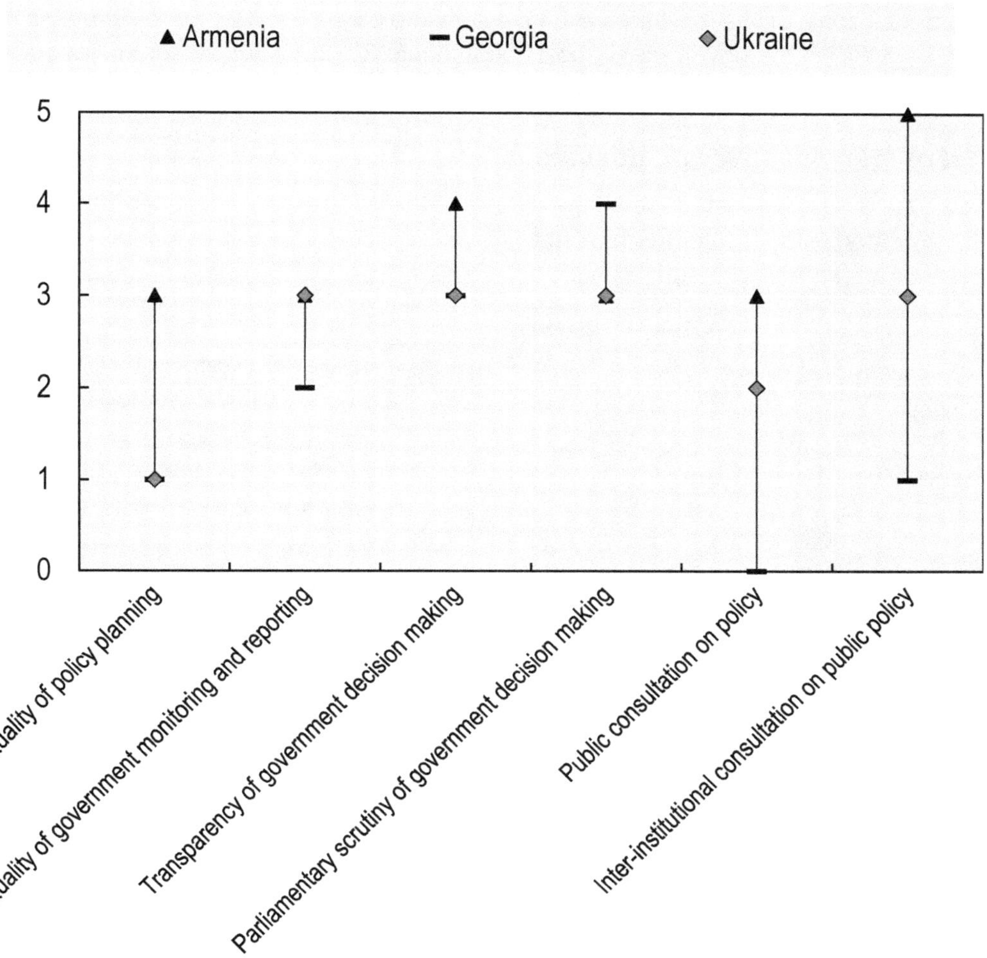

Source: OECD (2019[54]), *The Principles of Public Administration: Baseline Measurement Report: Armenia*, SIGMA, OECD Publishing, Paris, http://www.sigmaweb.org/publications/Baseline-Measurement-Armenia-2019.pdf; OECD (2018[58]), *The Principles of Public Administration: Baseline Measurement Report: Georgia*, SIGMA, OECD Publishing, Paris, http://www.sigmaweb.org/publications/Baseline-Measurement-Report-2018-Georgia.pdf; OECD (2018[59]), *The Principles of Public Administration: Baseline Measurement Report: Ukraine*, SIGMA, OECD Publishing, Paris, http://www.sigmaweb.org/publications/Baseline-Measurement-Report-2018-Ukraine.pdf

Armenia ranked 47th globally in 2020 on the World Bank Group's Ease of Doing Business Index, which measures protection of property rights and investors and the quality of business regulations, below its previous rankings (41st in 2019 and 38th in 2017) (World Bank, 2020[15]). Its neighbours, Georgia in particular, have outpaced Armenia's, but despite its drop in rankings, Armenia has made significant progress on improving investor protections and simplifying business operations. Armenia continues to make progress on rooting out corruption. In public procurement for infrastructure projects, Armenia should continue to introduce systematic centralised monitoring procedures and facilities to ensure impartial and technically adequate requirements and terms of reference (OECD, 2018[55]).

To analyse risks effectively and develop, screen and implement infrastructure projects, the institutional capacity of government bodies in infrastructure development need to be strengthened (World Bank, 2018[60]). In 2017 Armenia established the Centre for Strategic Initiatives, tasked with helping to shape the country's strategic development vision, attracting FDI, fostering public-private partnerships and bringing the developmental goals of line ministries and investors into alignment. Centre for Strategic Initiatives was, however, short-lived, as the government abolished it in late 2018. Its successor in strategic development planning and fostering investment is unclear.

List of relevant strategic documents

Table 1.4. Main strategic documents in force

	Status	Time Horizon	Sectoral Coverage	Main objectives
First Nationally Determined Contribution (NDC)	Submitted in 2017	2015-30	Economy-wide	• Conditional target: Limit total aggregate emissions between 2015 and 2050 to 633 million tCO_2e • Main sectors targeted for emission reduction: energy, transport, urban development, industrial processes, waste management, land use and forestry • Main adaptation tool: 'ecosystem approach' to climate change adaptation
Strategic Programme of Prospective Development (2014-2025)	Adopted in 2014	2014-25	Economy-wide	• Focus on job creation, development of human capital, improvement of the social protection system and modernisation of public administration and governance
Programme of the Government of the Republic of Armenia 2017-2022	Adopted in 2017	2017-22	Economy-wide	• Adopt new Law on Energy by 2020 • Develop long-term development programme for power system

Table 1.5. Other relevant documents

	Status	Time Horizon	Sectoral Coverage
National Strategy and Action Programme to Combat Desertification	Adopted in 2014	2015-20	Land use
Strategy and State Programme of Conservation and Use of Specially Protected Nature Areas	Adopted in 2014	2014-20	Ecosystems, biodiversity
Territorial Development Strategy	Adopted in 2016	2016-25	Economy-wide
Marz Development Strategies	Adopted in 2017	2017-25	Economy-wide
Territorial Development Operation Programme	Adopted in 2018	2018-20	Economy-wide
Household Waste Management Development Strategy	Adopted in 2017	2017-36	Waste

References

ADB (2019), *Technical Assistance: Transport and Trade Facilitation Strategy, 2020-2040 (Armenia)*, Asian Development Bank, Manila. [30]

Avetisyan, A. (2019), *Armenia cuts five ministries in government 'optimisation'*, OC Media, https://oc-media.org/armenia-cuts-five-ministries-in-government-optimisation/ (accessed on 12 August 2020). [57]

Benton, D. (2020), *Amulsar, the largest gold mine in Armenia, moves closer to production*, Mining Global, https://www.miningglobal.com/mining-sites/amulsar-largest-gold-mine-armenia-moves-closer-production (accessed on 12 August 2020). [51]

Bertelsmann Stiftung (2020), *BTI 2020 Country Report Armenia*, Bertelsmann Stiftung, https://www.ecoi.net/en/file/local/2029509/country_report_2020_ARM.pdf (accessed on 10 August 2020). [46]

EBRD (2019), *Armenia Diagnostic*, European Bank for Reconstruction and Development (EBRD), London, https://www.ebrd.com/publications/country-diagnostics. [34]

Energy Community (2019), *2019 Implementation Report*, https://www.energy-community.org/implementation/IR2019.html (accessed on 26 November 2019). [39]

Energy Community (2017), *Secretariat issues policy recommendations for Armenia*, Energy Community News, https://energy-community.org/news/Energy-Community-News/2017/07/31.html (accessed on 10 September 2020). [40]

EU4Climate (2020), *Armenia Country Profile*, https://eu4climate.eu/wp-content/uploads/countries/EU4Climate-ARMENIA.pdf (accessed on 26 February 2021). [56]

fDi Markets (2019), *fDi Markets: the in-depth crossborder investment monitor (database)*, https://www.fdimarkets.com/. [20]

Gabrielian, S. (2018), "Investment Firm Sues Armenia Over Railway Deal", *Radio Liberty*, https://www.azatutyun.am/a/29472531.html (accessed on 28 July 2020). [36]

GET Georgia (2016), *Trade between Georgia and Armenia: Business as usual?*, Georgian Economic Team Georgia (GET Georgia), Berlin, http://www.get-georgia.de (accessed on 16 July 2020). [11]

Gevorkyan, A. (2017), *Развитие и многообразие: «старая» и «новая» армянские диаспоры на современном этапе [Development and diversity: the contemporary state of the "old" and "new" Armenian diasporas*, Caucasus Institute, Yerevan, http://www.migrationpolicy.org/article/development-through-diversity-engaging-armenias-new-and-old-diaspora (accessed on 25 June 2020). [4]

Government of Armenia (2017), *Program of the Government of the Republic of Armenia 2017-2022*, Government of the Republic of Armenia, Yerevan, https://www.gov.am/files/docs/2219.pdf (accessed on 28 July 2020). [37]

Government of Armenia (2015), *Nationally Determined Contributions of the Republic of Armenia under the UN Framework Convention on Climate Change*, Ministry of Nature Protection of the Republic of Armenia, Yerevan. [22]

Government of Armenia (2014), *ՀԱՅԱՍՏԱՆԻ ՀԱՆՐԱՊԵՏՈՒԹՅԱՆ 2014-2025 ԹԹ. ՀԵՌԱՆԿԱՐԱՅԻՆ ԶԱՐԳԱՑՄԱՆ ՌԱԶՄԱՎԱՐԱԿԱՆ ԾՐԱԳԻՐ [Strategic Programme for the Future Development of the Republic of Armenia 2014-2025]*, Government of the Republic of Armenia, Yerevan, https://www.gov.am/files/docs/1322.pdf (accessed on 28 July 2020). [27]

Harutyunyan, S. (2019), *Iran Looks To Boost Gas Supplies To Armenia*, Radio Liberty, https://www.azatutyun.am/a/30045968.html (accessed on 10 August 2020). [43]

IAEA (2018), *IAEA Country Nuclear Power Profiles: Armenia, 2018 Edition*, International Atomic Energy Agency, Vienna, https://www-pub.iaea.org/MTCD/Publications/PDF/cnpp2018/countryprofiles/Armenia/Armenia.htm (accessed on 7 August 2020). [42]

IEA (2021), *Electricity Information 2020*, https://www.iea.org/data-and-statistics (accessed on 10 August 2020). [44]

IEA (2019), *The Future of Rail: Opportunities for energy and the environment*, International Energy Agency, Paris, https://dx.doi.org/10.1787/9789264312821-en. [32]

IEA (2019), *World Energy Balances 2019*, International Energy Agency, Paris, https://doi.org/10.1787/3a876031-en (accessed on 10 August 2020). [41]

IEA (2016), *Scaling Up Renewable Energy Program for Armenia (SREP Armenia)*, IEA/IRENA Renewables Policies Database, https://www.iea.org/policies/5674-scaling-up-renewable-energy-program-for-armenia-srep-armenia?country=Armenia&qs=armenia (accessed on 30 July 2020). [45]

IMF (2020), *IMF Executive Board Completes Third Review Under the Stand-By Arrangement for the Republic of Armenia and Approves US$36.9 Million Disbursement*, https://www.imf.org/en/News/Articles/2020/12/11/pr20371-armenia-imf-execboard-completes-3rd-review-under-sba-and-approves-us-36-9m-disbursement (accessed on 19 February 2021). [9]

IMF (2020), *World Economic Outlook: October 2020*, https://www.imf.org/external/datamapper/GGXCNL_NGDP@WEO/OEMDC/ADVEC/WEOWORLD. [2]

IMF (2019), *2019 Article IV Consultation and Request for a Stand-by Arrangement: Press Releases; Staff Report; and Statement by the Executive Director for the Republic of Armenia*, International Monetary Fund, Washington, D.C. [21]

IMF (2019), *IMF Executive Board Approves US$248.2 Million Stand-By Arrangement for Armenia*, https://www.imf.org/en/News/Articles/2019/05/17/pr19173-armenia-imf-executive-board-approves-stand-by-arrangement (accessed on 19 February 2021). [8]

ITF (2020), *Transport infrastructure investment and maintenance spending*, ITF Statistics: Transport: Transport Infrastructure, https://stats.oecd.org/Index.aspx?DataSetCode=ITF_INV-MTN_DATA (accessed on 26 February 2021). [28]

ITF (2019), *Transport Performance Indicators*, https://www.oecd-ilibrary.org/transport/data/itf-transport-statistics/transport-performance-indicators_2122fa17-en. [31]

Mejlumyan, A. (2020), “Armenia seeks to weaken environmental information law”, *Eurasianet*, https://eurasianet.org/armenia-seeks-to-weaken-environmental-information-law (accessed on 19 February 2021). [52]

Mejlumyan, A. (2020), “Armenia's new anti-corruption law draws skepticism”, *Eurasianet*, https://eurasianet.org/armenias-new-anti-corruption-law-draws-skepticism (accessed on 19 February 2021). [13]

Ministry of Environment of the Republic of Armenia (2020), *Armenia's Fourth National Communication on Climate Change under the United Nations Framework Convention on Climate Change*, Ministry of Environment of the Republic of Armenia, Yerevan, https://unfccc.int/sites/default/files/resource/NC4_Armenia_.pdf (accessed on 23 July 2020). [23]

Observatory of Economic Complexity (2020), *Armenia: Exports, Imports, and Trade Partners*, https://oec.world/en/profile/country/arm (accessed on 16 July 2020). [12]

OECD (2021), *COVID-19 and greening the economies of Eastern Europe, the Caucasus and Central Asia*, http://www.oecd.org/coronavirus/policy-responses/covid-19-and-greening-the-economies-of-eastern-europe-the-caucasus-and-central-asia-40f4d34f/ (accessed on 10 March 2021). [7]

OECD (2020), *COVID-19 crisis response in Eastern Partner countries*, OECD, Paris, https://www.oecd.org/coronavirus/policy-responses/covid-19-crisis-response-in-eu-eastern-partner-countries-7759afa3/ (accessed on 9 September 2020). [6]

OECD (2020), *Investment Promotion in Eurasia: A Mapping of Investment Promotion Agencies*, OECD Publishing, Paris, http://www.oecd.org/eurasia/competitiveness-programme/Investment-Promotion-in-Eurasia-A-Mapping-of-Investment-Promotion-Agencies-ENG.pdf (accessed on 11 February 2021). [19]

OECD (2020), *Trade Facilitation Index*, https://www.oecd.org/trade/topics/trade-facilitation/ (accessed on 9 September 2020). [29]

OECD (2019), *Baseline Measurement Report: The Principles of Public Administration: Armenia*, OECD Publishing, Paris, http://www.sigmaweb.org/publications/Baseline-Measurement-Armenia-2019.pdf (accessed on 12 August 2020). [54]

OECD (2019), *Mining and Green Growth in the EECCA Region*, OECD Green Growth Studies, OECD Publishing, Paris, https://dx.doi.org/10.1787/1926a45a-en. [50]

OECD (2018), *Anti-corruption reforms in Armenia: 4th round of monitoring of the Istanbul Anti-Corruption Action Plan*, OECD Publishing, Paris, https://www.oecd.org/corruption/acn/OECD-ACN-Armenia-4th-Round-Monitoring-Report-July-2018-ENG.pdf (accessed on 12 August 2020). [55]

OECD (2018), *Inventory of Energy Subsidies in the EU's Eastern Partnership Countries*, Green Finance and Investment, OECD Publishing, Paris, https://dx.doi.org/10.1787/9789264284319-en. [33]

OECD (2018), *The Principles of Public Administration Policy Development and Co-ordination: Baseline Measurement Report: Georgia*, OECD Publishing, Paris, http://www.sigmaweb.org/publications/Baseline-Measurement-Report-2018-Georgia.pdf (accessed on 13 August 2020). [58]

OECD (2018), *The Principles of Public Administration: Baseline Measurement Report: Ukraine*, OECD Publishing, Paris, http://www.sigmaweb.org/publications/Baseline-Measurement-Report-2018-Ukraine.pdf (accessed on 13 August 2020). [59]

OECD (2017), *Reforming Sanitation in Armenia: Towards a National Strategy*, OECD Studies on Water, OECD Publishing, Paris, https://dx.doi.org/10.1787/9789264268982-en. [53]

Office of the President of the Republic of Armenia and UNCTAD (2020), *Armenia Investment Promotion Strategy in Times of the Global Crisis and Beyond*, Office of the President of the Republic of Armenia & United Nations Conference for Trade and Development. [18]

Roser, M. et al. (2020), *Coronavirus Pandemic (COVID-19)*, OurWorldInData.Org, https://ourworldindata.org/coronavirus (accessed on 9 September 2020). [5]

Schneider, M. et al. (2018), *The World Nuclear Industry Status Report 2018*, https://www.worldnuclearreport.org/The-World-Nuclear-Industry-Status-Report-2018-HTML.html (accessed on 19 February 2021). [48]

State Commission for the Protection of Economic Competition of the Republic of Armenia (2018), *Response of RA Competition Authority to Armenian Revolutionary Federation - Dashnaktsutyun: there are no abuses in fuel market*, http://www.competition.am/index.php?page=news_cases&menu=&newsID=1489&lng=2 (accessed on 19 February 2021). [61]

Statistical Committee of the Republic of Armenia (2020), *1.2. Производство (услуги): 1.2.1. Промышленность [1.2. Production (services): 1.2.1. Industry]*, https://www.armstat.am/file/article/sv_06_20r_121.pdf (accessed on 10 August 2020). [47]

Statistical Committee of the Republic of Armenia (2020), *General purpose motor roads by indicators and years*, 4. Transport and tourism: 4.1 Transport, https://armstatbank.am/pxweb/en/ArmStatBank/ArmStatBank__4%20Transport%20and%20tourism__41%20Transport/TT-tr-15-2019.px/table/tableViewLayout2/?rxid=0b6965b2-7577-4b02-b9f3-be0a75ad66e2 (accessed on 26 February 2021). [35]

Transparency International (2019), *CPI 2019: Eastern Europe & Central Asia*, https://www.transparency.org/en/news/cpi-2019-eastern-europe-central-asia (accessed on 20 July 2020). [17]

UNCTAD (2019), *Investment Policy Review: Armenia*, United Nations Conference on Trade and Development, Geneva, https://unctad.org/en/PublicationsLibrary/diaepcb2019d3_en.pdf. [10]

US Department of State (2019), *2019 Investment Climate Statements: Armenia*, https://www.state.gov/reports/2019-investment-climate-statements/armenia/ (accessed on 20 July 2020). [16]

World Bank (2021), *World Development Indicators (database)*, https://datacatalog.worldbank.org/dataset/world-development-indicators. [1]

World Bank (2020), *Doing Business 2020*, World Bank Group, Washington, DC, http://dx.doi.org/10.1596/978-1-4648-1440-2. [15]

World Bank (2019), *Country Score Card: Logistics Performance Index*, https://lpi.worldbank.org/international/scorecard/ (accessed on 27 July 2020). [24]

World Bank (2018), *Georgia from Reformer to Performer*, World Bank, Washington DC, http://documents.worldbank.org/curated/en/496731525097717444/pdf/GEO-SCD-04-24-04272018.pdf. [60]

World Bank (2017), *Doing Business 2017: Equal Opportunity for All Doing Business*, World Bank, Washington, D.C., http://dx.doi.org/10.1596/978-1-4648-0948-4. [14]

World Bank (2017), *Future Armenia: Systematic Country Diagnostic*, https://elibrary.worldbank.org/doi/abs/10.1596/29791 (accessed on 22 July 2020). [3]

World Bank (2017), *Policy Note: Infrastructure Finance in Armenia*, World Bank Group, Washington, D.C. [26]

World Bank (2016), *Armenia: Strategic Mineral Sector Sustainability Assessment*, World Bank. [49]

World Bank (n.d.), *Enterprise Surveys: Infrastructure*, https://www.enterprisesurveys.org/en/data/exploretopics/infrastructure (accessed on 29 July 2020). [38]

World Economic Forum (2019), *The Global Competitiveness Report 2019*, World Economic Forum, Geneva, http://www3.weforum.org/docs/WEF_TheGlobalCompetitivenessReport2019.pdf (accessed on 23 July 2020). [25]

Notes

[1] The EU Eastern Partnership (EaP) is a joint initiative for strengthening the relationships between the European Union, its member states and six countries (hereafter the EaP countries): Armenia, Azerbaijan, Belarus, Georgia, Moldova and Ukraine.

[2] Confirmed case and death figures are underestimates of actual case and death numbers. Methodology and testing rates vary widely, and international comparisons are necessarily flawed.

[3] Estimates of the size of the Armenian diaspora in these countries are as follows: Russia, 1.2-2 million; France, 400-600 thousand (Gevorkyan, 2017[4]); the United States, 0.5-2 million; Lebanon, 4% of the population – or approximately 270 thousand. Cyprus officially recognises Armenian as a minority language.

[4] In this instance, 'electricity poor' and 'energy poor' households are those that spend more than 10% of their overall budget on electricity or energy.

[5] Diesel was exempt from VAT until 2018, when its excise tax was lowered from AMD 35 thousand per tonne to AMD 13 thousand per tonne (State Commission for the Protection of Economic Competition of the Republic of Armenia, 2018[61]).

[6] January to June 2020.

2. Azerbaijan's sustainable infrastructure investments

This chapter describes sustainable infrastructure planning in Azerbaijan and presents current trends in investment in large-scale infrastructure projects. It compares Azerbaijan's infrastructure plans in the energy, transport, industry and water sectors against its international commitments under the Paris Agreement on climate change and the Sustainable Development Goals (SDGs). The chapter also explores Azerbaijan's strategic documents for long-term economic development, sectoral development and the environment, including those related to climate change mitigation and adaptation. It identifies misalignments between stated goals and observed investment flows and provides recommendations to improve strategic planning for sustainable infrastructure.

State of play: economy, investment and climate change in Azerbaijan

Economy and trade

Table 2.1. Key indicators on Azerbaijan's economy

Population (2019)	10 023 318
Urbanisation rate (2019)	56.0%
Annual population growth (2019)	0.8%
Surface area	86 600 km^2
GDP (USD, current price, 2019)	48 048 million
GDP per capita (USD, current price, 2019)	4 794
Real GDP growth (year-on-year change, 2019, 2020)	2.2%, -4%
Inflation (average consumer price, y-o-y change, 2019)	2.6%
Exports of goods and services (% of GDP, 2019)	49.2%
Imports of goods and services (% of GDP, 2019)	36.9%
FDI, net inflows (% of GDP, 2019)	3.1%
General government net lending/borrowing (% of GDP, 2019, 2020)	8.1%, -6.3%
Unemployment (% of total labour force, 2020)	6.0%
Remittances (% of GDP, 2019)	2.7%
Transparency, accountability and corruption in the public sector rating (1= most corrupt, 6 = least corrupt, 2010)	2.5

Source: World Bank (2021[1]), *World Development Indicators (database)*, World Bank, https://datacatalog.worldbank.org/dataset/world-development-indicators; IMF (2020[2]), *World Economic Outlook: October 2020*, International Monetary Fund https://www.imf.org/external/datamapper/GGXCNL_NGDP@WEO/OEMDC/ADVEC/WEOWORLD

Economy and demographics

Azerbaijan is an upper-middle income country in the Caucasus. Its population, the largest in the south Caucasus, has grown steadily at annual rates of about 0.8%. Unlike in neighbouring Armenia and Georgia, Azerbaijan's population did not decline following the breakup of the Soviet Union, nor has the country ever experienced non-positive annual population growth rates.

The economy of Azerbaijan, on the other hand, followed a similar trajectory to other former Soviet Union countries. It shrank to less than half of its pre-independence levels, from USD 8.9 billion (in current USD) in 1990 to USD 3.1 billion in 1995, and then slowly recovered throughout the late 1990s and early 2000s. Rapid economic growth characterised the period from 2005 to 2014, followed by a major contraction ending in 2016 from which the economy has not fully recovered. In 2019 the country's GDP stood at USD 48 billion, more than five times larger than before independence.

Azerbaijan's economy, unlike other countries in the present study, depends more heavily on industry and construction (which accounted for 48.7% of GDP in 2019) than on services (37.4%) and agriculture (5.7%). The share of agriculture in Azerbaijan's economy is the lowest among EU Eastern Partnership (EaP)[1] countries (World Bank, 2021[1]).

Azerbaijan's territory consists of two unconnected areas separated by Armenia. Larger portion of Azerbaijan's territory is the only part of the southern Caucasus with access to the Caspian Sea, while the Nakhchivan Autonomous Republic, the country's exclave, is landlocked between Armenia, Iran and Turkey. Despite the ongoing closure of border crossings between Armenia and Azerbaijan, a 48-kilometre corridor guarantees safe transport links between the exclave and the rest of Azerbaijan. The corridor, which was established by a 2020 ceasefire agreement following renewed armed conflicts between Armenia and

Azerbaijan (see below), could improve connectivity between Azerbaijan's territories and facilitate trade between Azerbaijan and Turkey.

Azerbaijan has no diplomatic relations with Armenia due to the ongoing conflict over the Nagorno-Karabakh region of western Azerbaijan. The region and surrounding areas bordering Armenia declared independence in 1991 as the Republic of Artsakh (or the Nagorno-Karabakh Republic) during the First Nagorno-Karabakh War (1988-1994). To date, no UN member state has recognised the breakaway region's independence. In 1994 Armenia, Azerbaijan and representatives from the breakaway region signed a ceasefire agreement resulting in an uneasy period of relative peace characterised by intermittent border clashes. The 2020 Nagorno-Karabakh war re-escalated the conflict, and the new ceasefire agreement led to significant transfers of territorial control from the breakaway region to Azerbaijan.

As of February 2021, Azerbaijan has the lowest number of COVID-19 cases per capita among EaP countries. Azerbaijan has diagnosed 22.8 cases per thousand inhabitants compared to 56.6 in Armenia, 27 in Belarus, 65.4 in Georgia, 40.5 in Moldova and 29.3 in Ukraine. Azerbaijan's death rate (311 deaths per million inhabitants) is the second lowest in the region after Belarus (187), significantly lower than in Armenia (1 049), Georgia (817), Moldova (937) and Ukraine (562) (Roser et al., 2021[3]).[2] Azerbaijan's response to the outbreak included reinforced border restrictions, school closures and country-wide and localised lockdowns.

In 2020, as a result of the COVID-19 pandemic and decreased demand for Azerbaijan's primary export, crude oil, Azerbaijan's GDP fell by 4%. The economy is projected to experience modest growth of about 2% starting in 2021. Azerbaijan has announced a raft of economic stimulus measures to support the recovery, including a revised strategy for private sector development targeting micro, small and medium enterprises (OECD, 2021[4]).

Trade

Azerbaijan is an observer, not a member, of the World Trade Organisation. Unlike neighbouring Armenia, it is not a member of the Eurasian Economic Union. Azerbaijan is a target country of the European Union's European Neighbourhood Policy under the EaP initiative. This aim to deepen EU-Azerbaijan relations through actions focusing on economic development, governance, connectivity and people-to-people contact. Its trade relations with the EU have been governed by a Partnership and Cooperation Agreement since 1999, and negotiations began in 2017 to establish a more comprehensive trade agreement (European Commission, 2019[5]), Unlike Armenia, Georgia and Turkey, Azerbaijan has no formal relationship with the European Union's Energy Community.

The oil and gas industry produces all but a small fraction of Azerbaijan's exports (see Figure 2.1(c), where they are classified as 'mineral products'). The country's most important export by far is crude petroleum (80% of exports), followed by petroleum gas (7.6%) and refined petroleum (2.6%). Other than limited exports of metal, the share of other exports is very small. While Azerbaijan exports mostly raw hydrocarbon resources, it imports primarily finished manufactured goods and consumer goods. Its main imports are machinery (33%) and vehicles (9%, mostly cars which account for 3.7% of imports) as well as precious metals (12%), metals (11%), chemical products (7%) and foodstuffs (6%) (see Figure 2.1(d)).

Azerbaijan's main export market is the European Union (53% of exports), especially Italy (30%), the Czech Republic (5%), Germany (4%) and Portugal (3%) (see Figure 2.1(a)). Major non-EU export destinations include Turkey (9%) – with which Azerbaijan has close historical, cultural and linguistic ties, and Israel (7%). Azerbaijan's most important export destinations within the former Soviet Union are Russia (3%), its neighbour Georgia (2.5%) and Ukraine (1.8%). The European Union as a bloc is Azerbaijan's most important source of imports (17.4%), with Germany (5.1%), Italy (2.9%) and the Netherlands (1.7%) as the sources of most of Azerbaijan's EU imports. Azerbaijan's neighbours, the Russian Federation (16%) and Turkey (13%), are the most important countries for Azerbaijan's imports, followed by the United Kingdom (11%) and the People's Republic of China (5.7%) (see Figure 2.1(b)). Other than the Russian Federation,

Georgia (4%), Belarus (2%) and Kazakhstan (1.5%) are the former Soviet countries that export the most to Azerbaijan. Azerbaijan's *Strategic Road Map on the Development of Logistics Outcomes* set goals for increasing trade volumes by 2020 with specific regions and countries compared to 2015 (see section 2.3 on Azerbaijan's key strategic documents). Azerbaijan aimed to increase trade via the Black Sea with Central Asia by 40% and with Iran by 25%. It also aims to increase transit volumes for various routes: between Central Asia and Europe by 25%, between China and Europe by 3% and between the Russian Federation and Iran by 40% (President of Azerbaijan, 2016[6]).

Figure 2.1. Trade of Azerbaijan

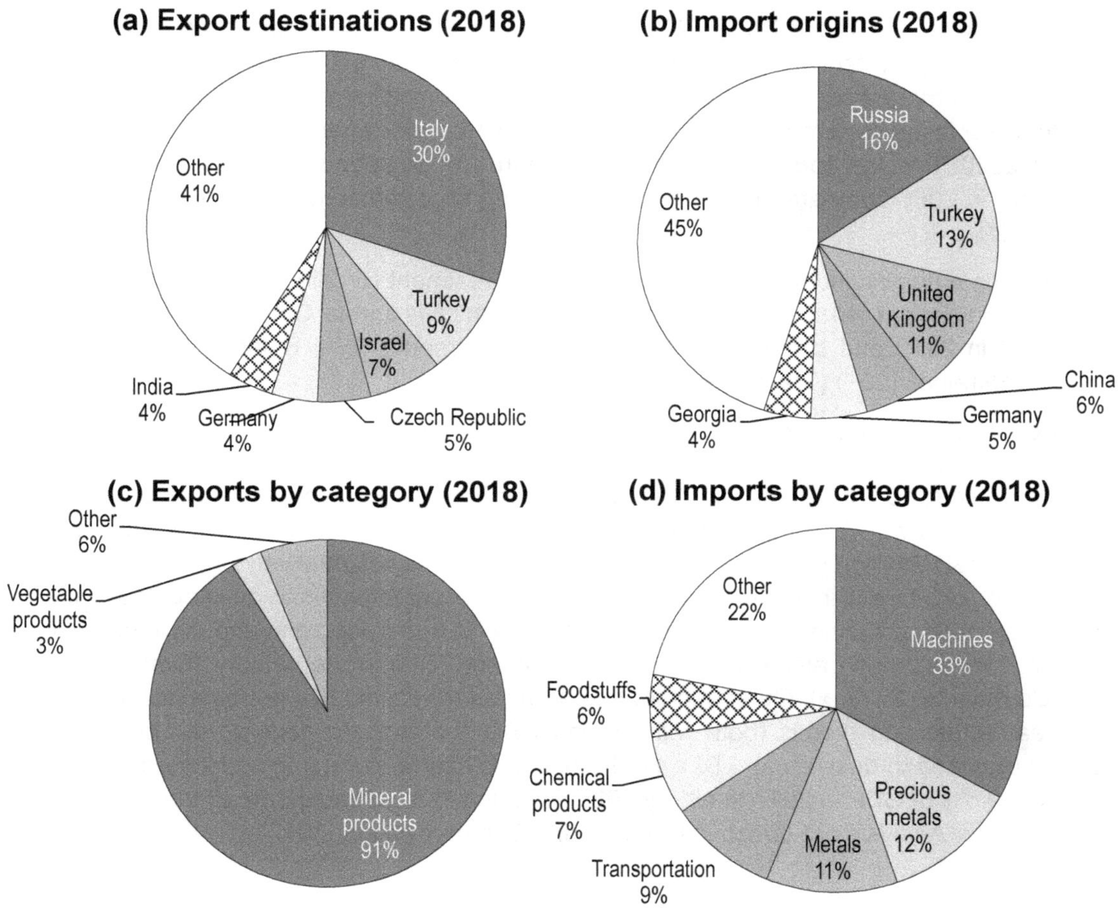

Source: Observatory of Economic Complexity (2020[7]), *Azerbaijan: Exports, Imports and Trade Partners*, Observatory of Economic Complexity, https://oec.world/en/profile/country/aze

Investment climate

In recent years, Azerbaijan has taken significant reforms to improve its investment climate by strengthening the institutional, regulatory and operational environment for companies to operate in the country. Such reforms and programmes are part of government's efforts to develop industry and improve the image of the country worldwide (OECD, 2019[8]).

A recent OECD survey in Azerbaijan also demonstrates positive business perceptions of the reforms in Azerbaijan, with over 50% of the businesses considering all reforms "good" or "very good" (OECD, 2019[8]). The reforms that have been well-received by businesses include the suspension of business inspections (with 86% of businesses responding good or very good), as well as the online licensing (82%), and visa services (77%). Other initiatives such as the simplification of the tax system and the simplification of the customs system have also been perceived as positive by businesses in Azerbaijan.

Yet, despite such reforms in improving the investment climate, Azerbaijan still needs to improve its ability to foster skills development, promote competition among firms and reduce uncertainty. Despite the improved regulatory framework, the current business environment still deters entry of new firms and the expansion of existing businesses (EBRD, 2019[9]). According to some companies surveyed by the OECD, there is volatility in the sectors targeted by the government for growth, which creates uncertainty for businesses and hampers the effectiveness of the initiatives (OECD, 2019[8]). Companies would welcome greater consistency and long-term commitment across the reform programme.

Azerbaijan ranks 34th in the World Bank's 2020 Ease of Doing Business report, second among its EaP peers after Georgia (6th). Protections for minority investors are the weakest point of Azerbaijan's regulatory system, with the country ranking 105th out of 190 countries. Azerbaijan's progress on other indicators has been consistent. For instance, it reduced the time required to open a business (105 days in 2004 compared to 3.5 days in 2020) and the complexity of the tax system (37 payments requiring over 750 hours on average per year in 2006 compared to 9 payments requiring approximately 160 hours per year in 2020) (World Bank, 2020[10]).

Corruption remains a significant problem for Azerbaijan's investment climate. Transparency International ranked Azerbaijan 129th out of 180 countries in the 2020 edition of its annual Corruption Perceptions Index, down from 126th in 2019 and below other EaP countries (Armenia, 77th; Belarus, 66th; Georgia, 44th; Moldova, 120th; Ukraine, 126th) (Transparency International, 2020[11]).

International data on announced greenfield FDI projects offer insights on cross-border investment by economic activity in Azerbaijan. Between 2003 and 2017, the economy attracted over USD 32.7 billion of greenfield FDI projects, 50% of which was directed towards the coal, oil and natural gas sectors (or USD 16.3 billion) (see Figure 2.2). Infrastructure-related investments, particularly in the transport sector attracted close to USD 5 billion (or 15% of total greenfield FDI), which is relatively high compared to other countries in the region. This is in line with the government's current priorities to develop new trade routes and transport corridors, including five logistics centres, the Alat free trade zone and the modernisation of the East-West Railway, which are expected to further attract FDI into the country (German-Azerbaijan Chamber of Commerce, 2018[12]). Other sectors that attracted greenfield FDI are financial services (USD 2.8 billion), real estate and metals (both with around USD 1 billion). In general, the government has acknowledged the need to diversify its FDI away from coal, oil and natural gas and increase the share of non-oil FDI from 2.6% of GDP in 2017 to 4% by 2025 as stated in the Strategic Road Map on the National Economy (Center for Analysis of Economic Reforms and Communication, 2017[13]).

Figure 2.2. Greenfield FDI in Azerbaijan by economic activity, 2003-2017

Cumulated greenfield FDI capital between January 2003 and September 2017 in USD million

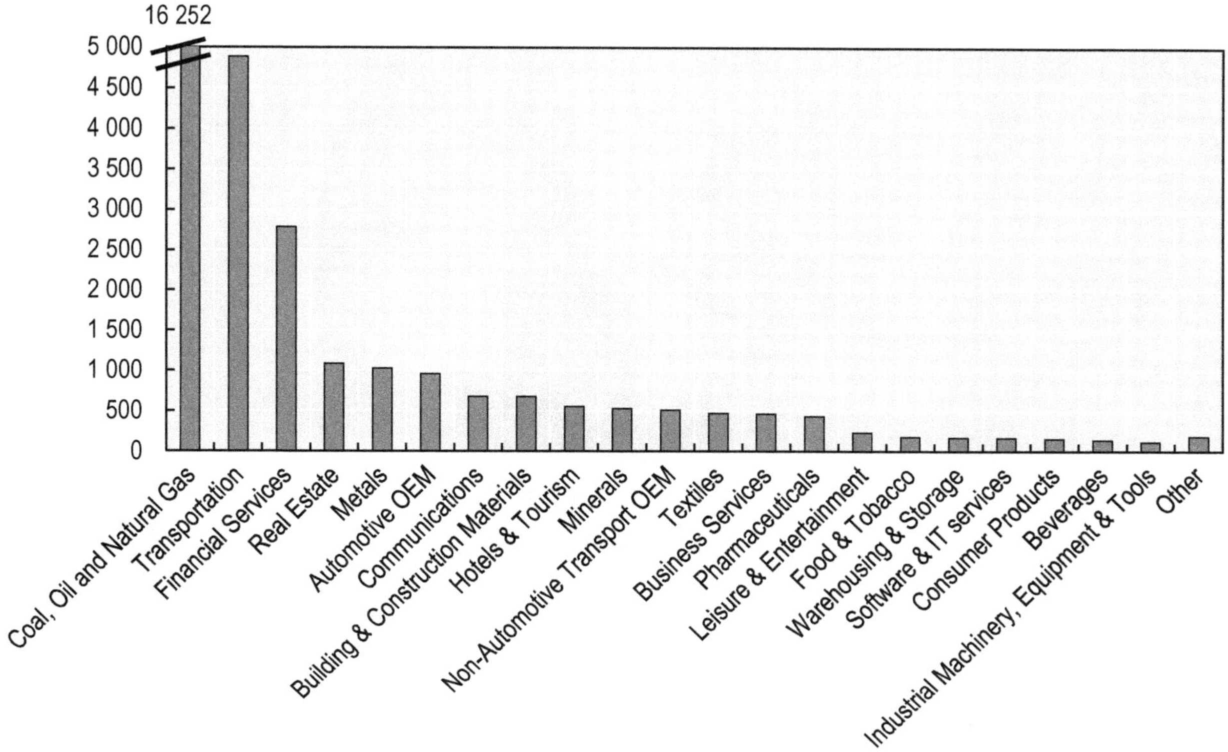

Source: OECD based on fDi Markets (2019[14]), fDi Markets: the in-depth crossborder investment monitor (database), fDi Markets, https://www.fdimarkets.com/

The United Kingdom is the most important source of foreign direct investment (FDI) in Azerbaijan, providing 27% of foreign investment in fixed capital between 2016 and 2019 (see Figure 2.3). The United Kingdom's interest in Azerbaijan centres on the country's oil and gas industry, in which BP actively participates. Azerbaijan's neighbour Turkey and international organisations (i.e. multilateral development banks) contribute a further 13% of FDI each. Azerbaijan's other important investors are geographically diverse: Malaysia (9%), Switzerland (6%), Iran (6%), Russia (6%), Japan (6%) and the United States of America (5%). Other than Russia, the former Soviet Union countries are not large investors.

Figure 2.3. Type title hereForeign capital directed to fixed capital in Azerbaijan by foreign countries, 2016-2019

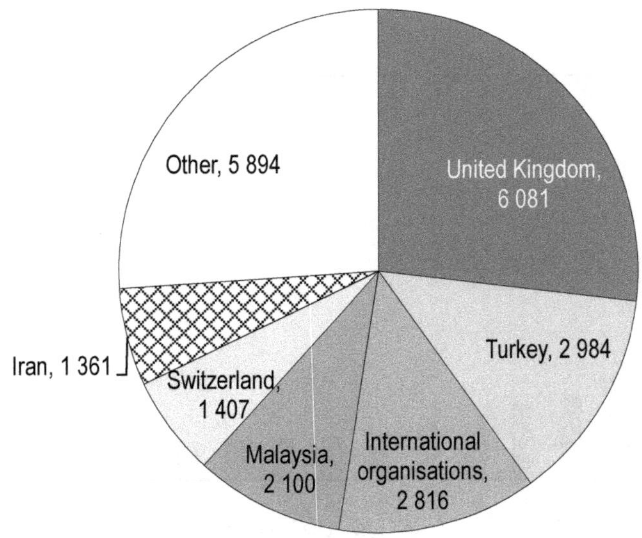

Source: State Statistical Committee of the Republic of Azerbaijan (2020[15]), "Fixed investments directed to fixed capital by foreign countries", https://www.stat.gov.az/source/construction/

Azerbaijan's public debt is considered to be at sustainable levels. However, given the country's reliance on oil revenue, shocks to demand and price fluctuations like those experienced in 2020 are set to worsen the country's fiscal and external positions (IMF, 2019[16]).

Climate change

Given the country's relatively small size, its total emissions amount to only 0.1% of total global greenhouse gas (GHG) emissions. Azerbaijan's GHG emissions and GDP both halved in the 1990s, following the breakup of the Soviet Union. Its GHG emissions fell from 78 $MtCO_2e$ in 1990 to 38 $MtCO_2e$ in 1997, while its GDP declined (see Figure 2.4). Over the past two decades, Azerbaijan's emissions have slowly increased but, as of 2012, they have not yet surpassed their 1990 levels. Azerbaijan's economy, on the other hand, has expanded rapidly since the late 1990s; by 2017, it was 2.5 larger than before independence. Consequently, the GHG intensity of Azerbaijan's economy decreased by more than half, from 3.5 $kgCO_2e$ per USD (in constant 2010 dollars) in 1990 to 1 $kgCO_2e$ per USD of GDP by 2012. While this figure is the lowest GHG intensity of the countries analysed in the present study, it is significantly higher than the OECD average (0.35 $kgCO_2e$ per USD in 2012) (World Bank, 2021[1]).

Azerbaijan's per capita emissions have also dropped from 10.9 tCO_2e in 1990 to 6.1 tCO_2e. While this figure is less than a third of other hydrocarbon-dependent economies like Kazakhstan and the Russian Federation and less than half the OECD average of 12.9 tCO_2 per capita, it is considerably higher than its neighbour Georgia's per capita emissions of 3.8 tCO_2e (World Bank, 2021[1]).

Figure 2.4. GHG emissions and GDP of Azerbaijan, 1990-2019

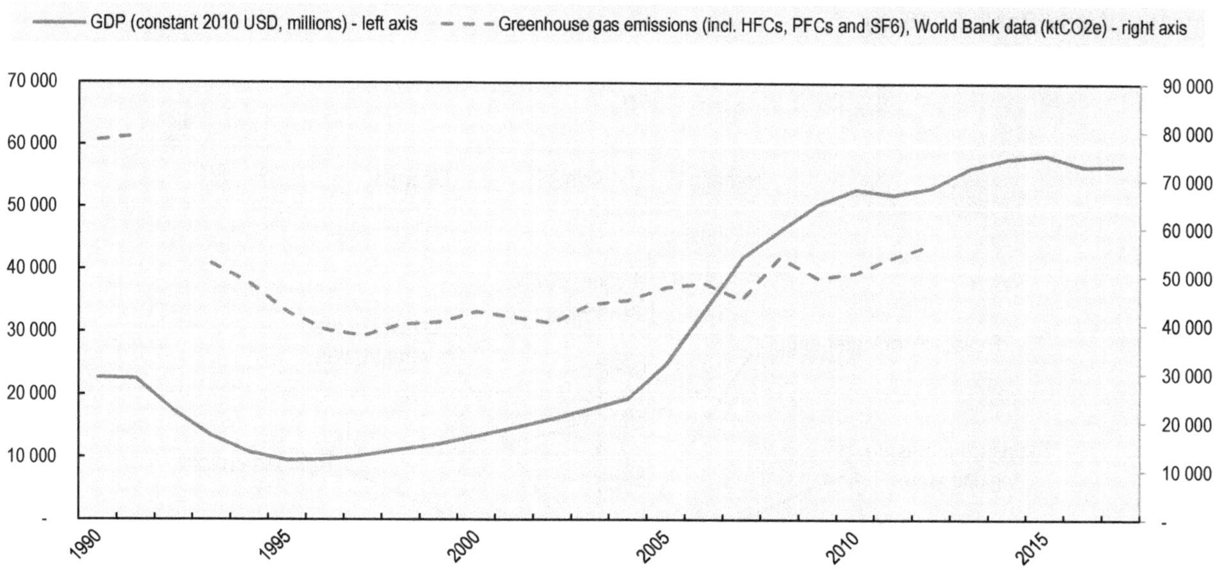

Source: World Bank (2021[1]), *World Development Indicators (database)*, World Bank, https://data.worldbank.org/

Energy (including fuel combustion for transport) accounts for the majority of Azerbaijan's greenhouse gas emissions, at 75.3% in 2012. While this is a sizeable share, it is smaller than in 1990 when energy accounted for 87.2% of total emissions. Azerbaijan's energy-related emissions were 38.5% lower than in 1990, while all other sources have gradually increased emissions since independence. Agriculture accounted for 13.6% of emissions in 2012, while industrial processes made up 5.8% and waste 4.8% (Ministry of Ecology and Natural Resources Republic of Azerbaijan, 2015[17]).

Current trends of decreasing precipitation and rising temperatures linked to climate change are already affecting Azerbaijan's agriculture industry, which employs 38% of the population Pastures and vital crops, such as wheat, cotton and grapes, are particularly vulnerable to these changes due to overgrazing. The country already faces a shortage of water to meet domestic needs, caused in part due to a disproportionate draw on water from large-scale agricultural enterprises, and projected decreases in water resources (rivers, lakes, reservoirs and glaciers) are set to deepen the deficit. The number of days with maximum temperatures exceeding 35 degrees Celsius in Azerbaijan has increased rapidly, from 3 in the period 1961-1990 to 16 in the 2000s. The capital Baku in 2010 registered 44 days of temperatures over 35 degrees Celsius resulting in increased sunstroke incidence and hospitalisation rates. Climate impacts on economic activity and human wellbeing are projected to worsen without adequate adaptation measures (Ministry of Ecology and Natural Resources Republic of Azerbaijan, 2015[17]).

Azerbaijan's infrastructure needs and current plans

Azerbaijan's infrastructure, especially its transportation infrastructure, is relatively high quality in comparison to other EaP countries and upper-middle income countries as a whole. Azerbaijan's road network as well as air and rail transport services are of higher quality than in neighbouring countries, but its power and water infrastructure systems underperform on certain metrics (see Figure 2.5). However, Azerbaijan's capital stock per capita is one of the lowest in the former Soviet Union, and much scope remains for increased infrastructure investment, particularly in modernising rail and improving irrigation as well as water supply and sanitation. Infrastructure service delivery varies considerably by region, with rural areas neglected in favour of the capital city region (World Bank, 2015[18]). Despite its relatively good infrastructure, Azerbaijan ranks poorly in the World Bank's Logistics Performance Index (123rd out of 167 countries) due primarily to its 'soft' trade infrastructure, such as the competence and quality of its logistics services (World Bank, 2018[19]).

Figure 2.5. Quality of infrastructure in Azerbaijan

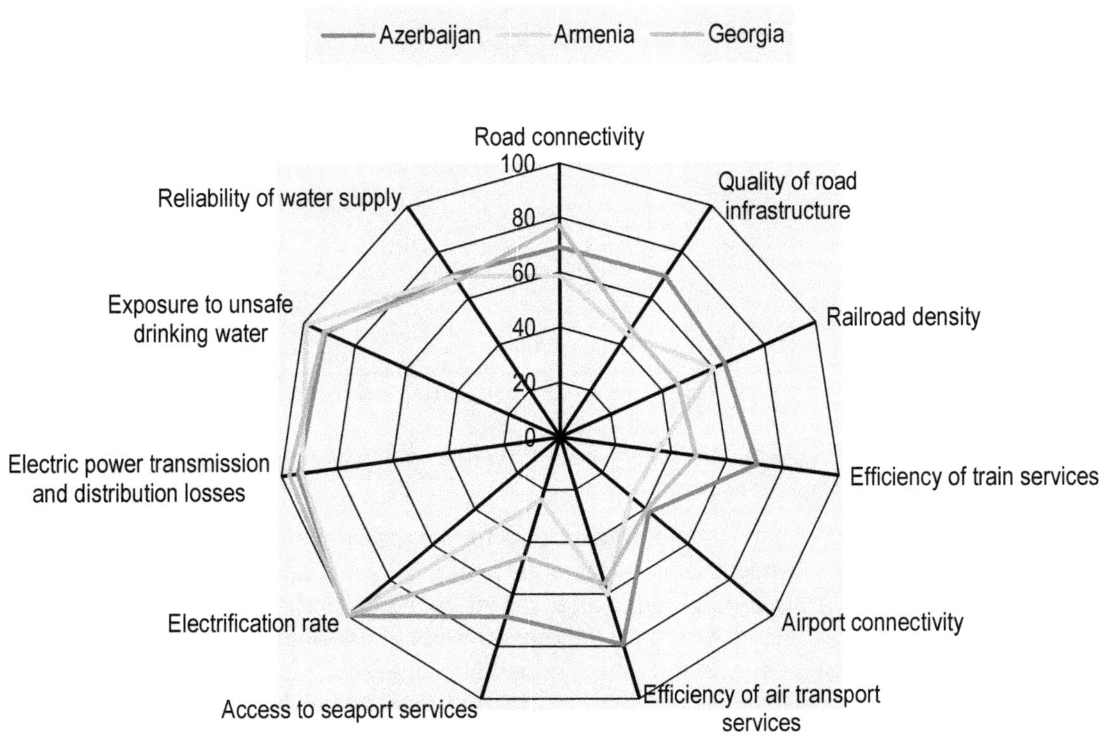

Source: World Economic Forum (2019[20]), *The Global Competitiveness Report 2019*, World Economic Forum, http://www3.weforum.org/docs/WEF_TheGlobalCompetitivenessReport2019.pdf

The OECD's database tracks 26 major infrastructure projects planned and under construction in Azerbaijan, with a cumulative value of USD 27.4 billion. By value, industry and mining projects account for over half of the investments (61%, USD 16.6 billion); energy and transport projects make up the second and third largest shares respectively (29%, USD 8.0 billion; 9%, USD 2.6 billion) (Figure 2.6). By comparison, water projects (1%, USD 234 million) represent much smaller shares of total investment in Azerbaijan's infrastructure.

Figure 2.6. Investment projects in Azerbaijan, by sector

Planned and under construction, in USD millon

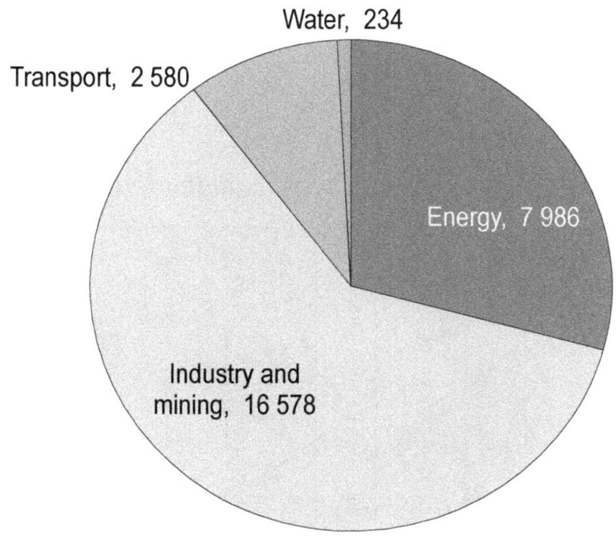

Source: OECD analysis based on accessed databases as of June 2020.

Transport

Transport costs are high in Azerbaijan, and domestic connectivity outside of the capital, Baku, presents a major barrier for rural residents' economic prospects. Azerbaijan's road and rail networks are in need of modernisation and increased spending on maintenance in order to take advantage of the country's position by the Caspian Sea and being in proximity to major markets such as Iran, the Russian Federation and Turkey (World Bank, 2015[18]). However, in recent years Azerbaijan's per capita spending on transport infrastructure has declined (see Figure 2.7). Road infrastructure investments account for almost all government spending on transport infrastructure, of which only about 3% is dedicated to maintenance of existing roads. Only 0.2% of inland infrastructure spending benefits the country's rail network (ITF, 2019[21]).

Figure 2.7. Inland transport infrastructure investment in Azerbaijan (2012-2018)

Modal share (%) of total inland infrastructure investment (left axis) and total inland transport infrastructure investment in current USD per capita (right axis)

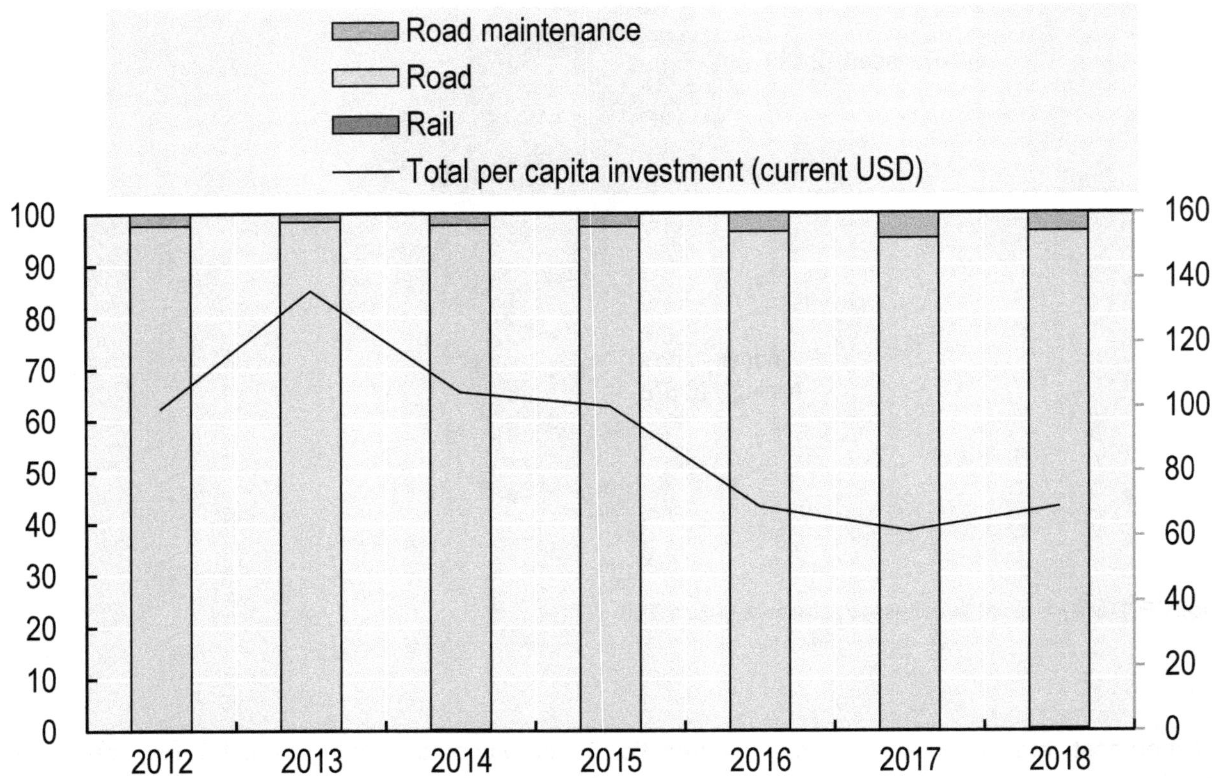

Source: ITF (2019[21]), *Transport performance indicators*, International Transport Forum, https://doi.org/10.1787/trsprt-data-en

Azerbaijan's inland transport modal split for freight has shifted towards road over time. In 2005, road only accounted for 44% of the country's freight, measured in tonne-kilometres, but by 2015 it had risen to 71% (15.5 billion tkm), while rail's share dropped from 56% to 29% (6.2 billion tkm). For passengers, road's dominance is even starker: in 2015, 98% of passenger transport (23.8 billion passenger-km, up from 15.3 billion pkm in 2009) occurred by road, compared to only 2% (0.5 billion pkm, down from 1.0 billion pkm in 2009) by rail (UNECE, 2018[22]).

In the road sector, the government's main development strategy, *Azerbaijan – 2020: View to the Future*, prioritises the development of two corridors: one running east-west from the capital Baku to Georgia and another north-south corridor from the Russian Federation to Iran (Government of Azerbaijan, 2012[23]). The World Bank, however, has recommended focusing on secondary and local roads to improve domestic connectivity and bring down travel and trade costs (World Bank, 2015[18]).

Azerbaijan's state-owned rail company, Azerbaijan Railways, owns and operates the country's rail network. Azerbaijan has international links with Georgia, Iran (only from the Nakhchivan exclave), the Russian Federation and Turkey (via the Kars-Tbilisi-Baku railway). No rail links exist with Armenia and, as a consequence, to date rail traffic between the majority of Azerbaijan and its exclave must bypass Armenia via Iran or Georgia and Turkey. However, the condition in the 2020 ceasefire agreement guaranteeing safe transport across Armenia between Nakhchivan and the rest of Azerbaijan could lead to the development of a rail link between Azerbaijan, its exclave and Turkey (Goble, 2020[24]).

Given its strategic position by the Caspian Sea and near large markets such as Turkey, Iran, Europe and Russia, Azerbaijan partakes in several international connectivity initiatives. Azerbaijan is a key component of the EU initiative TRACECA (Transport Corridor Europe-Caucasus-Asia), with its key Caspian Sea port (Baku) and well-established rail and road links to the Black Sea and onwards via Georgia and Turkey (TRACECA, 1998[25]). CAREC Corridor 2 also passes through Azerbaijan, linking Central Asia to the Caucasus via the port of Baku and onwards to Turkey and Europe through Georgia and its Black Sea ports (ADB, 2017[26]). Other initiatives include the Middle Corridor Trans-Caspian International Transport Route (2019[27]) (along with Georgia and Kazakhstan) and the South-West Transport Corridor (along with Georgia and Iran) (Financial Tribune, 2017[28]).

Azerbaijan's transport infrastructure projects planned and under construction account for around USD 3.8 billion. Road projects dominate investments in the transport sector (68%, USD 1.7 billion), followed by rail projects (31%, USD 801 million) (Figure 2.8). While rail and port infrastructure accounted for larger proportions of Azerbaijan's transport investments in the OECD's 2019 study of ongoing infrastructure projects (OECD, 2019[29]), their shares have diminished with the completion of two key projects. In rail, the Astara-Astara railway, which connects eastern Azerbaijan to Iran, was completed in 2018 and complemented with a series of terminals for oil and grain. In 2020, the expansion and modernisation of the new Port of Baku at Alat was completed (Port Technology International, 2020[30]). Investment projects in the roads sector are mainly focused on expanding or rehabilitating highways, which are important in order to further strengthen Azerbaijan's geographical position as an important link between the Black and Caspian seas and between Russia and Iran.

Figure 2.8. Transport projects in Azerbaijan, by sub-sector

Planned and under construction in USD million

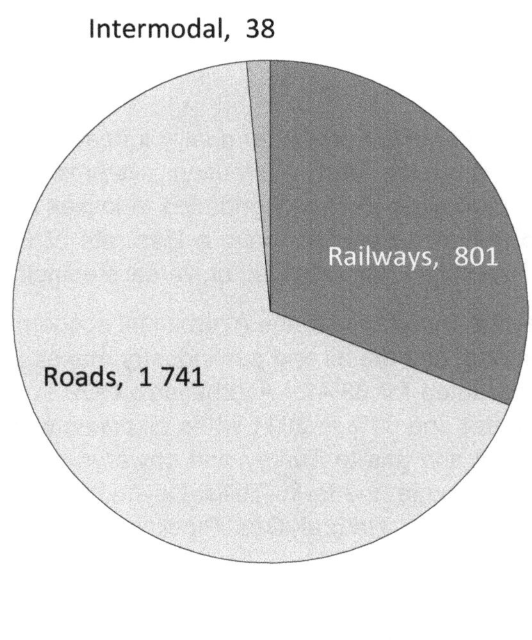

Source: OECD analysis based on accessed databases as of June 2020.

Refurbishment and rehabilitation of existing assets make up the majority of major transport investments in Azerbaijan (Table 2.2). Highest impact in terms of regional connectivity is the Railway Sector Development Programme, which aims to rehabilitate the Sumgait-Yalama rail line connecting Azerbaijan to Russia, which is also considered a key link in the North-South Railway Corridor of the CAREC corridors (ADB, n.d.[31]).

Table 2.2. Hotspot projects in the transport sector in Azerbaijan

Name	Sub-sector	Description	Project value (USD million)	Funding source	Type of investment	Status
Railway Sector Development Programme	Rail	The project will finance the rehabilitation of the line between Sumgait, near Baku, and Yalama, by the Russian border.	650	ADB, AFD, Government of Azerbaijan	Brownfield	Under construction
Highway III Project	Road	The project will improve safety and efficiency along the Baku-Shamakhi road by expanding sections to accommodate four lanes.	483	World Bank, Government of Azerbaijan	Brownfield	Under construction
Second Road Network Development Investment Programme	Road	The project aims to rehabilitate key sections of the Ujar-Zardab-Agjabedi road and construct 30-km road segment between Masalli and Jailabad.	130	ADB, Government of Azerbaijan	Brownfield	Under construction

Note: Refer to the Reader's guide for the present report's definition of 'hotspot' and other information on how the projects above were selected and prioritised. ADB = Asian Development Bank; AFD = French Development Agency (*Agence française de développement*).
Source: OECD database as of June 2020.

Energy

Overall, Azerbaijan's energy sector benefits from better quality infrastructure than other strategic sectors, but the country's electricity transmission and distribution systems underperform compared to its neighbours. While neighbouring Georgia's electricity grids led to losses of 7.3% of electricity output, the Azerbaijani transmission and distribution networks have a loss rate of 9.7% (IEA, 2019[32]). Like other former Soviet Union countries, Azerbaijan has achieved universal electricity access.

The energy sector is of fundamental importance to the Azerbaijani economy. Petroleum products account for over 90% of Azerbaijan's exports, and the oil and gas industry makes up a large but fluctuating share of the economy. Oil and gas accounted for 33% of Azerbaijan's GDP in 2016 when oil prices were low (USD 46.4 per barrel of Brent crude) and 50% in 2011 when oil prices were higher (USD 112 per barrel) (Deloitte, 2017[33]). To export its oil and gas to Turkey and onwards to Europe, Azerbaijan has several pipelines that cross its neighbour, Georgia: the Baku-Tbilisi-Ceyhan (BTC) pipeline, Baku-Tbilisi-Erzurum (BTE) pipeline and the Trans-Anatolian Natural Gas Pipeline (TANAP) (Emerging Markets Forum, 2019[34]).

Azerbaijan's electricity generation relies on its hydrocarbon resources; natural gas-fired power plants generate 93% of the country's electricity (Figure 2.9). Historically, Azerbaijan relied more heavily on oil-fired power plants than on cleaner burning natural gas-fired plants. The former accounted for 66% of generated electricity in 1995 compared to just 16.9% for natural gas, but by the 2000s natural gas-fired electricity generation had surpassed oil-fired power. Hydroelectric dams are also an important part of Azerbaijan's electricity mix, although their share has varied considerably in the past decade. Hydro accounted for 6% (1.6 TWh) of the country's electricity in 2019, which is considerably less than in 2010

(18%, 3.4 TWh). Azerbaijan also began generating electricity from waste incineration in the 2010s; since 2016 waste accounts for 1% of power generation. Other renewables also account for small but increasing fractions of Azerbaijan's electricity mix: Wind and solar photovoltaics (PV) generated 105 MWh (0.4%) and 44 MWh (0.17%) respectively in 2019 compared to 1 MWh (0.005%) in 2010 for wind and 5 MWh (0.02%) in 2015 for solar PV (IEA, 2018[35]).

Figure 2.9. Electricity generation by fuel (GWh, 2019)

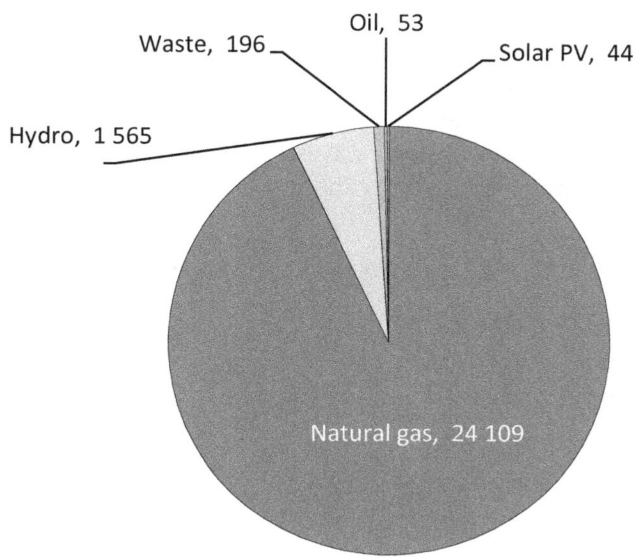

Source: IEA (2020[36]), *Electricity Information 2019*, International Energy Agency.

Azerbaijan, as a result of its hydrocarbon reserves, is a net energy exporter and does not face the same energy security concerns as its neighbour Georgia. It exported 33 Mt of oil in 2017 making it the third largest oil exporter in the former Soviet Union after the Russian Federation and Kazakhstan. It is also an exporter of oil products (1.1 Mtoe in 2017), natural gas (7.4 Mtoe in 2017) and electricity (0.1 Mtoe in 2017) (IEA, 2019[37]).

Although the government of Azerbaijan identifies economic diversification and strengthening of the 'non-oil sector' as key priorities in its development strategy *Azerbaijan-2020*, many of its energy-related goals support the continued dominance of oil and gas in the energy sector and economy more widely. *Azerbaijan-2020* singles out Phase 2 of the Shah Deniz gas field and its connection to the Trans-Anatolian natural gas pipeline (TANAP) as priorities (Government of Azerbaijan, 2012[23]). Since the OECD's last review of Azerbaijan's infrastructure plans, both projects have reached completion.

The government has set a number of targets related to renewable energy use and energy efficiency. The *National Strategy of Azerbaijan on the Use of Alternative and Renewable Energy Sources (2015-2020)* aimed to increase the share of renewables in electricity generation to 20% and in total energy consumption to 9.7% by 2020 (EaPGREEN, 2016[38]). Renewables development by 2020 fell short of these targets. The *Strategic Roadmap on Development of Utilities* sets the following goals for diversifying the country's installed capacity for electricity generation: 350 MW of wind, 50 MW of solar and 20 MW of bioenergy by 2020 (President of Azerbaijan, 2016[39]). By 2019, installed capacity was well below targets: 66 MW of wind, 35 MW of solar, 44 MW of solid waste incineration and 1 MW of biogas (State Statistical Committee of the Republic of Azerbaijan, 2020[40]). In 2020, the Ministry of Energy of Azerbaijan announced that its new target is to increase the share of renewables in installed capacity to 30% by 2030 (Ministry of Energy of the Republic of Azerbaijan, 2020[41]).

Azerbaijan's large-scale energy infrastructure projects planned and under construction total around USD 8.0 billion. Upstream oil and gas projects account for 80% (USD 6.4 billion), and electricity generation projects (16%, USD 1.2 billion) and transmission and distribution projects (USD 325 million) make the remainder (Figure 2.10). A single capital-intensive project, Azeri Central East platform, is responsible for the majority of upstream oil and gas's large share. The joint project between Azerbaijan's state oil company SOCAR and BP-Azerbaijan seeks to build a new exploration platform to further explore the offshore Azeri-Chirag-Guneshli oilfields.

As for electricity generation, all of the currently tracked projects are in wind power (). The push towards renewables development stems from two very different motivations. First, increased power generation capacity from renewable sources will help Azerbaijan meet its domestic targets and international commitments. Second, more renewable power will help Azerbaijan meet its rising domestic energy demand, which has been threatening natural gas exports (O'Byrne, 2020[42]).

Figure 2.10. Energy projects in Azerbaijan, by sub-sector

Planned and under construction in USD million

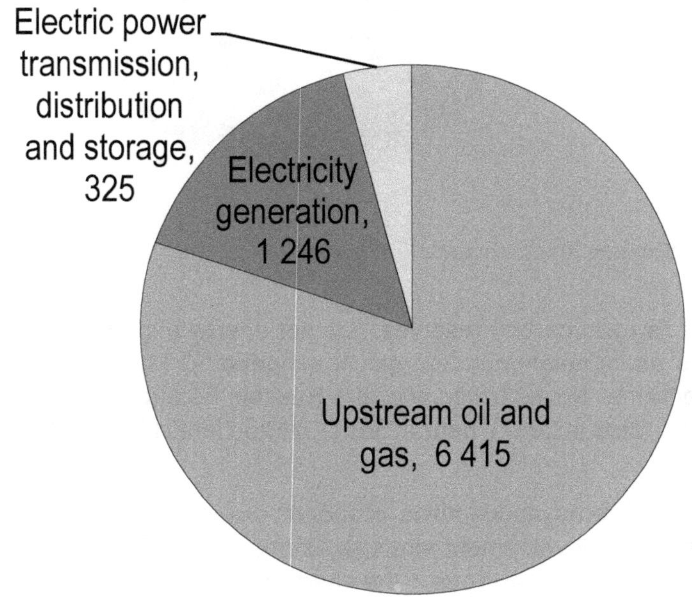

Source: OECD analysis based on accessed databases as of June 2020.

Table 2.3. Hotspot projects in the energy sector in Azerbaijan

Name	Sub-sector	Description	Project value (USD million)	New capacity (MW)	Funding source	Type of investment	Status
Azeri Central East platform	Upstream oil and gas	The project will construct an offshore platform to further explore the Azeri-Chirag-Guneshli oilfield.	6 000	N/A	SOCAR, BP-Azerbaijan, Chevron, INPEX, Equinor, ExxonMobil	Greenfield	Under construction
Pirallahi Island Wind Farm Project	Electricity generation (wind)	The project entails the construction of a 200 MW wind power station to provide stable electricity to Pirallahi and Chilov islands	430	200	Greenfield	Government of Azerbaijan	Planned
Power Distribution Enhancement Investment Program - Tranche 1	Electric power transmission and distribution	The project involves the upgrading of power distribution networks in secondary cities and rural areas to provide more reliable electricity to households. Overall, the project is expected to benefit 1.4 million consumers and stimulate the overall economy.	325	N/A	ADB	Brownfield	Under construction

Note: Refer to the Reader's guide for the present report's definition of 'hotspot' and other information on how the projects above were selected and prioritised.

Source: OECD database as of June 2020.Industry, mining and water

Mining and quarrying, primarily the extraction of crude petroleum and natural gas, account for 70% of Azerbaijan's industrial output, while manufacturing makes up a further 25% (Figure 2.11). Historically, these proportions were reversed: In 1990, manufacturing accounted for 90% of the country's output compared to only mining and quarrying's 5% share. The manufacture of food products, both historically and today, is the country's most important manufacturing industry (8% of industrial output in 2019; 25% in 1990), closely followed by the production of refined petroleum products (6% of industrial output in 2019). Other important manufacturing industries include the production of construction materials (2%), chemicals (1%) and the metallurgy industry (1%). Azerbaijan's remaining industrial input is split between electricity, gas, steam and air conditioning supply (4%) and water supply, sewerage, waste management and remediation activities (1%).

Azerbaijan's large-scale industry infrastructure projects planned and under construction total around USD 16.6 billion. The SOCAR GPC project is by far the largest active investment in the country's industrial sector, valued at USD 15 billion. It aims to increase the production of polyethylene and propylene, primarily for export to Turkey, the EU and China, allowing Azerbaijan to move up the petroleum value chain and diversify from crude oil exports. Current investments in water supply and sanitation tracked in the OECD database are modest, amounting to USD 234 million.

Figure 2.11. Industrial output by NACE* subsector

2019, percentage of total output

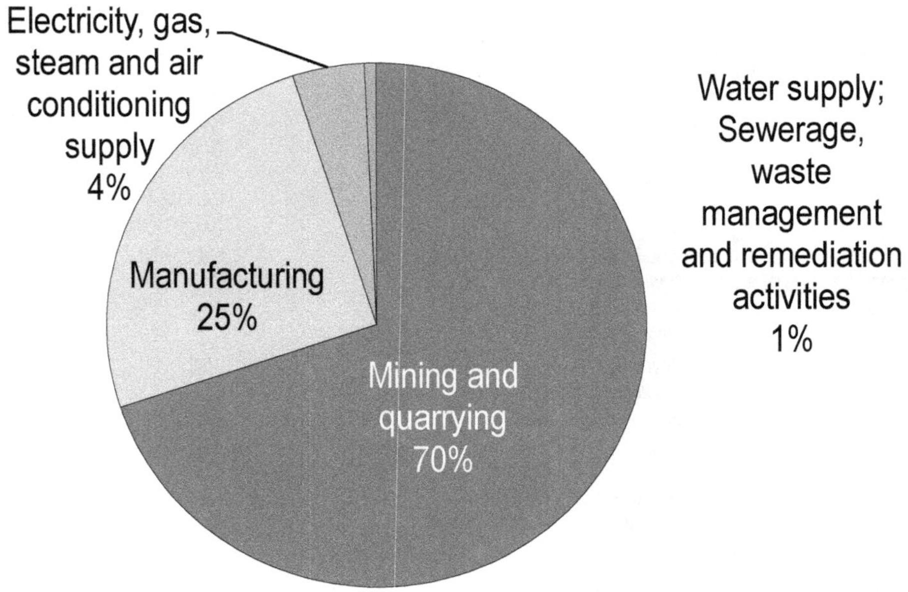

Note: * NACE = Nomenclature statistique des activités économiques dans la Communauté européenne [Statistical Classification of Economic Activities in the European Community]
Source: State Statistical Committee of the Republic of Azerbaijan (2020[43]), "Industry of Azerbaijan - Sectoral structure of industry, 2019", https://www.stat.gov.az/source/industry/

Strategic planning and links between long-term goals, infrastructure plans and environmental considerations

Azerbaijan adopted a long-term development strategy in 2012, *Azerbaijan 2020: A Look to the Future*, which describes the government's vision for strengthened economic growth, diversification away from fossil fuels and the development of key sectors, including information and communications technologies (ICT) and logistics. The government complemented this document in 2016 with its *Strategic Road Map on the National Economy* and a series of twelve sectoral road maps for key economic sectors, including industry, agriculture, transport and housing, with quantitative targets for 2020, 2025 and some unspecified for post-2025. A follow-up strategy, *National Priorities for Socio-Economic Development - Azerbaijan-2030*, is set to be adopted in 2021.

Azerbaijan needs a longer-term development strategy, preferably to the mid-century, to plan its transition towards other economic activities. While *Azerbaijan 2020* and the *Strategic Road Map* both discuss environmental challenges, they do not articulate a clear action plan to achieve the greenhouse gas emissions reduction goals expressed in the country's Nationally Determined Contribution (NDC) or the long-term sustainability of the country's transport and energy systems. Azerbaijan would benefit from a coherent document with a strong environmental focus and, crucially, a sufficiently long time horizon to evaluate the synergies and trade-offs associated with different infrastructure investments.

Azerbaijan also lacks formal strategies, instead it has set strategic directions for certain key sectors. One of the *Strategic Road Map*'s primary objectives is to strengthen the non-oil sectors of the economy through increases in foreign direct investment (FDI) flows, support for export-oriented non-oil industries and increased employment in services (particularly tourism) and commodities manufacturing (e.g. industry and food production). The *Strategic Road Map* also calls for the government to reduce its budgetary dependence on transfers from SOFAZ, Azerbaijan's energy-related sovereign wealth fund, from about 50% in 2016 to 15% by 2025. However, despite these goals of economic diversification, the oil and gas sector still looms large in the country's development vision, most notably with the construction of the new Azeri Central East platform for oil exploration.

Among the sectoral road maps that accompanied Azerbaijan's *Strategic Road Map on the National Economy* were strategies relating to upstream oil and gas, the *Strategic Road Map on Oil and Gas Development,* and the end use of energy (both from hydrocarbons and other sources), the *Strategic Roadmap on Development of Utilities*. However, Azerbaijan does not have a strategy for the energy sector as a whole and currently lacks legislation on energy efficiency standards. The government is drafting a National Energy Efficiency Action Plan (NEEAP) and is expected to adopt a draft Law on the Efficient Use of Energy Resources and Energy Efficiency.

In the transport sector, both *Azerbaijan-2020* and the *Strategic Road Map on the Development of Logistics Outcomes* set goals relating to the development of transport, primarily in terms of international connectivity and trade facilitation. Neither document presents a holistic development plan for the transport sector including improved secondary and rural roads to improve domestic connectivity, which has been identified as a barrier to regional economic development (World Bank, 2015[18]).

Institutional set-up and decision making processes

As noted in the OECD's previous review of Azerbaijan's infrastructure-related institutional set-up, Azerbaijan abolished the State Agency for Alternative and Renewable Energy Sources in 2019. In late 2020, the Azerbaijan Renewable Energy Agency was established by presidential decree under the Ministry of Energy. The Ministry has subsequently announced more ambitious renewables development targets (30% of electricity generation capacity by 2030) (Ministry of Energy of the Republic of Azerbaijan, 2020[41]).

Azerbaijan is a party to the Convention on Environmental Impact Assessment (EIA) in a Transboundary Context (the Espoo Convention), and in 2018 Azerbaijan adopted a Law on Environmental Impact Assessment. However, the parties to the Convention have signalled that Azerbaijan's existing legislation and current lack of secondary legislation relating to EIA do not comply with the articles of the Convention (UNECE, 2019[44]).

Unlike neighbouring Georgia, Azerbaijan is not a signatory of the Protocol on Strategic Environmental Assessment (SEA). However, Azerbaijan in conjunction with the EaP-GREEN programme carried out a pilot SEA of the *National Strategy on the Use of Alternative and Renewable Energy Source (2015-2020)* (EaPGREEN, 2016[38]). EaP GREEN has also supported training programmes and workshops in Azerbaijan as well as the publication of Azeri-language documents on SEA's benefits to encourage the tool's adoption and use (UNECE, n.d.[45]).

List of relevant strategic documents

Table 2.4. Main strategic documents in force

	Status	Time Horizon	Sectoral Coverage	Main objectives
First Nationally Determined Contribution (NDC)	Submitted in 2017	2017-2030	Economy-wide	• Target: to achieve a 35% reduction in total greenhouse gas emissions compared to 1990 levels by 2030 • Main sectors for emission reduction: Energy sector (ensure the development of legislative acts and regulatory documents for the energy sector, replace existing technology with modern, environmentally friendly technology, reconstruct energy distribution networks for example to reduce gas distribution losses by 1% by 2020), Transport sector (promote the use of electric vehicles for public transportation, ensure the electrification of railway lines), Waste management sector (develop a modern solid waste management system)
Azerbaijan – 2020: A Look to the Future	Adopted in 2012	2011-2020	Governance, transport, energy, water, industry	• Achieve a per capita GDP of USD 13 000 by 2020 • Reach highest positions in group of countries with high human development in accordance with the human development classification of the UN Development Programme • Ensure an increase in the construction and use of renewable and alternative energy sources • Modernise 6 international airports • Provide villages and cities with water purifying installations and ensure regular water quality monitoring to improve the water supply service • Modernise the petrochemical industry • Ensure the diversification of the economy, moving away from the oil and gas sector
Strategic Roadmap on the National Economy	Adopted in 2016	2016-2025	Governance, energy, industry, transport	• Further strengthen the judicial system • Improve the business environment • Ensure the adoption of the most appropriate and competitive tax and tariff rates • Develop regional scale transport-logistics corridors • Minimise the energy used to produce each unit of GDP by increasing the share of renewable energy sources
Strategic Roadmap for Development of Logistics and Trade in the Republic of Azerbaijan	Adopted in 2016	2016-2025	Governance, energy, industry, transport	• Transform Azerbaijan into a regional logistics hub • Conduct feasibility studies for increasing the number of free trade zones

	Status	Time Horizon	Sectoral Coverage	Main objectives
				• Increase the volume of trade and promote higher value added trade to help diversify the economy • Elevate the role of the private sector within the economy
National Strategy of Azerbaijan on the Use of Alternative and Renewable Energy Sources (2015-2020)	Adopted in 2015	2015-2020	Governance, Energy	• Increase the share of renewable energy within the energy sector • Organise centralised management structures in the renewable energy sector • Establish a normative legal framework for the use within the alternative and renewable energy sector • Improve the tariff policy for renewable energy
Strategic Roadmap on Oil and Gas Development	Adopted in 2016	2016-2025	Energy, Industry	• Ensure national energy security, for example through the protection of offshore energy infrastructure • Diversify gas transportation options • Develop relationships with Caspian states and European states in the oil and gas sector
Strategic Roadmap on Development of Utilities	Adopted in 2016	2016-2025	Energy, Water	• Increase investment in alternative and renewable energy sources • Increase the country's generation capacity by 1 000 MW in the next 5-10 years, 420 MW being generated by renewable energy sources (wind: 350 MW, solar: 50 MW, bioenergy: 20 MW) • Revision of tariffs in the energy market
Strategic Roadmap on Development of Heavy Industry and Machinery	Adopted in 2016	2016-2025	Industry	• Implement energy saving technology which also meets environmental standards • Increase heavy industry production output

Table 2.5. Other relevant documents

	Status	Time Horizon	Sectoral Coverage
Strategic Roadmap for Development of Specialised Tourism Industry in the Republic of Azerbaijan	Adopted in 2016	2016-2025	Multi-sector
Action Plan on the Improvement of the Ecological Situation for 2010-2014	Adopted in 2010	2010-2014	Multi-sector
National Programme on Environmentally Sustainable Social and Economic Development for the period 2003–2010	Adopted in 2003	2003-2010	Multi-sector
State Programme for the Socioeconomic Development of the Regions of Azerbaijan for the period 2009–2013	Adopted in 2009	2009-2013	Multi-sector, primarily energy and water
State Programme on Reforestation and Afforestation for the period 2003–2008	Adopted in 2003	2003-2008	Multi-sector
State Programme on Summer/Winter Pastures, Effective Use of Meadows and Desertification Prevention for the period 2004–2010	Adopted in 2004	2004-2010	Multi-sector
State Programme for the Development of Fuel Energy Complex for the period 2005–2015	Adopted in 2005	2005-2015	Energy
Hydrometeorology Development Programme for the period 2004–2010	Adopted in 2004	2004-2010	Water
State Strategy on Hazardous Waste Management for the period 2004–2010	Adopted in 2004	2004-2010	Waste Management

References

ADB (2017), *The CAREC Corridors - Linking the Russian Federation with South Asia and the Middle East*, https://www.adb.org/news/infographics/carec-corridors-linking-russian-federation-south-asia-and-middle-east. [26]

ADB (n.d.), *Azerbaijan: Railway Sector Development Program*, https://www.adb.org/projects/48386-004/main. [31]

Center for Analysis of Economic Reforms and Communication (2017), *Azerbaijan Economic Reforms Review*, http://www.vusalmusayev.com. [13]

Deloitte (2017), *Business Outlook in Azerbaijan*, https://www2.deloitte.com/content/dam/Deloitte/ru/Documents/research-center/business-outlook-in-Azerbaijan-2017.pdf. [33]

EaPGREEN (2016), *Strategic Environmental Assessment of the National Strategy of Azerbaijan on the use of Alternative and Renewable Energy*, http://www.unece.org/fileadmin/DAM/env/eia/documents/EaP_GREEN/1_Homepage/Azerbaijan/SEA_report_Azerbaijan_Executive_Summary_October_2016.pdf. [38]

EBRD (2019), *Azerbaijan Country Strategy 2019-2024*, https://www.ebrd.com/news/2019/ebrd-approves-new-strategy-for-azerbaijan.html. [9]

Emerging Markets Forum (2019), *The Impact of the Belt and Road Initiative in Central Asia and the South Caucasus: "'Inside-out" Perspectives of Experts from the Region*, Emerging Markets Forum, Gerzensee, http://www.research.pmcg-i.com/images/banners/The%20Belt%20and%20Road%20Initiative%20in%20the%20South%20Caucasus%20Region.pdf. [34]

European Commission (2019), *Azerbaijan: Trade picture*, http://ec.europa.eu/trade/policy/countries-and-regions/countries/azerbaijan/. [5]

fDi Markets (2019), *fDi Markets: the in-depth crossborder investment monitor (database)*, https://www.fdimarkets.com/. [14]

Financial Tribune (2017), *Georgia, Iran, Azerbaijan to Launch Transport Corridor*, https://financialtribune.com/articles/economy-domestic-economy/66042/georgia-iran-azerbaijan-to-launch-transport-corridor. [28]

German-Azerbaijan Chamber of Commerce (2018), *EU Business Climate Report Azerbaijan 2018*, https://eeas.europa.eu/sites/eeas/files/business_climate_report_-2018.pdf. [12]

Goble, P. (2020), *A 'Railway War' Is About to Break out in the South Caucasus*, Eurasia Daily Monitor, https://jamestown.org/program/a-railway-war-is-about-to-break-out-in-the-south-caucasus/ (accessed on 6 February 2021). [24]

Government of Azerbaijan (2012), *Концепция развития Азербайджан 2020: взгляд в будущее [The concept of development Azerbaijan 2020: view to the future]*, https://president.az/files/future_ru.pdf. [23]

IEA (2020), *Electricity Information 2019*, https://www.iea.org/reports/electricity-information-2019 (accessed on 10 August 2020). [36]

IEA (2019), *World Energy Balances 2019*, International Energy Agency, Paris, https://doi.org/10.1787/3a876031-en (accessed on 10 August 2020). [37]

IEA (2019), *World Energy Statistics 2019*, International Energy Agency, Paris, https://doi.org/10.1787/2e828dea-en. [32]

IEA (2018), *IEA World Energy Balances 2018*, https://webstore.iea.org/world-energy-balances-2018. [35]

IMF (2020), *World Economic Outlook: October 2020*, https://www.imf.org/external/datamapper/GGXCNL_NGDP@WEO/OEMDC/ADVEC/WEOWORLD. [2]

IMF (2019), *Republic of Azerbaijan : 2019 Article IV Consultation-Press Release; Staff Report; and Statement by the Executive Director for Republic of Azerbaijan*, International Monetary Fund (IMF), Washington, D.C., https://www.imf.org/en/Publications/CR/Issues/2019/09/18/Republic-of-Azerbaijan-2019-Article-IV-Consultation-Press-Release-Staff-Report-and-Statement-48684 (accessed on 6 February 2021). [16]

ITF (2019), *Transport Performance Indicators*, https://www.oecd-ilibrary.org/transport/data/itf-transport-statistics/transport-performance-indicators_2122fa17-en. [21]

Ministry of Ecology and Natural Resources Republic of Azerbaijan (2015), *Third National Communication to the United Nations Framework Convention on Climate Change: Republic of Azerbaijan*, https://unfccc.int/sites/default/files/resource/azenc3.pdf. [17]

Ministry of Energy of the Republic of Azerbaijan (2020), *The Use of Renewable Energy Resources in Azerbaijan*, https://minenergy.gov.az/en/alternativ-ve-berpa-olunan-enerji/azerbaycanda-berpa-olunan-enerji-menbelerinden-istifade (accessed on 7 February 2021). [41]

Observatory of Economic Complexity (2020), *Azerbaijan: Exports, Imports, and Trade Partners*, https://oec.world/en/profile/country/aze (accessed on 20 August 2020). [7]

O'Byrne, D. (2020), *Azerbaijan looks to renewables to meet growing power demand*, Eurasianet, https://eurasianet.org/azerbaijan-looks-to-renewables-to-meet-growing-power-demand (accessed on 7 February 2021). [42]

OECD (2021), *COVID-19 and greening the economies of Eastern Europe, the Caucasus and Central Asia*, http://www.oecd.org/coronavirus/policy-responses/covid-19-and-greening-the-economies-of-eastern-europe-the-caucasus-and-central-asia-40f4d34f/ (accessed on 10 March 2021). [4]

OECD (2019), *Azerbaijan: Linking Domestic Suppliers with Foreign Investors*, OECD, Paris, http://www.oecd.org/eurasia. [8]

OECD (2019), *Sustainable Infrastructure for Low-Carbon Development in Central Asia and the Caucasus: Hotspot Analysis and Needs Assessment*, Green Finance and Investment, OECD Publishing, Paris, https://dx.doi.org/10.1787/d1aa6ae9-en. [29]

Port Technology International (2020), *Baku completes port expansion as Azerbaijan looks to transform economy*, Port Technology International, https://www.porttechnology.org/news/baku-completes-port-expansion-as-azerbaijan-looks-to-transform-economy/ (accessed on 6 February 2021). [30]

President of Azerbaijan (2016), *Azərbaycan Respublikasında kommunal xidmətlərin (elektrik və istilik enerjisi, su və qaz) inkişafına dair Strateji Yol Xəritəsi [Strategic Roadmap for the Development of Utility Services (electricity, heat, water and gas) in the Republic of Azerbaijan]*, https://mida.gov.az/documents/Kommunal_xidm%C9%99tl%C9%99rin_inki%C5%9Faf%C4%B1na_dair_Strateji_Yol_X%C9%99rit%C9%99si_.pdf. [39]

President of Azerbaijan (2016), *Azərbaycan Respublikasında logistika vəticarətin inkişafına dair Strateji Yol Xəritəsi [Strategic Roadmap for Development of Logistics Outcomes in the Republic of Azerbaijan]*, https://static.president.az/pdf/38542.pdf. [6]

Roser, M. et al. (2021), *Coronavirus Pandemic (COVID-19)*, OurWorldInData.Org, https://ourworldindata.org/coronavirus (accessed on 9 September 2020). [3]

State Statistical Committee of the Republic of Azerbaijan (2020), *5.3 Plant capacity, MW*, https://www.stat.gov.az/source/balance_fuel/en/005_3en.xls (accessed on 7 February 2021). [40]

State Statistical Committee of the Republic of Azerbaijan (2020), *Foreign investments directed to fixed capital by foreign countries*, https://www.stat.gov.az/source/construction/ (accessed on 6 February 2021). [15]

State Statistical Committee of the Republic of Azerbaijan (2020), *Industry of Azerbaijan: "Sectoral structure of industry"*, https://www.stat.gov.az/source/industry/?lang=en (accessed on 7 February 2021). [43]

TITR (2019), *Trans-Caspian International Transport Route: History of Company*, http://titr.kz/en/about-the-association/history-en. [27]

TRACECA (1998), *TRACECA- Restoration of the Historic Silk Road*, http://www.traceca-org.org/en/countries/azerbaijan/azerbaijan-in-traceca/. [25]

Transparency International (2020), *Corruption Perceptions Index 2020*, https://www.transparency.org/en/cpi/2020/index/ (accessed on 20 July 2020). [11]

UNECE (2019), *Decision IS/1c on compliance by Azerbaijan with its obligations under the Convention in respect of its national legislation*, UNECE, Geneva, http://www.unece.org/fileadmin/DAM/env/documents/2019/ece/Meeting_of_Parties_-_2019/adopted_decisions/IS.1.c_ADOPTED_07.02.2019_advance_unedited.pdf. [44]

UNECE (2018), *2018 Transport Statistics Infocards*, UNECE, http://www.unece.org/trans/main/wp6/infocards.html. [22]

UNECE (n.d.), *Azerbaijan: Environmental Policy*, http://www.unece.org/environmental-policy/conventions/environmental-assessment/about-us/protocol-on-sea/enveiaabouteap-green/azerbaijan.html. [45]

World Bank (2021), *World Development Indicators (database)*, https://datacatalog.worldbank.org/dataset/world-development-indicators. [1]

World Bank (2020), *Doing Business 2020*, World Bank Group, Washington, DC, http://dx.doi.org/10.1596/978-1-4648-1440-2. [10]

World Bank (2018), *Logistics Performance Index*, https://lpi.worldbank.org/international/aggregated-ranking. [19]

World Bank (2015), *Azerbaijan Systematic Country Diagnostic*, World Bank, Washington DC, https://openknowledge.worldbank.org/bitstream/handle/10986/23105/Azerbaijan000S00country0diagnostic0.pdf?sequence=1&isAllowed=y. [18]

World Economic Forum (2019), *The Global Competitiveness Report 2019*, World Economic Forum, Geneva, http://www3.weforum.org/docs/WEF_TheGlobalCompetitivenessReport2019.pdf (accessed on 23 July 2020). [20]

Notes

[1] The EU Eastern Partnership (EaP) is a joint initiative for strengthening the relationships between the European Union, its member states and six countries (hereafter the EaP countries): Armenia, Azerbaijan, Belarus, Georgia, Moldova and Ukraine.

[2] Confirmed case and death figures are underestimates of actual case and death numbers. Methodology and testing rates vary widely, and international comparisons are necessarily flawed.

3. Trends in sustianable infrastructure investment in Belarus

This chapter describes sustainable infrastructure planning in Belarus and presents current trends in investment in large-scale infrastructure projects. It compares Belarus's infrastructure plans in the energy, transport, industry and water sectors against its international commitments under the Paris Agreement on climate change and the Sustainable Development Goals (SDGs). The chapter also explores Belarus's strategic documents for long-term economic development, sectoral development and the environment, including those related to climate change mitigation and adaptation. It identifies misalignments between stated goals and observed investment flows and provides recommendations to improve strategic planning for sustainable infrastructure.

State of play: economy, investment and climate change in Belarus

Economy and trade

Table 3.1. Key indicators on Belarus's economy

Population (2019)	9 466 856
Urbanisation rate (2019)	79.0%
Annual population growth (2018)	-0.2%
Surface area	207 600 km2
GDP (USD, current price, 2018)	63 080 million
GDP per capita (USD, current price, 2019)	6 663
Real GDP growth (year-on-year change, 2019, 2020)	1.2%, -3%
Inflation (average consumer price, y-o-y change, 2020)	5.6%
Exports of goods and services (% of GDP, 2019)	66.4%
Imports of goods and services (% of GDP, 2018)	66.9%
FDI, net inflows (% of GDP, 2019)	2.0%
General government net lending/borrowing (% of GDP, 2019, 2020)	0.6%, -4.6%
Unemployment (% of total labour force, 2019)	4.2%
Remittances (% of GDP, 2019)	2.2%
Transparency, accountability and corruption in the public sector rating	n.a.

Source: World Bank (2021[1]), *World Development Indicators (database)*, World Bank, https://datacatalog.worldbank.org/dataset/world-development-indicators; IMF (2020[2]), *World Economic Outlook: October 2020*, International Monetary Fund https://www.imf.org/external/datamapper/GGXCNL_NGDP@WEO/OEMDC/ADVEC/WEOWORLD

Economy and demographics

Belarus is a landlocked, upper-middle income country in Eastern Europe. It borders Russia to the northeast, Ukraine to the south and European Union member states Poland, Lithuania and Latvia to the west and northwest. It has the highest GDP per capita in the EU Eastern Partnership (EaP).[1] Like many countries in Eastern Europe, Belarus has a shrinking national population (-6% between 1999 and 2019). Although Belarus's urban population experienced positive growth (+5% between 1999 and 2019) including from net immigration, its rural population has declined dramatically (-31% between 1999 and 2019) (Belstat, 2020[3]). Current trends are expected to continue. Belarus's population is projected to decrease from 9.4 million in 2019 to 8.6 million by 2050, with the share of individuals aged 65 or older increasing from 15.6% (2020) to 24% (2050) (UNDESA, 2019[4]).

Following independence in 1991, Belarus's GDP fell from USD 31.2 billion in 1991 (in constant 2010 USD) to USD 20.6 billion in 1995. In real terms, the country's GDP grew rapidly until the late 2010s, increasing over three-fold in size from USD 20.6 billion to USD 63 billion by 2014. The economic downturn in neighbouring Russia beginning in 2014 has had a major impact on Belarus's economy, resulting in a sharp drop in GDP (to USD 59 billion in 2016) from which the country has since recovered (USD 63.2 billion in 2019) (World Bank, 2021[1]). Due to the ongoing COVID-19 pandemic, Belarus's economy expected to contract by 3% in 2020 and return to positive growth in 2021 (IMF, 2020[5]).

As of February 2021, Belarus had diagnosed 27 COVID-19 cases per thousand inhabitants, marginally more than in Azerbaijan (22.8) and slightly fewer than neighbouring Ukraine (29.3), while the other three EaP countries have considerably higher confirmed infection rates: Armenia (56.6), Georgia (65.4) and Moldova (40.5). Belarus's death rate (187 deaths per million inhabitants) is the lowest in the Eastern Partnership (Roser et al., 2020[6]).[2] Belarus implemented less stringent containment measures than its neighbours. Although it curtailed international travel and imposed quarantine restrictions on infected individuals and close contact, Belarus continued to permit mass gatherings and events as well as in-person education (OECD, 2020[7]).

Some of Belarus's stimulus measures to encourage a swift recovery from the economic downturn could have potentially negative impacts on the environment, while others could align well with its green economy-related goals. For instance, the government postponed the introduction of a tariff on heat and gas supply that was initially planned for 1 May 2020 by one year to avoid overburdening its citizens already facing economic hardship due to the pandemic. The government has also highlighted investments in renewable energy and low-emission technologies as potential ways to stimulate the economy (OECD, 2021[8]).

Belarus is a service-oriented economy (48.8% of GDP) with a sizeable manufacturing sector (21.3%) and a particularly small industrial and construction sector (1.4%). Agriculture accounts for 6.8% of GDP, less than in neighbouring Ukraine (9%) and Moldova (9.9%) (World Bank, 2021[1]).

Trade

Belarus, along with Azerbaijan, is one of only two EaP countries that are not members of the World Trade Organisation (WTO). Although its Working Party for eventual accession to the organisation was established in 1993, Belarus is currently an observer country. During its Working Party's 12th meeting in 2019, Belarus reaffirmed its commitment to join the WTO and aimed to do so by the 2020 Ministerial Conference (WTO, 2019[9]). Due to the COVID-19 pandemic, these plans have been postponed.

Belarus was a founding member of the Eurasian Economic Community and its Customs Union along with Kazakhstan and Russia. The Eurasian Economic Union replaced these regional structures in 2015, with Armenia and Kyrgyzstan joining the Union and its integrated single market. In 1999, before the Eurasian Economic Union's founding, Belarus had already established an integrated single market with Russia through the Union State of Russia and Belarus, which initially included the explicit but as yet unrealised goals of creating a single currency and coordinated foreign and defence policies.

Belarus and the European Union concluded a Partnership and Cooperation Agreement in 1995, but the European Union never ratified it, which makes Belarus the only EaP country without a Partnership and Cooperation Agreement (or a more comprehensive agreement, such as an Association Agreement) in force. The European Union's Eastern Partnership (EaP) is a key initiative for continued cooperation between the EU, its member states and Belarus. Negotiations between the European Union and Belarus have been ongoing since 2016 to define the Partnership Priorities.

Belarus participates in practical cooperation with the Northern Dimension, a joint policy between the European Union, Russia, Norway and Iceland initiated in 1999 and renewed in 2006 focused on economic integration and sustainable development in Northern Europe. Belarus participates in two of the Northern Dimension's four partnerships: on ecology and on transport and logistics. In 2020, Belarus held the chairmanship of the Northern Dimension Partnership on Transport and Logistics (NDPTL), which seeks to encourage market integration through improved transport connectivity. A key initiative is the development of the NDPTL Regional Transport Network, which aims to integrate the Trans-European Transport Network (TEN-T) with the transport networks of Belarus, Norway and Russia across all modes of transport.

Belarus has also been an observer state to the Council of Baltic Sea States since 2009 and has taken part in a number of its initiatives, such as the Baltic Energy Ring, which aims to develop a united energy system for the Baltic region states, as well as projects on environmental protection, radiation safety, health and migration.

Unlike Georgia, Moldova and Ukraine, Belarus is not a Contracting Party of the European Union's Energy Community, but it applied for Observer status in 2016. No decision on this application has been communicated yet. If granted, this would allow Belarus to attend institutional meetings of the Energy Community with a view for closer collaboration and eventual integration into a pan-European energy market. Observers, like Armenia, also benefit from policy guidance from the Energy Community Secretariat on potential reforms.

Russia is Belarus's most important trade partner by a wide margin, accounting for 60% of Belarus's imports and 38% of its exports (Figure 3.1(a) and (b)). Belarus's trade relationships with the other members of the Eurasian Economic Union are considerably less consequential, although Kazakhstan is a non-negligible export market (2.4%). In terms of exports, Belarus's most important markets are Ukraine (13%), the United Kingdom (9%) and the European Union (over 19%), particularly Germany (4%), the Netherlands (4%) and neighbouring Poland (4%). While Russia imports a variety of products from Belarus, refined petroleum dominates the mix of Belarusian exports to the United Kingdom, Ukraine and European Union countries. China (2%) and Brazil (2%) are also important export markets, particularly for fertilisers. Belarus sources 6% of its imports from China, 4% from Ukraine, 2% from Turkey and about 14% from the European Union – primarily Germany (5%), Poland (5%) and Lithuania (3%).

Mineral products make up the largest share of Belarus's imports (31%) and exports (27%) (Figure 3.1(c) and (d)). Belarus imports crude petroleum (19% of its imports, exclusively from Russia) and exports refined petroleum (20% of exports). Russia also supplies Belarus with petroleum gas (8% of imports) and refined petroleum (4%). Belarus's other major exports are chemical products (14%), especially fertilisers (8%); transport (9%), especially delivery trucks (5%) and tractors (2%) for the markets of the former Soviet Union; and animal products (9%), especially cheese (2%), almost exclusively for export to Russia. In addition to mineral products, Belarus's major imports are machines (17%), metals (10%), chemical products (8%) and transport (6%), especially cars (2%), mostly from Russia and Germany.

Figure 3.1. Trade of Belarus

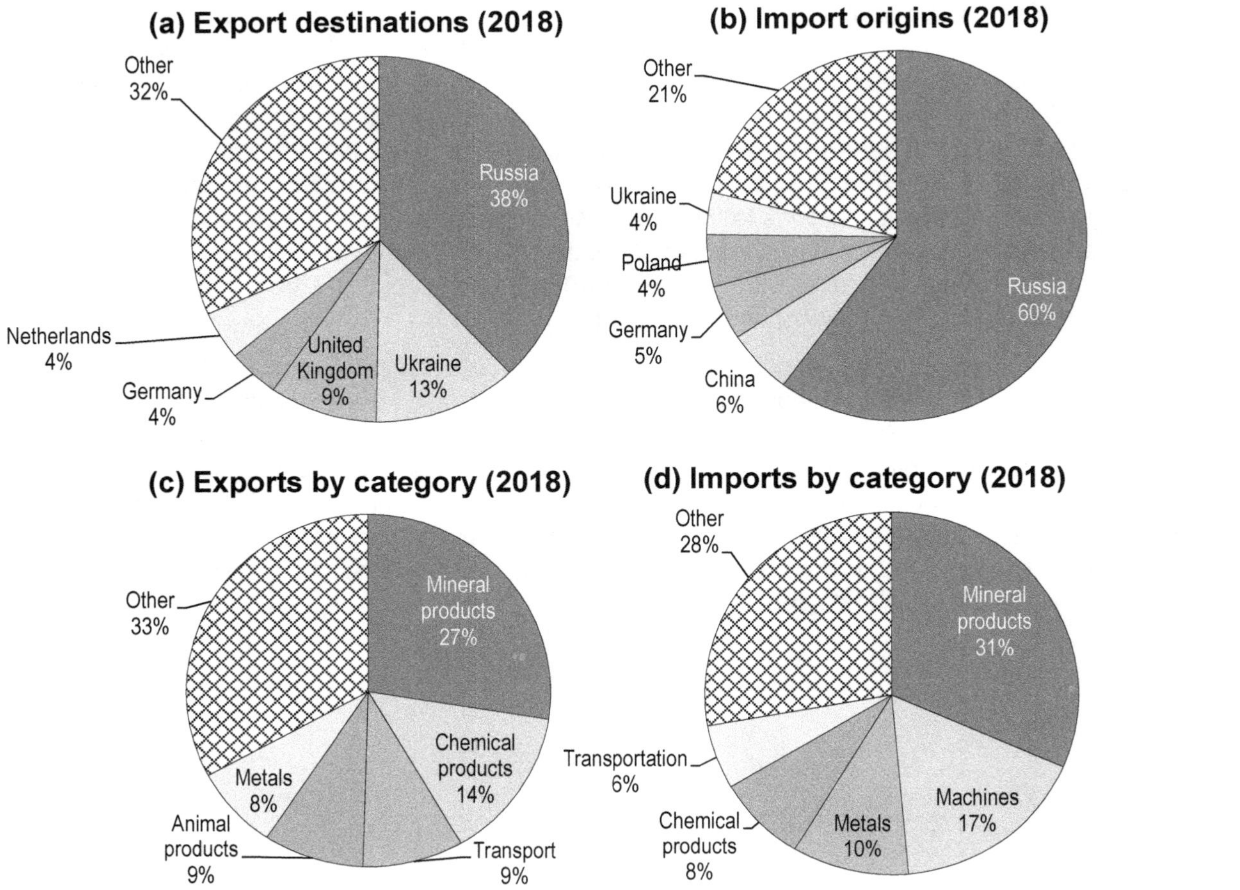

Source: Observatory of Economic Complexity (2018[10]), *Armenia: Exports, Imports and Trade Partners*, Observatory of Economic Complexity, https://oec.world/en/profile/country/blr

Investment climate

Belarus actively seeks foreign investment in strategic export-oriented sectors such as pharmaceuticals, nanotechnologies and manufacturing of electrical equipment, ICT technologies, home appliances and vehicles. Actual foreign direct investment (FDI) flows benefit primarily sectors dominated by state-owned enterprises (SOEs) (US Department of State, 2020[11]). SOEs play an outsized role in the Belarusian economy. According to the National Statistical Office (Belstat), the state sector accounts for just under a third of value added, but its definition of the state sector excludes all joint-stock companies, even when the state is the only shareholder. Other sources, notably the European Bank for Reconstruction and Development, estimate that the state sector accounts for closer to 70% of the Belarusian economy (Papko and Kozarzewski, 2020[12]). Foreign companies active in Belarus report that selective law enforcement and informal practices continue despite legislation establishing equal treatment for domestic and foreign investors, and the judiciary is not considered to be fully independent (US Department of State, 2020[11]).

According to its draft *National Strategy for Socioeconomic Development for the period to 2035*, Belarus aims to rank among the top 30 countries in the World Bank's annual Doing Business survey by 2030, compared to its ranking in 2016 of 37th. However, by 2020 Belarus had backslid in the rankings to 49th place, behind Armenia (47th), Azerbaijan (34th), Georgia (7th) and Moldova (48th). Belarus has improved its score on individual Doing Business indicators in recent years, but its progress has been outpaced by more comprehensive reforms elsewhere. Whereas it took 80 days and 17 procedures on average to open a business in 2004, Belarus had streamlined the process to four procedures taking 8.5 days by 2020. Belarus's tax system is particularly onerous and remains burdensome despite improvements. In 2006, businesses spent 987 hours annually on their taxes, which were collected in 125 payments per year. By 2020, the tax regime required only 7 payments amounting to about 170 hours per year (World Bank, 2020[13]).

Corruption is a major concern in Belarus. In 2019, the Council of Europe's Group of States against Corruption declared that Belarus had consistently failed to meet its anti-corruption standards and was deemed non-compliant. It noted that corruption appeared particularly rampant in procurement processes for state-run enterprises (OECD, 2020[14]). According to Transparency International's Corruption Perceptions Index, however, the situation in Belarus has improved markedly over the past decade: Belarus ranked 123rd out of 176 countries in 2012 and 63rd out of 180 in 2020. This places Belarus ahead of most other countries in the Eastern Partnership, including Moldova (115th), Ukraine (117th) and Azerbaijan (129th) (Transparency International, 2019[15]).

In 2010, Belarus created an investment promotion agency, the National Agency of Investment and Privatisation, to provide essential services to potential investors in Belarus. The agency is charged with several functions including carrying out government investment policy, public-private partnerships and privatisations as well as searching for and attracting foreign investors, improving the image of Belarus abroad as a destination for investment and managing a centralised information portal on investment-related matters. However, the agency juggles too many mandates, including policy-making, treaty negotiations and public concession management, which reduces the overall quality of service delivery. On paper, the agency is also responsible for acting as a "one-stop shop" to access all government services necessary for starting and running a company in Belarus, but it does not offer essential services such as work permits or assistance with utilities. Despite its large number of mandates, the National Agency of Investment and Privatisation has only a small staff of about 30 employees, compared to a median of over 110 employees in OECD investment promotion agencies that are responsible for fewer mandates on average. If functions beyond investment promotion and facilitation were transferred to the purview of the Ministry of Economy, the National Agency of Investment and Privatisation could function more effectively and credibly (OECD, 2020[14]). Currently reforms to the Agency's functions are under consideration.

The Chinese-Belarus Industrial Park Great Stone, a large-scale manufacturing hub under development near Minsk within the framework of the China-Belarus intergovernmental cooperation agreement signed in 2011, acts as a free economic zone with its own unique investment climate. Any company, regardless of country of capital origin, can act as a resident of the industrial park. To compete for investors in the world market, Belarus has created a favourable investment climate for industrial park residents, as guaranteed by national law as well as special international agreements and obligations. It offers favourable tax conditions and is administered by a dedicated state institution that reports to the Government of Belarus. This institution, through its One Station Investor Services Department, offers comprehensive investor support services. By providing ready-made engineering and transport infrastructure and duty-free access to the Customs Union of the Eurasian Economic Union, the park aims to boost investment into high-value sectors of the Belarusian economy (Great Stone Industrial Park, n.d.[16]).

Inward FDI stocks have increased over the past decade in Belarus, increasing from 10% of GDP in 2007 to 23% in 2019. FDI stocks in Belarus remain below the EU average and its EaP peers, which indicates room for growth (OECD, 2020[14]).

According to the OECD FDI Restrictiveness Index, which measures barriers to foreign direct investment such as foreign equity limitations and operational restrictions, Belarus has the second most restrictive FDI rules in the Eastern Partnership after Ukraine. In 2019, on a scale from 0 (open) to 1 (closed), Belarus scored 0.086, more restrictive than the regional average for the Eastern Partnership (0.064) and slightly more closed than OECD countries (0.085). Restrictions in Belarus, like in Azerbaijan, apply primarily to the media sector as well as business and financial services.

Between 2003 and 2017, Belarus attracted USD 12.1 billion of FDI to greenfield projects across a wide variety of sectors, including communications (11%), automotive original equipment manufacturing (11%), transportation (11%) and financial services (8%) (Figure 3.2). Belarus's energy sector, especially alternative/renewable energy sources (7%) but also fossil fuels (5%), benefited from considerable greenfield FDI inflows.

Figure 3.2. Greenfield FDI in Belarus by economic activity, 2003-2017

Cumulated greenfield FDI capital between January 2003 and September 2017 in USD million

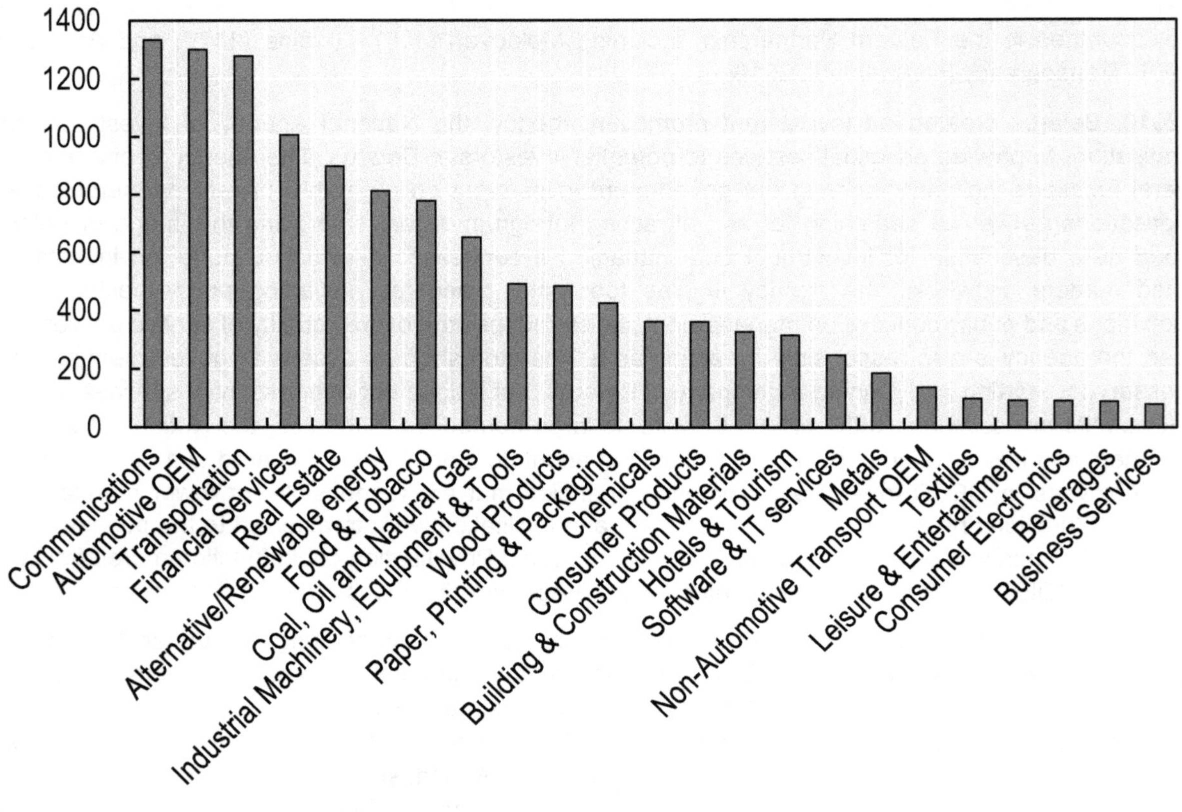

Source: OECD based on fDi Markets (2019[17]), fDi Markets: the in-depth crossborder investment monitor (database), fDi Markets, https://www.fdimarkets.com/

Not only is Russia Belarus's most important trade partner, it also invests more in Belarus's economy than any other country. In 2019, Russia invested USD 4.6 billion in Belarus, accounting for 32% of the country's FDI (Figure 3.3). A large share of Cyprus's 20% likely derives from offshore Russian concerns (Balas et al., 2018[18]). Belarus's other foreign investors are much smaller in scale: the Netherlands (4%), Austria (4%), Turkey (4%) and China (3%) (National Bank of the Republic of Belarus, 2020[19]). Much of Belarus's industries remain dominated by state-owned enterprises, which seek FDI by forming joint ventures with foreign investors. About half of the foreign capital that Belarus receives is funnelled into joint ventures with SOEs (Balas et al., 2018[18]).

Figure 3.3. Belarus's FDI inflows by country of origin, 2019

USD million

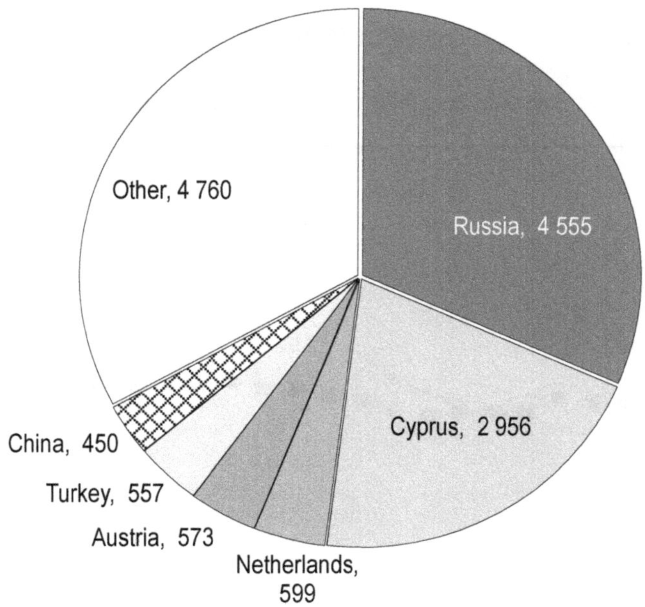

Source: National Bank of the Republic of Belarus (2020[19]), "Foreign direct investments in the reporting economy for 2010-2019", https://www.nbrb.by/engl/statistics/foreigndirectinvestments

The vast majority (about 90% in 2018) of Belarus's public debt is denominated in foreign currencies, which makes it particularly vulnerable to exchange rate fluctuations and external shocks. According to the IMF, external observers have advised caution about Belarus's rising public debt, which is high (52% of GDP) and expected to rise (55% by 2022). The IMF has encouraged reforms to macroeconomic policies and the country's large state-owned enterprises to boost economic resilience (IMF, 2018[20]).

Climate change

Belarus emits about 0.2% of global greenhouse gas (GHG) emissions. Prior to independence, Belarus's annual GHG emissions over 50% greater than over the past decade. Total emissions declined dramatically in the 1990s following the breakup of the Soviet Union, falling from 138 (or 185 according to World Bank data) $MtCO_2e$ in 1990 to 78 (or 83) $MtCO_2e$ by 2002, before rising again over the past two decades (92 $MtCO_2e$ by 2018) (Figure 3.4). While Belarus's GDP also declined over the 1990s, it has since expanded to over twice its pre-independence levels in real terms (USD 63 billion in 2019 in constant 2010 USD compared to USD 31.6 billion in 1990) despite contractions in 2014-2016 (due to the economic situation in Russia).

As emissions have fallen and the economy has grown, the GHG intensity of Belarus's GDP dropped from approximately 4 $kgCO_2e$ per USD (in constant 2010 dollars) in 1990 to about 1.5 $kgCO_2e$ per USD by 2018. However, the GHG intensity of Belarus's economy is well above the OECD average (0.35 $kgCO_2e$ per USD in 2012) and its per capita emissions (9.7 tCO_2e in 2018) are the highest in the Eastern Partnership (Ministry of Natural Resources and Environmental Protection of the Republic of Belarus, 2018[21]).

Figure 3.4. GHG emissions and GDP of Belarus, 1990-2019

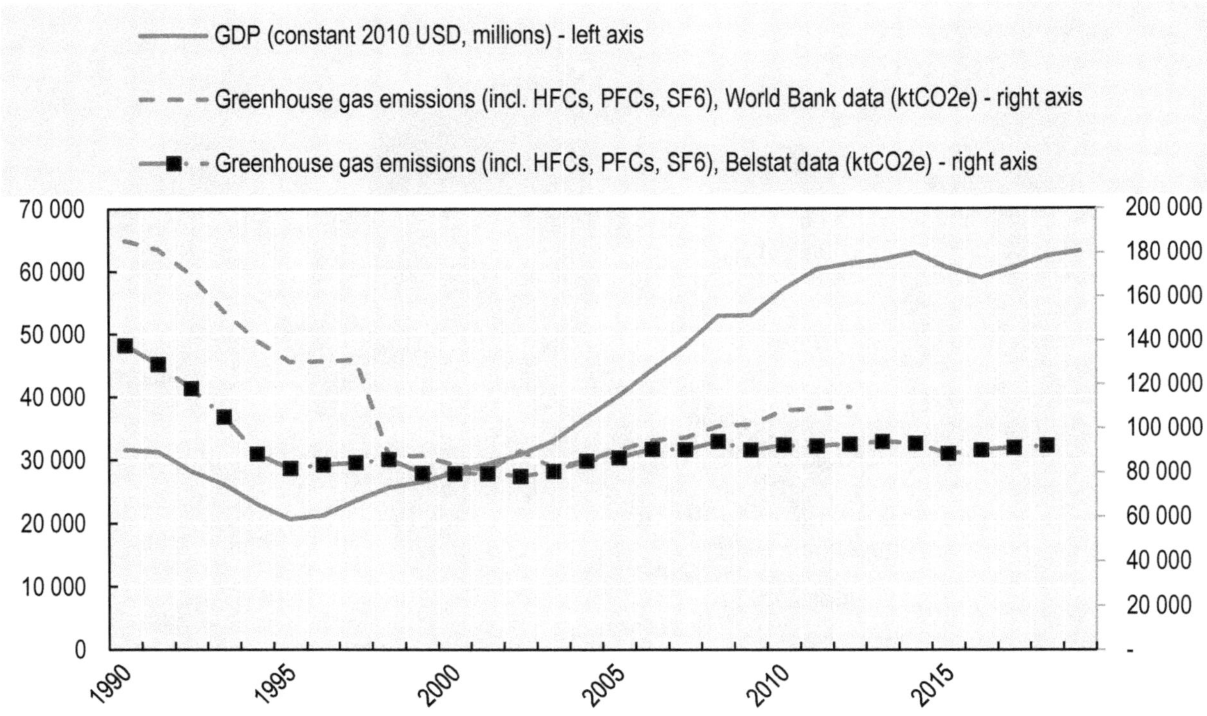

Source: World Bank (2021[1]), World Development Indicators (database), World Bank, https://data.worldbank.org/indicator/EN.ATM.GHGT.ZG; National Statistical Committee of the Republic of Belarus (2020[22]), B.3. Greenhouse gas emissions, Environment: Shared Environmental Information System Indicators, https://www.belstat.gov.by/en/ofitsialnaya-statistika/macroeconomy-and-environment/okruzhayuschaya-sreda/the-shared-environmental-information-system/b-slimate-change/b3-greenhouse-gas-emissions/

Energy (including fuel combustion from transport) has accounted for the largest, but declining, share of Belarus's GHG emissions since independence. 71% of the country's emissions (97.9 $MtCO_2e$) were from energy in 1990, declining somewhat to 62% (57 $MtCO_2e$) by 2015. Emissions from agriculture also decreased (from 30.6 $MtCO_2e$ to 22.5 $MtCO_2e$) over the same period, but their share of overall emissions expanded (from 22% to 24%). Emissions from Industrial processes and products use as well as waste both increased in absolute terms (from 6.1 $MtCO_2e$ and 3.2 $MtCO_2e$ to 6.2 $MtCO_2e$ and 6.3 $MtCO_2e$) and as a share of total emissions (from 4% and 2% respectively to 7% for both sectors) (Ministry of Natural Resources and Environmental Protection of the Republic of Belarus, 2018[21]).

Belarus ranks 40th in the Climate Change Performance Index (CCPI) for 2020, an aggregate rating of climate action of selected economies based on GHG emissions, renewable energy integration, energy use and climate policy. While this ranking places Belarus in the "low" category, Belarus performs better than Russia (52nd, "very low" category) and several OECD countries, including its neighbour Poland (50th, "very low" category) (Burck et al., 2020[23]).

The effects of climate change are already evident in Belarus. Average air temperatures nationally over the period of 1989 to 2016 were about 1.3°C above previously recorded trends (1881-1988), and heatwaves leading to dry conditions – including during the vegetation period, crucial for agricultural productivity – have increased in regularity from about 5 times a decade (before 1989) to 7 times a decade (after 1989). As a result of these changes, which have and will continue to have uneven impacts across the country's regions, Belarus's current agro-climatic zones are projected to undergo sweeping changes that will impact which crops are suitable. Crops currently viable in southern Belarus may be better suited to the country's north by 2030 or 2050 (Ministry of Natural Resources and Environmental Protection of the Republic of Belarus, 2018[21]). As a result, projected yields vary considerably from region to region and crop to crop. By 2050, barley, rapeseed and maize yields could decline by as much as 15-25% compared to 2010 levels in some areas, while maize yield in the northwest could increase by 10-20% (Clima East, 2017[24]).

Belarus's infrastructure needs and current plans

The overall quality of Belarus's infrastructure is adequate for most services, but infrastructure assets are often oversized and, due to age, in need of refurbishment or replacement. Most of the population has access to key infrastructure services, such as safe drinking water (99.5%), sanitation (98.7%), mobility (99.9% of the rural population lives within 2 km of a year-round road) and communal solid waste disposal services (95.5%) (Belstat, 2020[25]).

Belarus has the potential to capitalise on its strategic location between the European Union and Russia by ensuring that its infrastructure, particularly its logistics and transport infrastructure, facilitates the smooth movement of goods and people. However, according to the World Bank's Logistics Performance Index, Belarus's has fallen in the global rankings from 91st place in 2012 to 103rd in 2018. In particular, its infrastructure score has deteriorated, dropping from 2.78 (65th best in the world) to 2.44 (92nd) (Figure 3.5).

Figure 3.5. Belarus in the Logistics Performance Index, 2012 and 2018

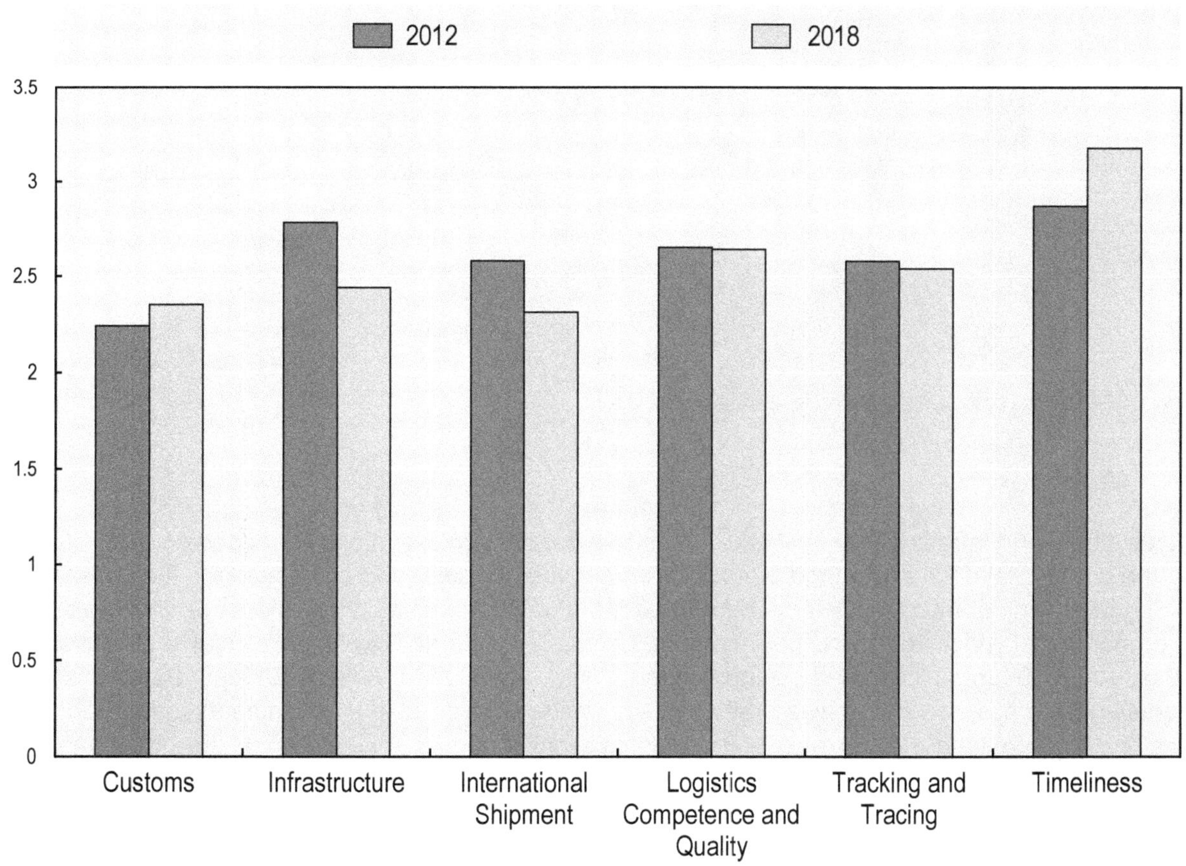

Source: World Bank (2019[26]), Country Score Card: Logistics Performance Index, https://lpi.worldbank.org/international/scorecard/

The strategic goal of Belarus's investment policy is to attract investment to fixed capital, particularly in priority industries. Priorities for the government include innovation, high value-added production and the development of human capital and industries that support environmental and socioeconomic security for the country. One of the criteria to measure progress towards this goal is the number of infrastructure investment projects carried out on the basis of public-private partnerships (PPPs). The government aims to increase the proportion of PPPs in infrastructure projects to at least 10% by 2030 (Government of Belarus, 2017[27]).

The OECD's database tracks 26 major infrastructure projects planned or under construction in Belarus with a cumulative value of USD 14.8 billion. By value, energy projects account for bulk of Belarus's infrastructure investments (78%, USD 11.5 billion), with transport (12%, USD 1.7 billion), industry and mining (6%, USD 0.8 billion) and water (4%, USD 0.7 billion) making up the remainder (Figure 3.6).

Figure 3.6. Investment projects in Belarus, by sector

Planned and under construction, in USD million

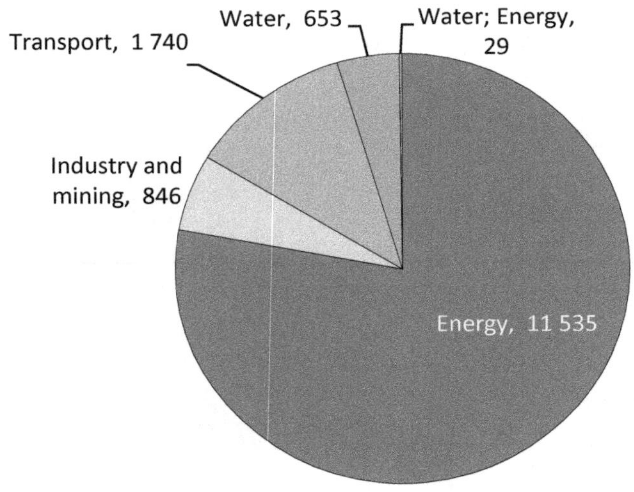

Source: OECD analysis based on accessed databases as of June 2020.

Transport

Belarus's transport infrastructure network is extensive but modernisation and increased connectivity could help the country take full advantage of its position between Russia (and other markets further east) and the European Union. In 2019, Belarus had 5 480 km of railways, of which 22.4% were electrified. While the proportion of electrified track has increased since 2000 (from 15.8%), the total rail network has decreased by 53 km as little-used sections of track were abandoned (Belstat, 2020[28]; Belstat, 2012[29]). Belarusian Railways, the state-owned rail company, made considerable improvements to its rolling stock in the 2010s, acquiring 12 163 new units. Belarus's public highway network, on the other hand, has increased in coverage from 74 thousand km in 2000 to 87 thousand km in 2019, but the proportion of paved public highways has fallen from 89% to 87% (Belstat, 2020[28]; Belstat, 2012[29]).

While the highway network has grown only modestly, the volumes of freight that it carries have has increased sharply over the past two decades. 31.4 billion tonne-kilometres (tkm) of cargo travelled by rail and 5 billion tkm by road in 2000, but 48.2 billion tkm and 28.5 billion tkm of cargo passed through Belarus's rail and road networks in 2019 (Belstat, 2020[28]; Belstat, 2012[29]). Rehabilitation of Belarus's internal, domestically oriented transport network would boost connectivity and connect domestic producers located away from the main transportation corridors with markets (World Bank, 2018[30]). As suggested by the trends in infrastructure development described above, a modal shift is underway in Belarus away from rail towards road transport for both cargo and passengers. In 2000, Belarus's railways carried 86.1% of cargo (excluding pipelines) and roads carried the remainder (13.8%), but by 2019 rail's modal share had dropped to 62.8% as road's increased to 37.1%. In terms of passenger turnover (measured in passenger-kilometres, pkm), the shift away from rail is even starker. In 2000, rail accounted for 54.6% (17.7 billion pkm) of passenger turnover, but passenger rail has since decreased in both absolute and relative terms, falling to 6.3 billion pkm and 22.8% of total turnover. Travel by bus has increased marginally (9.2 billion pkm to 10.9 billion pkm, growing from 28.5% to 39.5%) and air travel has increased more than tenfold (513 million pkm to 6.0 billion pkm, growing from 1.6% to 21.6% of passenger turnover). Some forms of urban public transport (e.g. tramways, trolleybuses and metro systems) have seen decreased turnover (4.8 billion pkm in 2000, 4.1 billion pkm in 2019 (Belstat, 2020[28]; Belstat, 2012[29]).

Belarus's per capita investments in its transport infrastructure system, at USD 153 on average between 2005 and 2018, are among the highest in the Eastern Partnership (Figure 3.7). By comparison, Azerbaijan and Georgia, two countries that have made their transport networks priorities for national development, invested USD 126 and USD 101 respectively over a comparable period (2008 to 2016) (ITF, 2019[31]). In line with cargo and passenger demand, rail accounts for a small and broadly declining share of inland transport investments.

Figure 3.7. Inland transport infrastructure investment in Belarus (2005-2018)

Modal share (%) of total inland infrastructure investment (left axis) and total inland transport infrastructure investment in current USD per capita (right axis)

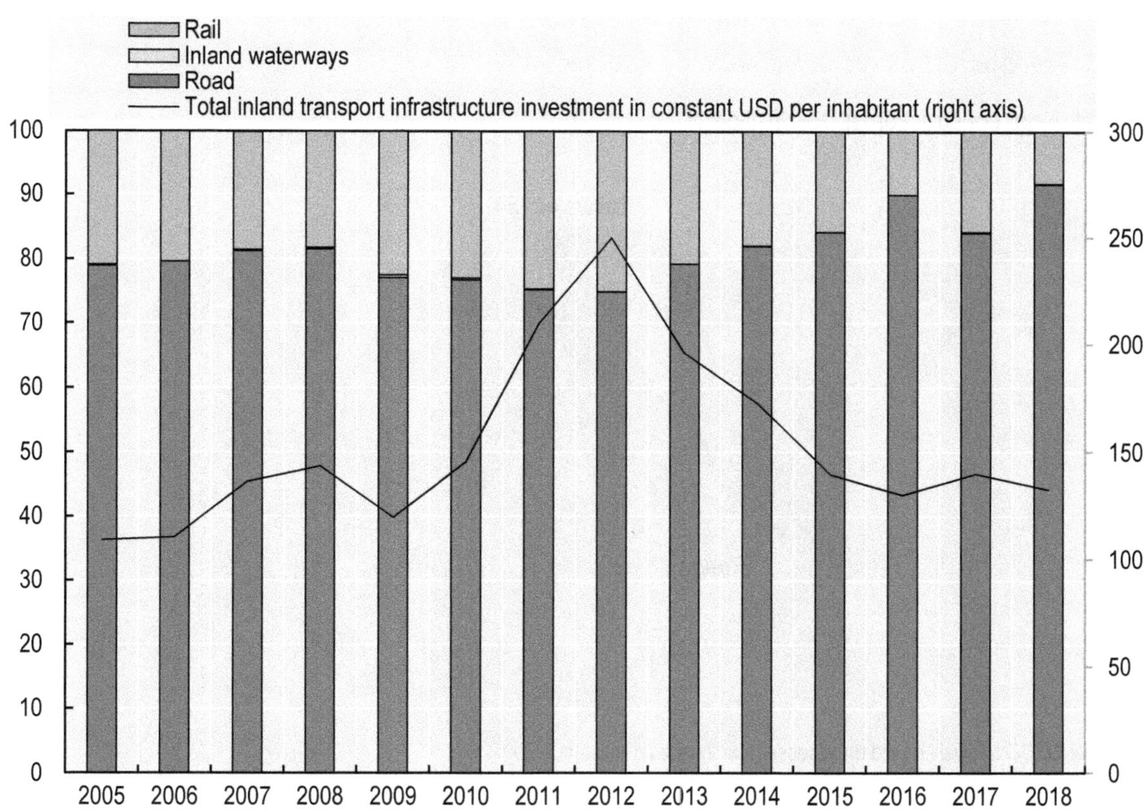

Source: ITF (2019[31]), *Transport performance indicators*, International Transport Forum, https://doi.org/10.1787/trsprt-data-en

The *National Strategy for Socioeconomic Development for the period to 2035* lays out a vision for the development of Belarus's transport system and increase the country's potential to support export-oriented sectors and the transit of goods, notably through the digitalisation of transport and logistics services. The strategy aims to increase cargo turnover by 20% and passenger turnover by 40% between 2016 and 2030. For the rail sector, the strategy explicitly references partnerships with Chinese companies for the improvement of Belarus's rail system and improvements to its transit capacity for trade between China and Europe. It aims to electrify all rail lines along international transport corridors. Belarus plans to prepare the road network for higher cargo volumes by creating a network of roads with the capacity to withstand single axle loads of 11.5 tonnes or more and speeds of 120 km/h or greater. Belarus aims to increase the share of paved roads to 88% by 2025 and 90% by 2030, and ensure access to the paved road network for all citizens and agricultural enterprises (Government of Belarus, 2017[27]).

A key component of the strategy's vision for Belarus's transport sector is the inclusion of more private sector actors, especially through private-public partnerships, and levelling the playing field by eliminating cross-subsidies for transport. The government also aims to simplify certification procedures and remove artificial barriers to entry for new firms (Government of Belarus, 2017[27]). The government is in the process of drafting a National Infrastructure Plan to 2025, which will include a list of priority transport and logistics infrastructure projects.

Belarus's large-scale transport infrastructure investments planned and under construction amount to around USD 1.7 billion, concentrated predominantly in road projects (97% or USD 1.69 billion) (Figure 3.8). All but one project tracked by the OECD's database are brownfield road improvement projects concentrated on international corridors (Table 3.2). While Belarus's transport projects seem to broadly align with its goals of increasing the carrying capacity of its international road network, its domestic connectivity and rail improvement goals are not addressed in the current pipeline of large-scale transport infrastructure projects.

Figure 3.8. Transport projects in Belarus, by sub-sector

Planned and under construction in USD million

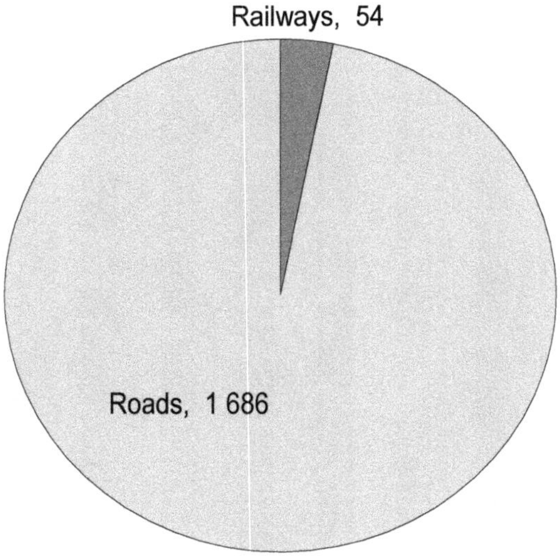

Source: Source: OECD analysis based on accessed databases as of June 2020.

Table 3.2. Hotspot projects in the transport sector in Belarus

(a) Under construction

Name	Sub-sector	Description	Project value (USD million)	Source	Type of investment
Belarus Transport Connectivity Project, composed of (1) Transport Corridor Modernisation Project and (2) Reconstruction and Modernisation of M-7/E28 (see components below)	Road	The project aims to rehabilitate stretches of the M6 highway between Minsk and the Polish border and the M7 highway between Minsk and the Lithuanian border.	380	EIB, World Bank, Government of Belarus	Brownfield
→(1) Transit Corridor Improvement Project	Road	With a view to improve transport connectivity, the project will improve border crossing procedures and safety by shoring up sections of the M6 Minsk-Grodno corridor.	270	Government of Belarus, World Bank	Brownfield
→(2) Reconstruction and Modernisation of M-7/E28	Road	The project aims to reconstruct and modernise over 100 km of the M7 highway and improve cross-border and trade infrastructure on the Belarusian side of the Lithuanian border.	110	EIB	Brownfield
Regional Bridges and M3 Road Rehabilitation Project	Road	The project aims to rehabilitate and modernise 12 bridges and sections of the M3 highway between Minsk and Vitebsk as part of the North-South corridor.	354	EBRD	Brownfield
Transit Corridor Improvement Project	Road	With a view to improve transport connectivity, the project will improve border crossing procedures and safety by shoring up sections of the M6 Minsk-Grodno corridor.	270	Government of Belarus, World Bank	Brownfield

(b) Planned

Name	Sub-sector	Description	Project value (USD million)	Source	Type of investment
M10 Highway Reconstruction PPP Project	Road	The project aims to reconstruct and maintain five sections of the M10 highway, which links Kobryn, Grodno and the Russian border.	212	EBRD, IFC, EDB	Brownfield
M1/E30 Brest (Kozlovichi) – Minsk – Redky	Road	The project aims to reconstruct the entirety (610 km) of the M1 (E30) highway in Belarus	TBD	TBD	Brownfield

Note: Refer to the Reader's guide for the present report's definition of 'hotspot' and other information on how the projects above were selected and prioritised. EBRD = European Bank for Reconstruction and Development; EDB = Eurasian Development Bank; EIB = European Investment Bank; IFC = International Finance Corporation.
Source: OECD database as of June 2020.

Energy

Belarus is one of the least energy self-sufficient countries in the world. Domestic production covers only about 15% of Belarus's energy demand with imports, primarily from a single supplier, Russia, covering the shortfall (IEA, 2020[32]). In 2018, Belarus imported 20 billion cubic metres (15 megatonnes of oil equivalent, Mtoe) of natural gas for domestic consumption, its primary fuel for electricity and heat generation, and produced only 128 ktoe domestically. Belarus's crude oil supply, which feeds the country's large refining industry (36th largest in the world), follows a similar pattern, with 18.2 Mtoe imported, 1.6 Mtoe exported and 1.7 Mtoe produced locally (IEA, 2019[33]). Due to increasing concerns about supply disruptions in the case of a dispute with Russia, Belarus has begun seeking to diversify its suppliers (S&P Global Platts, 2020[34]). Thanks to its large refining capacity, Belarus is a net exporter of oil products, exporting ten times more than it imports (11.9 Mtoe vs. 453 ktoe). Imports (974 ktoe) and domestic production (544 ktoe) each cover about half of Belarus's domestic demand for coal and peat, which are mainly used for heat generation, and Belarus exports small quantities of coal and peat (541 ktoe). Belarus both imports and exports limited amounts of electricity (280 ktoe and 365 ktoe respectively) (IEA, 2019[33]).

State-owned enterprises (SOEs) mainly reporting directly to the Ministry of Energy monopolise most of the Belarus's energy sector. The State Production Association "Belenergo" functions as a vertically integrated state-owned monopoly of Belarus's power sector. "Belorusneft" is the primary upstream gas producer in Belarus, while the State Production Association "Beltopgaz" operates the country's gas distribution network and provides gas to end-users. Gazprom Transgaz Belarus, wholly owned by Russia's Gazprom, wields exclusive rights to import gas from Russia for consumption in Belarus.

Like other former Soviet Union countries, Belarus has achieved universal electricity access. Its electricity supply is quite reliable, with businesses reporting few power outages per year (World Bank, 2020[13]). Distribution and transmission losses amounted to 8.9% in 2017, lower than in neighbouring Ukraine (10%) and Moldova (18.8%). Its electricity grid is linked to the networks of Russia, Ukraine and its EU neighbours Latvia, Lithuania and Poland. Belarus also maintains an extensive network of natural gas infrastructure, including over 7.9 thousand km of pipelines, 13 compressor stations and 226 gas distribution stations. As a key transit country for Russian natural gas, Belarus has interconnections with the gas networks of Lithuania, Poland, Russia and Ukraine. Although Belarus aims to diversify its gas supply, the contractual arrangements between Russia's Gazprom and Belarus's Gazprom Transgaz Belarus do not permit reversing the flow of Belarus's pipelines to import natural gas from other suppliers like Lithuania and Poland (Energy Community Secretariat, 2018[35]).

Belarus generates almost all of its electricity (94%) from imported natural gas, with various renewables (3%) accounting for almost all of the remainder (Figure 3.9 (a)). Belarus has begun integrating renewable power generation, particularly from hydroelectric power plants, biomass incineration and solar photovoltaics (Figure 3.9 (b)).

Figure 3.9. Electricity generation by source

GWh, 2019

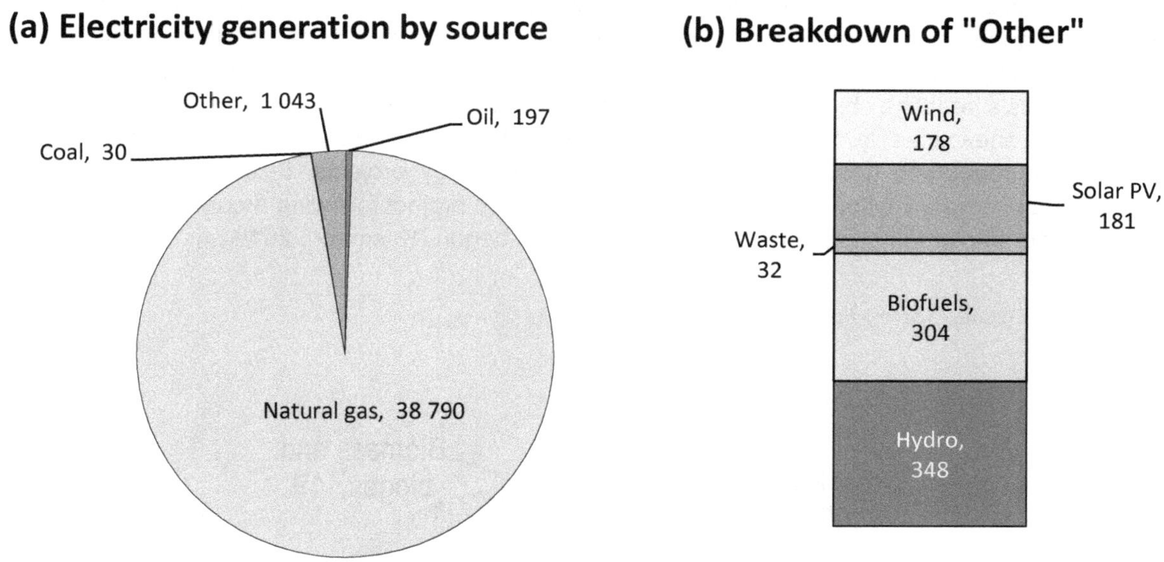

Source: IEA (2021[36]), *Electricity Information 2020*, International Energy Agency, https://www.iea.org/data-and-statistics

Energy self-sufficiency concerns are the driving force behind Belarus's strategy for the development of its energy sector. To bolster energy self-sufficiency, Belarus aims to improve energy efficiency, support renewables development and, most consequentially, integrate nuclear power into its energy mix. The *National Strategy for Socioeconomic Development for the period to 2030* identifies priority projects for each goal, including the construction of two nuclear reactors (with a combined generation capacity of 2 400 MW), modernising improvements to existing thermal power plants and the construction of three renewable energy projects (two hydroelectric power plants and a wind energy park). By 2030, Belarus aims to reduce the energy intensity[3] of its economy, increase the share of renewables in total energy consumption from 5.6% in 2015 to 8% by 2030 and use domestically extracted energy resources to cover 18% of total energy consumption by 2030 (compared to 14.2% in 2015) (Government of Belarus, 2017[27]). The draft *Concept for Developing Power Generation Facilities and Power Grids to 2030* forecasts that Belarus will generate slightly over 4% of electricity using renewable energy sources by 2030, meaning the majority of renewables use will instead be in heat production, primarily moving away from natural gas-fired heating towards biomass (Government of Belarus, 2020[37]). Belarus already succeeded in increasing the share of renewables in its total energy consumption to 7.1% in 2019, but its energy intensity has remained largely unchanged (Belstat, 2020[38]). of According to the *Concept on Energy Security*, Belarus intends to reduce the share of natural gas in electricity generation and heating to 60% by 2025 (IEA, 2020[32]).

According to the OECD's database of large-scale infrastructure projects planned and under construction, by value Belarus's current energy investments are overwhelmingly concentrated in new power generation projects (USD 11.3 billion, 98%). This is partially due to the capital-intensive nature of a single nuclear power project, the two reactors at the 2 400-MW Belarusian Nuclear Power Plant, which alone accounts for over 21% of energy investments in Belarus. Although listed as 'under construction' in the OECD database, the project passed international inspections and began generating electricity in November 2020, despite the Lithuanian opposition (Euronews, 2020[39]). Lithuania objected to the selected site, since it is located only 40 km away from Vilnius, and submitted concerns about the cross-border environmental impact assessment (EIA) process required by the UNECE Espoo Convention to the Convention's Implementation Committee (Ministry of Foreign Affairs of the Republic of Lithuania, 2018[40]).

The database's two non-generation projects are a large-scale energy efficiency project aimed at heating systems (USD 202 million) and a low-voltage substation in a town near Minsk (USD 21.7 million). In terms of new power generation capacity, the proposed nuclear power plant is by far the largest project (94%), but renewable projects, particularly in solar (4%), are also advancing (Figure 3.10). These projects align well with Belarus's headline objectives to increase energy self-sufficiency and, to a lesser degree, increase the share of renewables in the national energy mix (Table 3.3). However, foreign investors have encountered bureaucratic barriers developing renewable energy projects. In one notable instance, a German energy company withdrew from a 160-MW wind farm project following a conflict with the Ministry of Defence after implementation of the project had already begun (Kasmach, 2016[41]).

Figure 3.10. New electricity capacity in Belarus, by energy source

In MW

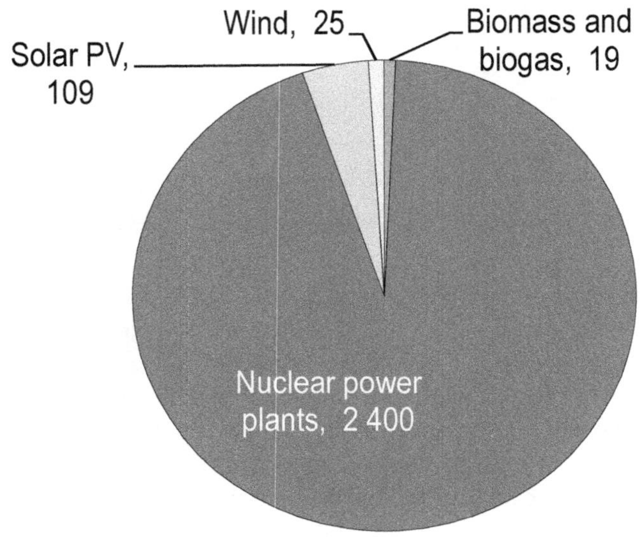

Source: OECD analysis based on accessed databases as of June 2020.

Table 3.3. Hotspot projects in the energy sector in Belarus

Name	Sub-sector	Description	Project value (USD million)	New capacity (MW)	Source	Type of investment
(a) Under construction						
Belarusian Nuclear Power Plant	Nuclear power plants	This project, in Grodno oblast, consists of two 1 200-MW units and will constitute the first nuclear power plant in Belarus.	11 000	2 400	Government of Russia, Government of Belarus	Greenfield
Blizhnyaya Rechitsa Solar PV Project	Solar PV	This project will construct a solar voltaic over 200 hectares in Mogilev oblast. Once completed, it will be the largest renewable energy generation facility in Belarus.	170	109	Solar Land	Greenfield
Biomass for Centralised Heat Generation Project	Energy efficiency, Biomass	This project aims to replace natural gas with biomass in heat generation facilities.	90	N/A	IBRD	Brownield
(b) Planned						
Name	Sub-sector	Description	Project value (USD million)	New capacity (MW)	Source	Type of investment
Sustainable Energy Scale-Up Project	Energy efficiency, biomass	This project aims to improve energy efficiency by reducing heat losses in multi-apartment buildings and replace natural gas with wood biomass in select district heating systems.	202	N/A	EIB, IBRD	Brownfield
Guris Wind Farm Project	Wind power	This project will provide electricity to 20 000 households in Vitebsk oblast.	40	25	Guris Construction and Engineering	Greenfield
Belarus Environmental Infrastructure Facility	Biogas-fired power plant, Water	This project has a dual purpose: improving water quality on the West Dvina/Daugava river and the construction of a biogas generation plant using wastewater sludge.	29		EBRD	Greenfield

Note: Refer to the Reader's note for the present report's definition of 'hotspot' and other information on how the projects above were selected and prioritised. EBRD = European Bank for Reconstruction and Development, EIB = European Investment Bank, IBRD = International Bank for Reconstruction and Development.
Source: OECD database as of June 2020

Industry, mining and water

SOEs, including those wholly owned by the state and those with partial state ownership, remain a dominant force in Belarus's economy. They account for a third of total employment and gross value added. Micro, small and medium enterprises (MSMEs), on the other hand, collectively account for 29% of gross value added while employing 47% of Belarusians. MSMEs are concentrated in non-innovative industries characterised by low productivity; 36% of MSMEs operate in wholesale and retail trade or vehicle repair (OECD et al., 2020[42]). SOEs also dominate the industry sector in Belarus, both for domestic and export markets. Many of the SOEs date back to the Soviet era; their advantage has derived from their sheer size rather than inherent competitiveness via investment in intellectual property or strategic positioning within global value chains (World Bank, 2018[30]). Belarus seeks to reorient its industrial sector towards high-tech, innovative industries, particularly pharmaceuticals, aerospace, fibre optics, medical devices and measuring equipment. By 2030, Belarus aims to increase the share of high-tech industries in its industrial production to 8% (Government of Belarus, 2017[27]).

Manufacturing accounts for nearly the totality (89%) of Belarus's industrial output (Figure 3.11). Food products and beverages, particularly meat and dairy products, are the largest category of manufacturing (27% of industrial output), followed by refined oil products (16%), chemical products (10%), metal production (8%), rubber and plastic products (8%) and vehicles and tractors (5%). SMEs account for small shares of key production categories: 13% of chemicals, 14% of food products and 18% of vehicles. Unlike in Ukraine or the countries in the Caucasus, mining plays only a minor (1%) role in Belarus's industrial production. Water supply and sanitation (WSS) and waste management and electricity, gas, steam and air conditioning supply accounted for the remaining 2% and 8% of industrial output respectively.

Figure 3.11. Industrial output by NACE* subsector

2019

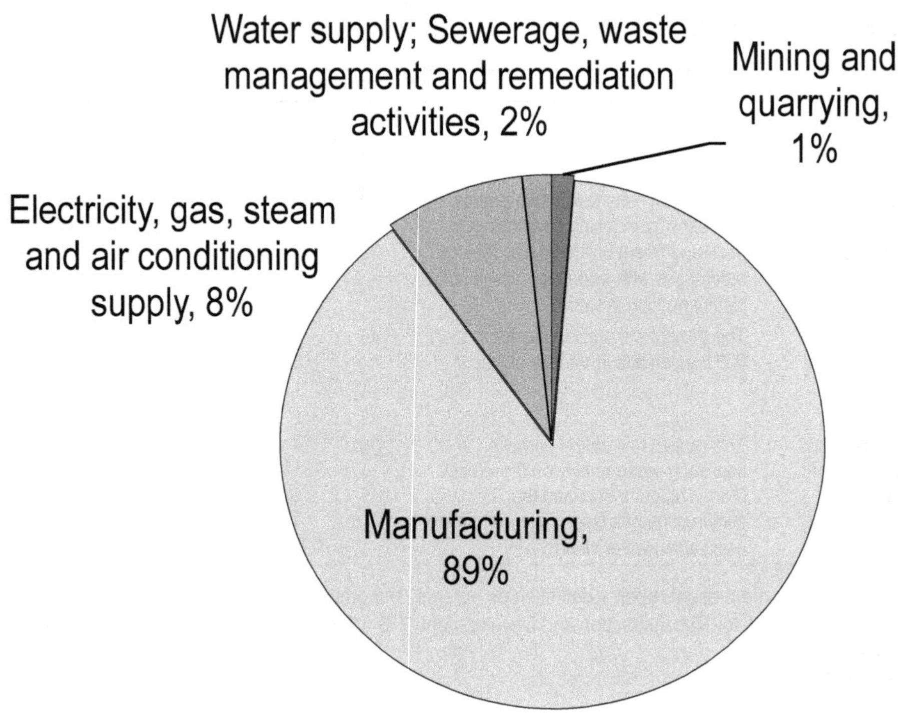

Note: * NACE = Nomenclature statistique des activités économiques dans la Communauté européenne [Statistical Classification of Economic Activities in the European Community]
Source: Belstat (2020[43]), *Industry of the Republic of Belarus*, National Statistics Committee of the Republic of Belarus, https://www.belstat.gov.by/upload/iblock/88c/88ca482411a706f47c7da68ae873fff7.pdf

Belarus has achieved high levels of access to water supply and sanitation (WSS) and waste services. 99.5% of Belarusians enjoy access to safe drinking water and 98.7% have access to sanitation, although disparities persist between rural and urban populations. The proportion of Belarusians that use communal solid waste disposal services has increased rapidly in the past few years, from 75% in 2016 to 95.5% in 2019 (Belstat, 2020[25]).

Solid municipal waste makes up an increasing share of Belarus's total waste generation, rising from 15.6% 2015 to 22.5% in 2019. In 2019, 850 900 tonnes of secondary material resources were collected in 2019 (46.1% higher than in 2015), and 25 500 tonnes of electrical and electronic equipment (almost six times higher than in 2016). Currently, there are seven garbage processing plants in five regional centers (Brest,

Gomel, Grodno, Mogilev, Minsk) and two regional cities (Baranovichi and Novopolotsk), as well as 80 lines for sorting municipal waste. Collection of recyclable materials from the industrial sector (e.g. waste paper and cardboard, glass, plastics, rubber-containing waste, including worn tires) on average in the country is over 94%. According to the results of 2019, about 23% of solid municipal waste was recycled, which is 2.5 times more than in 2010. The proportion of the population using the solid municipal waste disposal service on a regular basis in 2019 was 95.5%, compared to 75.3% in 2016 (Belstat, 2020[25]).

Belarus's draft *Water Strategy in the Context of Climate Change for the Period until 2030* sets improving water security as its primary objective through more effective water management and incentives for sustainable consumption patterns, including through the progressive adoption of energy- and resource-saving technological processes and the improvement of the pricing system for water use (OECD, 2020[44]).

The OECD database tracks USD 1.5 billion worth of infrastructure projects in industry and WSS in Belarus. By number, WSS projects represent almost two-thirds of total projects, but due to their smaller average value they cumulatively amount to 44% of all investments (Figure 3.12). All but one of the current large-scale WSS projects are brownfield investments aimed at improving water treatment facilities, primarily in urban areas; the remaining project consists of 70 new iron-removal facilities in rural settlements of Vitebsk *oblast*. Such facilities are essential for rural drinking water supply, since the iron level in the water abstracted from 70% of the boreholes in Belarus exceeds the maximum allowable concentration of 0.3 mg/L and therefore requires iron removal to satisfy water quality guidelines (OECD, 2020[44]). With no mining projects in the OECD database, manufacturing projects account for the remaining 56% of Belarus's industry projects. The four manufacturing projects in the database represent four industries: potash fertilisers, steel, textiles and chemicals. These projects align more closely with historic industrial production than with the government's objectives for innovative, high-tech industrial development.

Figure 3.12. Industry, mining and water infrastructure projects in Belarus, by sub-sector

Planned and under construction in million USD

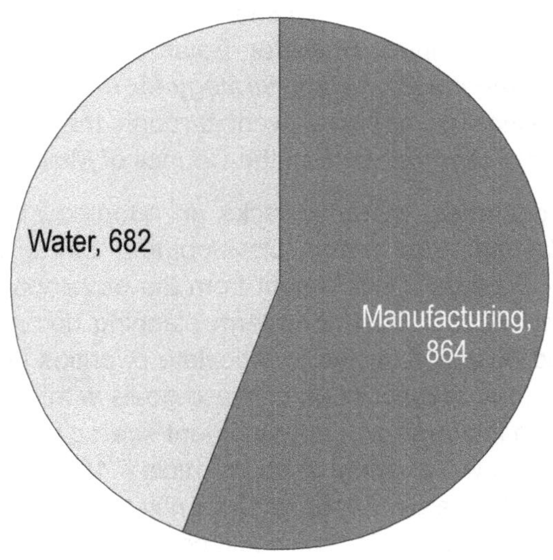

Source: OECD analysis based on accessed databases as of June 2020.

Strengths and weaknesses of existing institutional set-up for sustainable infrastructure planning

Strategic planning and links between long-term goals, infrastructure plans and environmental considerations

Belarus has a system of strategic planning documents for economic development is well defined in Belarusian law, which sets out a three-tier system of strategic cascading from long-term strategies of socioeconomic development (10-15 years), mid-term programmes for socioeconomic development (5 years) and short-term annual forecasting documents. Sectoral development planning has adopted an analogous approach.

Belarus's current top-level strategy is the *National Strategy for Socioeconomic Development for the period to 2030*, adopted in 2017, which replaced the previous socioeconomic development strategy (2004-2020). It improves upon the previous strategy in its implementation monitoring procedures that require annual monitoring and publicly available biannual implementation reports. Belarus re-established the National Commission on Sustainable Development to oversee monitoring and report preparation. Lower-level strategies, including the Programme for Socio-Economic Development 2016-2020 and its 2021-2025 follow-up currently under development, are the main mechanisms for implementation, translating long-term goals into mid-term development plans (UNECE, 2016[45]). Belarus has drafted a *National Sustainable Development Strategy to 2035*, which will replace the 2030 strategy.

Belarus has also carried out a pilot assessment of infrastructure needs in the long term and, in 2015, the Inter-Agency Infrastructure Coordination Committee approved the National Infrastructure Plan for 2016-2030. The Plan identifies 100 infrastructure projects for the implementation period, including projects with the potential to be realised through public-private partnerships. In 2017, the National Infrastructure Strategy was updated.

The draft *National Sustainable Development Strategy to 2035* integrates green economy principles, including the use of economic instruments for sustainable resource use and the introduction of green technologies and circular economy principles. However, Belarus's current top-level strategy dedicated to environmental issues, the *Environmental Protection Strategy for the period to 2025* has weaker political buy-in than originally planned, since its approval went through the Board of the Ministry of Natural Resources and Environmental Protection rather than the Council of Ministers (UNECE, 2016[45]).

Belarus, like many other EaP countries, currently lacks an adopted strategic document that extends beyond 2030, and its draft *National Sustainable Development Strategy to 2035* does not adopt a significantly longer time horizon. Belarus could benefit from the development of a longer-term vision for the country's transition, perhaps to 2050. Such long-term planning documents enable countries to look beyond shorter-term political and business cycles to articulate priorities in terms of economic and social development as well as, crucially, the reconciliation of these goals with environmental concerns. Belarus is currently developing a long-term low-emission development strategy for the period to 2050 (LT-LEDS), as all Parties to the Paris Agreement were invited to do in Article 4.19 (Belta, 2020[46]). It is expected to be completed by 2022 (Government of Belarus, 2018[47]). Currently Ukraine is the only EaP country that has communicated its LT-LEDS to the UNFCCC. Belarus could consider complementing the LT-LEDS process by developing an economic development strategy with a mid-century timeframe, like *Armenia Transformation Strategy 2050* or *Kazakhstan-2050,* aligned with the SDGs, its draft long-term low-emission development strategy and its existing sectoral documents.

Belarus has adopted a wide array of sectoral strategic documents. Although many expire in 2020 and have not yet been replaced, draft strategies covering 2021-2025 are in an advanced stage of development. In the energy sector, Belarus's guiding documents are the *Concept of Energy Security*, the *Comprehensive Plan for the Development of Electric Energy to 2025* and the *Concept for Developing Power Generation*

Facilities and Power Grids to 2030, which acts as the main mechanism for implementing the energy security strategy. In transport, Belarus has dedicated strategies and state programmes extending to 2020 for reducing transport-related air pollution, the development of the overall transport system and the development and maintenance of roads. Sectoral strategies vary in their integration of green economy principles. For instance, the power generation strategy focused primarily on self-reliance from nuclear power generation and foreseeing only a modest increase in Belarus's electricity generation capacity from renewable sources, meaning that the integration of renewables called for by the top-level economic development strategy will be achieved almost exclusively through switching from natural gas to biomass as a fuel for heating. As Belarus moves towards drafting the post-2020 editions of its transport-related and other sectoral strategies, it should ensure that they are mutually reinforcing and aligned with the country's top-level development strategy and the draft LT-LEDS.

A promising development in the integration of environmental concerns into sectoral documents is Belarus's draft *Water Strategy in the Context of Climate Change for the Period until 2030*. The strategy features expanded sections on minimising the impact on water resources and ecosystems as well as the potential impacts of climate change. Although strategic environmental assessments (SEAs) are not widely used in Belarus and the country is not yet a Party to the Protocol on Strategic Environmental Assessment to the Espoo Convention, the 2030 Water Strategy underwent a pilot strategic environmental assessment (SEA) through the EU Water Initiative Plus (EUWI+) programme. The process, which includes a transparent and open consultation process, led to considerable improvements to the draft strategy such as more robust sections on wetlands, the expansion of protected areas and the consequences of climate change for water-dependent economic sectors and natural ecosystems (OECD, 2020[44]).

Belarus should consider adopting the more regular use of SEAs in its development of strategic documents. Since 2019, one of the main work areas of the EU-funded EU4Environment programme, the successor to the EaP GREEN programme, is supporting reforms and improvements to the environmental assessment processes in Belarus and other EaP countries. The programme is jointly implemented by the OECD, UNECE, UNEP, UNIDO and the World Bank.

Belarus is a Party to several multilateral environmental agreements, including the UN Environment Programme's Cartagena Protocol on Biosafety, the Montreal Protocol on the Ozone Layer, the Stockholm Convention on Persistent Organic Pollutants, the Basel Convention on the Control of Transboundary Movements of Hazardous Wastes and Their Disposal, the Protocol on Biosafety and the Convention on Biological Diversity.

Institutional set-up and decision making processes

Unlike in many EaP countries, the institutional set-up of Belarus's government has been remarkably stable, with many infrastructure-related ministries experiencing few structural changes since independence and even before. In the case of the Ministry of Natural Resources and Environmental Protection, its relative stability and its status as a ministry (rather than an agency or state committee, as is common in the former Soviet Union), has facilitated the integration of environmental considerations into legislation as well as strategies across the government (UNECE, 2016[45]). Since 2017, the National Council on Sustainable Development has been in charge of facilitating inter-agency coordination for achieving the SDGs.

While strong centralised governance, including exclusive controls over economic activities, has been credited with Belarus's success in avoiding asset stripping during the fallout from the dissolution of the Soviet Union in the 1990s, the persistent role of the central government in economic affairs has emerged as a barrier to growth and development. Large SOEs still dominate much of the Belarusian economy and, since their independence in decision-making processes is limited by state interference, Belarus has proven less adaptable and innovative than its regional peers (World Bank, 2018[30]).

List of relevant strategic documents

Table 3.4. Main strategic documents in force

	Status	Time Horizon	Sectoral Coverage	Main objectives
First Nationally Determined Contribution (NDC)	Submitted in 2016	2016-2030	Economy-wide	• Unconditional Target: 28% reduction of GHG emissions by 2030 compared to 1990 excluding LULUCF • Main sectors for emission reduction: energy, IPPU, agriculture, waste Adaptation priorities: forestry and agriculture
Draft National Sustainable Development Strategy to 2035	Developed, adoption expected in 2021	2021-2035	Economy-wide	• Improve Belarus's rankings in international metrics, including the World Bank's annual Doing Business survey • Achieve an LPI ranking of 50th or better Improve energy self-sufficiency
National Strategy for Socio-Economic Development of the Republic of Belarus for the period to 2030	Adopted in 2017	2017-2030	Economy-wide	• Join top 30 countries in the World Bank's annual Doing Business survey by 2030 • Increase quality of road network (90% paved roads by 2030) • Increase energy self-sufficiency (integration of nuclear energy, 8% renewables in total energy consumption by 2030, 18% local energy resources in total energy consumption by 2030)
Concept for Developing Power Generation Facilities and Power Grids to 2030	Adopted in 2020	2020-2030	Energy	• Increase electricity exports by developing power grid • Commission Belarusian Nuclear Power Plant • Reduce the share of natural gas in electricity generation and heat production to 60% by 2025 Expand electric vehicle charging infrastructure
Environmental Protection Strategy of the Republic of Belarus for the period to 2025	Adopted in 2011	2011-2025	Economy-wide	• Improve air quality and water quality, e.g. gradually introduce standards on mobile pollution sources in line with EU standards Strengthen regulations protecting environmental health and biodiversity; improve waste management
Strategy for the Development of the Geological Sector and the Intensification of Exploitation of the Minerals and Raw Materials of the Republic of Belarus to 2025	Adopted in 2013	2013-2025	Mining	• Improve information base and monitoring processes of subsoil resources Increase domestic production and reduce imports
Strategy for the Reduction of the Negative Impact of Transport on Air of the Republic of Belarus for the period to 2020	Adopted in 2013	2013-2020	Transport	• Reduce mobile source emissions from 72% to 65% by 2020 • Increase share of green and electric vehicles in public transport fleets of cities with populations larger than 100 000 to 50% by 2020 Improve fuel standards of vehicles and environmental performance of rail stock
State Programme for the Development of the Transport Complex of the Republic of Belarus 2016-2020	Adopted in 2016	2016-2020	Transport	Increase cargo and passenger turnover by 6.8% and 2.4% respectively compared to 2015 levels by 2020
Energy Security Concept	Adopted in 2015	2015-2035	Energy	Improve energy self-reliance, including through reduction of the share of natural gas in power generation and heat generation to 60% by 2025

Table 3.5. Other relevant documents

	Status	Time Horizon	Sectoral Coverage
National Strategy for Socio-Economic Development of the Republic of Belarus for the period to 2020	Adopted in 2004	2004-2020	Multi-sector
National Action Plan on Green Economy Development in the Republic of Belarus to 2020	Adopted in 2016	2016-2020	Multi-sector
State Programme for the Development and Maintenance of Roads in the Republic of Belarus 2017-2020	Adopted in 2017	2017-2020	Transport
State Programme "Small and Medium Enterprises in the Republic of Belarus" 2021-2025	To be adopted in 2021	2021-2025	Multi-sector
State Programme "Environmental Protection and Sustainable Use of Natural Resources" for 2021-2025	To be adopted in 2021	2021-2025	Multi-sector
State Programme on Energy Saving for 2021-2025	Adopted in 2016	2016-2020	Energy, Energy Efficiency
State Programme the Development of Agricultural Businesses 2016-2020	Adopted in 2016	2016-2020	Agriculture
State Programme "Belarusian Forest" for 2021-2025	To be adopted in 2021	2021-2025	Forestry
State Programme for the Development of Vehicle Manufacturing for 2017-2020	Adopted in 2017	2017-2020	Industry
State Programme for the Development of the Transport Complex of the Republic of Belarus 2021-2025	To be adopted in 2021	2021-2025	Transport

References

Balas, P. et al. (2018), *Foreign Direct Investment between the EU and EAEU: Challenges and Opportunities of Economic Integration within a Wider European and Eurasian Space*, International Institute for Applied Systems Analysis, Vienna. [18]

Belstat (2020), *Energy Balance of the Republic of Belarus: Statistical Book*, National Statistics Committee of the Republic of Belarus, https://www.belstat.gov.by/upload/iblock/484/484d69a59d489c53b25079a3c088e5c6.pdf (accessed on 14 November 2020). [38]

Belstat (2020), *Industry of the Republic of Belarus*, National Statistics Committee of the Republic of Belarus, Minsk, https://www.belstat.gov.by/upload/iblock/88c/88ca482411a706f47c7da68ae873fff7.pdf (accessed on 14 November 2020). [43]

Belstat (2020), *Transport in the Republic of Belarus*, National Statistics Committee of the Republic of Belarus, Minsk, https://www.belstat.gov.by/upload/iblock/e58/e58620b44fc739884f156af60bf23ae1.pdf (accessed on 14 November 2020). [28]

Belstat (2020), *Беларусь на пути достижения Целей устойчивого развития [Belarus on the path to achieving the Sustainable Development Goals]*, National Statistics Committee of the Republic of Belarus, Minsk, http://www.sdgplatform.belstat.gov.by (accessed on 14 November 2020). [25]

Belstat (2020), *B.3. Greenhouse gas emissions*, National Statistical Committee of the Republic of Belarus, https://www.belstat.gov.by/en/ofitsialnaya-statistika/macroeconomy-and-environment/okruzhayuschaya-sreda/the-shared-environmental-information-system/b-slimate-change/b3-greenhouse-gas-emissions/ (accessed on 18 February 2021). [22]

Belstat (2020), *Общая численность населения, численность населения по возрасту и полу, состоянию в браке, уровню образования, национальностям, языку, источникам средств к существованию по Республике Беларусь [Overall population, population by age and sex, marital status, education level, ethnicity, language, source of income in the Republic of Belarus]*, National Statistics Committee of the Republic of Belarus, Minsk, https://belstat.gov.by/ofitsialnaya-statistika/publications/izdania/public_bulletin/index_17853/ (accessed on 13 November 2020). [3]

Belstat (2012), *Транспорт и связь в Республике Беларусь, 2012 [Transport and communications in the Republic of Belarus, 2012]*, National Statistics Committee of the Republic of Belarus, Minsk, https://www.belstat.gov.by/ofitsialnaya-statistika/realny-sector-ekonomiki/transport/ofitsialnye-publikatsii_11/index_288/ (accessed on 14 November 2020). [29]

Belta (2020), *В Беларуси разрабатывают стратегию развития с низким уровнем парниковых газов до 2050 года [In Belarus a strategy for low-GHG development to 2050 is being developed]*, Belta, https://www.belta.by/society/view/v-belarusi-razrabatyvajut-strategiju-razvitija-s-nizkim-urovnem-parnikovyh-gazov-do-2050-goda-404421-2020/ (accessed on 14 November 2020). [46]

Burck, J. et al. (2020), *Climate Change Performance Index (CCPI): Results 2020*, Germanwatch, NewClimate Institute and Climate Action Network International, https://newclimate.org/wp-content/uploads/2019/12/CCPI-2020-Results_Web_Version.pdf (accessed on 18 February 2021). [23]

Clima East (2017), *Strategy for Adaptation of Agriculture to Climate Change in the Republic of Belarus (Preliminary Version)*, Clima East and Zoi Environment Network. [24]

Energy Community Secretariat (2018), *Energy Governance in Belarus: Policy Recommendations*, Energy Community, Vienna, http://enercommunities.eu/wp-content/uploads/2018/07/ECS_Belarus_042018-%CE%98%CE%95%CE%9F%CE%94%CE%A9%CE%A1%CE%91-%CE%A4%CE%A3%CE%A9%CE%9A%CE%9F%CE%A5.pdf. [35]

Euronews (2020), *Belarus' first nuclear power plant launches despite Baltic unease*, Euronews, https://www.euronews.com/2020/11/05/belarus-first-nuclear-power-plant-launches-despite-baltic-unease (accessed on 14 November 2020). [39]

fDi Markets (2019), *fDi Markets: the in-depth crossborder investment monitor (database)*, https://www.fdimarkets.com/. [17]

Government of Belarus (2020), *Концепция развития электрогенерирующих мощностей и электрических сетей на период до 2030 года [Concept for Developing Power Generation Facilities and Power Grids to 2030]*, Ministry of Energy of the Republic of Belarus, Minsk. [37]

Government of Belarus (2018), *План мероприятий по реализации положений Парижского соглашения к Рамочной конвенции Организации Объединенных Наций об изменении климата [Action Plan for the Realisation of the Paris Agreement under the UNFCCC]*, https://www.minpriroda.gov.by/uploads/folderForLinks/plan-ps-2019.pdf (accessed on 18 February 2021). [47]

Government of Belarus (2017), *Национальная стратегия устойчивого социально-экономического развития Республики Беларусь на период до 2030 года [National Strategy for Sustainable Socioeconomic Development of the Republic of Belarus for the period to 2030]*, http://www.economy.gov.by/uploads/files/NSUR2030/Natsionalnaja-strategija-ustojchivogo-sotsialno-ekonomicheskogo-razvitija-Respubliki-Belarus-na-period-do-2030-goda.pdf (accessed on 14 November 2020). [27]

Great Stone Industrial Park (n.d.), *General Information*, https://en.industrialpark.by/o-parke/obshhaya-informaciya/ (accessed on 18 February 2021). [16]

IEA (2021), *Electricity Information 2020*, https://www.iea.org/data-and-statistics (accessed on 10 August 2020). [36]

IEA (2020), *Belarus energy profile*, https://www.iea.org/reports/belarus-energy-profile#key-energy-data (accessed on 14 November 2020). [32]

IEA (2019), *World Energy Balances 2019*, International Energy Agency, Paris, https://doi.org/10.1787/3a876031-en (accessed on 10 August 2020). [33]

IMF (2020), *Real GDP growth*, World Economic Outlook (October 2020), https://www.imf.org/external/datamapper/NGDP_RPCH@WEO/OEMDC/ADVEC/WEOWORLD (accessed on 14 November 2020). [5]

IMF (2020), *World Economic Outlook: October 2020*, https://www.imf.org/external/datamapper/GGXCNL_NGDP@WEO/OEMDC/ADVEC/WEOWORLD. [2]

IMF (2018), *2018 Article IV Consultation-Press Release; Staff Report; and Statement by the Executive Director for Republic of Belarus*, International Monetary Fund, Washington, D.C., https://www.imf.org/en/Publications/CR/Issues/2019/01/18/Republic-of-Belarus-2018-Article-IV-Consultation-Press-Release-Staff-Report-and-Statement-by-46526 (accessed on 14 November 2020). [20]

ITF (2019), *Transport Performance Indicators*, https://www.oecd-ilibrary.org/transport/data/itf-transport-statistics/transport-performance-indicators_2122fa17-en. [31]

Kasmach, L. (2016), *Renewable vs Nuclear: The Fate of Green Energy in Belarus*, BelarusDigest, https://belarusdigest.com/story/renewable-vs-nuclear-the-fate-of-green-energy-in-belarus/ (accessed on 14 November 2020). [41]

Ministry of Foreign Affairs of the Republic of Lithuania (2018), *Statement by the Ministry of Foreign Affairs on Astravets Nuclear Power Plant under construction in Belarus*, https://www.urm.lt/default/en/news/statement-by-the-ministry-of-foreign-affairs-on-astravets-nuclear-power-plant-under-construction-in-belarus- (accessed on 14 November 2020). [40]

Ministry of Natural Resources and Environmental Protection of the Republic of Belarus (2018), *Седьмое национальное сообщение Республики Беларусь в соответствии с обязательствами по Рамочной конвенции ООН об изменении климата [Seventh national communication of the Republic of Belarus in accordance with the obligations under the UN Framework Convention on Climate Change]*, Ministry of Natural Resources and Environmental Protection of the Republic of Belarus, Minsk, https://unfccc.int/sites/default/files/resource/92104765_Belarus-NC7-1-AI_BLR_NC7.pdf (accessed on 14 November 2020). [21]

National Bank of the Republic of Belarus (2020), *Foreign Direct Investments*, https://www.nbrb.by/engl/statistics/foreigndirectinvestments (accessed on 14 November 2020). [19]

Observatory of Economic Complexity (2018), *Belarus: Exports, Imports, and Trade Partners*, https://oec.world/en/profile/country/blr (accessed on 16 July 2020). [10]

OECD (2021), *COVID-19 and greening the economies of Eastern Europe, the Caucasus and Central Asia*, http://www.oecd.org/coronavirus/policy-responses/covid-19-and-greening-the-economies-of-eastern-europe-the-caucasus-and-central-asia-40f4d34f/ (accessed on 10 March 2021). [8]

OECD (2020), *COVID-19 crisis response in Eastern Partner countries*, OECD, Paris, https://www.oecd.org/coronavirus/policy-responses/covid-19-crisis-response-in-eu-eastern-partner-countries-7759afa3/ (accessed on 9 September 2020). [7]

OECD (2020), *Investment Perspectives in Eastern Partnership Countries*, http://www.oecd.org/investment/Investment-perspectives-in-Eastern-Partner-countries.pdf. [14]

OECD (2020), *Towards Water Security in Belarus: A Synthesis Report*, OECD Studies on Water, OECD Publishing, Paris, https://dx.doi.org/10.1787/488183c4-en. [44]

OECD et al. (2020), *SME Policy Index: Eastern Partner Countries 2020: Assessing the Implementation of the Small Business Act for Europe*, SME Policy Index, OECD Publishing, Paris/European Union, Brussels, https://dx.doi.org/10.1787/8b45614b-en. [42]

Papko, A. and P. Kozarzewski (2020), “The evolution of Belarusian public sector: From command economy to state capitalism?”*, 12*, No. 136, Centre for Social and Economic Research (CASE), Warsaw, https://www.case-research.eu/files/?id_plik=6381 (accessed on 18 February 2021). [12]

Roser, M. et al. (2020), *Coronavirus Pandemic (COVID-19)*, OurWorldInData.Org, https://ourworldindata.org/coronavirus (accessed on 9 September 2020). [6]

S&P Global Platts (2020), *Belarus President pledges new oil, gas infrastructure by 2025*, https://www.spglobal.com/platts/en/market-insights/latest-news/oil/080420-belarus-president-pledges-new-oil-gas-infrastructure-by-2025 (accessed on 14 November 2020). [34]

Transparency International (2019), *CPI 2019: Eastern Europe & Central Asia*, https://www.transparency.org/en/news/cpi-2019-eastern-europe-central-asia (accessed on 20 July 2020). [15]

UNDESA (2019), *World Population Prospects 2019, Volume II: Demographic Profiles*, United Nations Department of Economic and Social Affairs Population Division, https://population.un.org/wpp/Publications/Files/WPP2019_Volume-II-Demographic-Profiles.pdf (accessed on 14 November 2020). [4]

UNECE (2016), *Environmental Performance Reviews: Belarus, Third Review*, United Nations Economic Commission for Europe, New York and Geneva. [45]

US Department of State (2020), *2020 Investment Climate Statements: Belarus*, https://www.state.gov/reports/2020-investment-climate-statements/belarus/ (accessed on 20 July 2020). [11]

World Bank (2021), *World Development Indicators (database)*, https://datacatalog.worldbank.org/dataset/world-development-indicators. [1]

World Bank (2020), *Doing Business 2020*, World Bank Group, Washington, DC, http://dx.doi.org/10.1596/978-1-4648-1440-2. [13]

World Bank (2019), *Country Score Card: Logistics Performance Index*, https://lpi.worldbank.org/international/scorecard/ (accessed on 27 July 2020). [26]

World Bank (2018), *Systematic Country Diagnostic: Towards a Competitive, Inclusive and Dynamic Belarus*, World Bank, Washington, D.C., https://openknowledge.worldbank.org/bitstream/handle/10986/29599/Belarus-SCD-03072018.pdf (accessed on 14 November 2020). [30]

WTO (2019), *Belarus reaffirms intent to complete WTO accession by next Ministerial Conference*, World Trade Organisation: News and events, https://www.wto.org/english/news_e/news19_e/acc_blr_11jul19_e.htm (accessed on 14 November 2020). [9]

Notes

[1] The EU Eastern Partnership (EaP) is a joint initiative for strengthening the relationships between the European Union, its member states and six countries (hereafter the EaP countries): Armenia, Azerbaijan, Belarus, Georgia, Moldova and Ukraine.

[2] Confirmed case and death figures are underestimates of actual case and death numbers. Methodology and testing rates vary widely, and international comparisons are necessarily flawed.

[3] The strategy aims to reduce energy intensity from 372 kg of coal equivalent (approximately 0.26 tonnes of oil equivalent) to 220 kg of coal equivalent (approximately 0.15 toe) in 2030 per million Belarusian rubles between 2015 and 2030.

4. Sustainable infrastructure investment in Georgia

This chapter describes sustainable infrastructure planning in Georgia and presents current trends in investment in large-scale infrastructure projects. It compares Georgia's infrastructure plans in the energy, transport, industry and water sectors against its international commitments under the Paris Agreement on climate change and the Sustainable Development Goals (SDGs). The chapter also explores Georgia's strategic documents for long-term economic development, sectoral development and the environment, including those related to climate change mitigation and adaptation. It identifies misalignments between stated goals and observed investment flows and provides recommendations to improve strategic planning for sustainable infrastructure.

State of play: economy, investment and climate change in Georgia

Economy and trade

Table 4.1. Key indicators on Georgia's economy

Population (2019)	3 720 382
Urbanisation rate (2019)	59.0%
Annual population growth (2019)	-0.2%
Surface area	69 700 km^2
GDP (USD, current price, 2019)	17 477 million
GDP per capita (USD, current price, 2019)	4 698
Real GDP growth (year-on-year change, 2019, 2020)	5.1%, -5%
Inflation (average consumer price, y-o-y change, 2019)	4.9%
Exports of goods and services (% of GDP, 2019)	54.8%
Imports of goods and services (% of GDP, 2019)	63.8%
FDI, net inflows (% of GDP, 2019)	7.3%
General government net lending/borrowing (% of GDP, 2019, 2020)	-1.8%, -8.1%
Unemployment (% of total labour force, 2019)	14.7%
Remittances (% of GDP, 2019)	12.9%
Transparency, accountability and corruption in the public sector rating (1= most corrupt, 6 = least corrupt, 2013)	3.5

Source: World Bank (2021[1]), *World Development Indicators (database)*, World Bank, https://datacatalog.worldbank.org/dataset/world-development-indicators; IMF (2021[2]), *World Economic Outlook: October 2018*, International Monetary Fund https://www.imf.org/external/datamapper/GGXCNL_NGDP@WEO/OEMDC/ADVEC/WEOWORLD

Economy and demographics

Georgia is an upper-middle income country in the Caucasus. Its population shrank dramatically from 4.9 million in 1993 to 3.7 million in 2013 but has since stabilised. After two decades of nearly uninterrupted negative population growth, growth turned positive in 2014 (at 0.05%). Since then, Georgia's population growth rate has hovered around 0% (0.01% in 2017, -0.04% in 2018, -0.17 in 2019).

The Georgian economy initially followed a similar trajectory to its population immediately after the breakup of the Soviet Union, falling from USD 7.8 billion in 1990 in current USD to USD 2.5 billion in 1994. It then recovered over the next two decades to USD 17.5 billion in 2019.

Georgia's government only has effective control over about 80% of its internationally recognised territory (Ellyatt, 2019[3]). Two regions, Abkhazia in the northwest and South Ossetia in the north, declared themselves independent republics and, receiving support from neighbouring Russia, gained control of their claimed territories through a series of armed conflicts beginning right after independence (1991-1992 in South Ossetia, 1992-1993 in Abkhazia) and culminating in the Russo-Georgian War of 2008. Only a few UN member countries (Nauru, Nicaragua, the Russian Federation, Syria and Venezuela) recognise the independence of the two breakaway regions, while the rest of the world recognises them as integral parts of Georgia.

Personal remittances are an increasingly important source of funds for some Georgian households. Since 2003, personal remittances as a percentage of GDP has increased from 6.2% to 12.9% in 2019. This is the second highest figure among EaP countries after Moldova (16%) and only slightly higher than in Armenia (11.2%) and Ukraine (10.4%) (World Bank, 2021[1]).

Georgia has the most service sector-oriented economy among the countries of the EU Eastern Partnership (EaP).[1] Services accounted for 60.8% of GDP in 2019, compared to 20.3% for industry and construction, 8.9% for manufacturing and only 6.5% for agriculture (World Bank, 2021[1]).

Although Georgia initially avoided widespread propagation of COVID-19 in the first wave of the pandemic, as of February 2021 Georgia has the highest number of COVID-19 cases per capita among EaP countries. Georgia has diagnosed 65.4 cases per thousand inhabitants compared to 56.6 in Armenia, 22.8 in Azerbaijan, 27 in Belarus, 65.4 in Georgia, 40.5 in Moldova and 29.3 in Ukraine. Georgia's death rate (817 deaths per million inhabitants) is the third highest in the region after Armenia (1 049) and Moldova (890), significantly higher than in Azerbaijan (311), Belarus (187) and Ukraine (562) (Roser et al., 2021[4]).[2] Georgia's response to the outbreak included a strict country-wide lockdown, reinforced border restrictions (including a ban on non-residents from entering) and school closures.

As a result of the pandemic and associated containment measures, Georgia's GDP contracted by 5% in 2020. In part, this steep decline is due to the large share of Georgia's economy linked to the travel and tourism industries (26% of GDP), by far the largest in the former Soviet Union. Its growth projections for 2021 onwards are the highest among EaP countries (IMF, 2021[2]). Some economic stimulus measures announced by the Georgian government, such support for greening small and medium enterprises and green job creation programmes, could help Georgia's transition towards a greener economy, while other measures, such as moratoria on environmental inspections during lockdown, could have potentially negative consequences on the environment (OECD, 2021[5]).

Trade

Georgia has been a member of the World Trade Organisation since 2000 and has close ties with the European Union, being a target country of the European Union's European Neighbourhood Policy under the Eastern Partnership (EaP) policy initiative. These initiatives aim to deepen EU-Georgia relations through actions focusing on economic development, governance, connectivity and people-to-people contact (European Commission, 2019[6]). In 2014, Georgia and the European Union signed an Association Agreement and established a Deep and Comprehensive Free Trade Area (DCFTA) (European Commission, 2017[7]).

In 2017, Georgia became a Contracting Party of the EU's Energy Community, thereby committing to implement the EU's energy-related *acquis communautaires* and liberalise its energy markets. The Energy Community's Secretariat supports Georgia's implementation of reforms in the energy sector, including on energy efficiency, renewable energy development and environmental protection, and Georgia has made steady progress. The Secretariat rated Georgia's overall implementation as 36% complete in 2020, up from 24% in 2019 (Energy Community, 2020[8]).

Georgia exports a more diversified array of products than other countries in the Caucasus (Figure 4.1c). Its most important export categories by value are foodstuffs (19% of exports; particularly wine, rolled tobacco and hard liquor, accounting for 5.2%, 4% and 3% respectively), mineral products (17% of exports; primarily copper ore, which alone accounts for 13.6% of total exports), metals (15% of exports; mostly ferroalloys, 9%), transportation (12% of exports; cars alone account for 10%) and chemical products (10%). Georgia's main import categories are machines (19%), mineral products (16%), transportation (10%), chemical products (9%) and foodstuffs (9%) (Figure 4.1d). Georgia's imports of fuels (refined petroleum and petroleum gas account for 9% and 3% of imports respectively) explain the comparatively large share of mineral products in the country's import mix. Georgia imports gas primarily from Azerbaijan (93%), but its oil suppliers are more diverse (Romania, 22%; Russia, 20%; Turkmenistan, 17%; Azerbaijan, 12%; Bulgaria, 11%; Greece, 11%).

Most of Georgia's largest export and import markets are its geographical neighbours, especially Russia (12% of exports, 11% of imports), Turkey (6% of exports, 16% of imports) and Azerbaijan (13% of exports, 5% of imports), and, to a lesser extent, Armenia (7% of exports, 1% of imports), Iran (2% of exports, 2%

of imports) and Ukraine (4% of exports, 5% of imports) (Figure 4.1a and b). Although individual European countries account for only small shares of Georgia's trade, as a bloc, the European Union makes up 24% of exports and 26% of imports. Bulgaria is Georgia's most important EU export destination (8%), while Germany is its most important import origin country (5%). Beyond the EU and its direct neighbours, Georgia also maintains important trading relationships with the People's Republic of China (6% of exports, 10% of imports) and the United States (5% of exports, 3% of imports).

Figure 4.1. Trade of Georgia

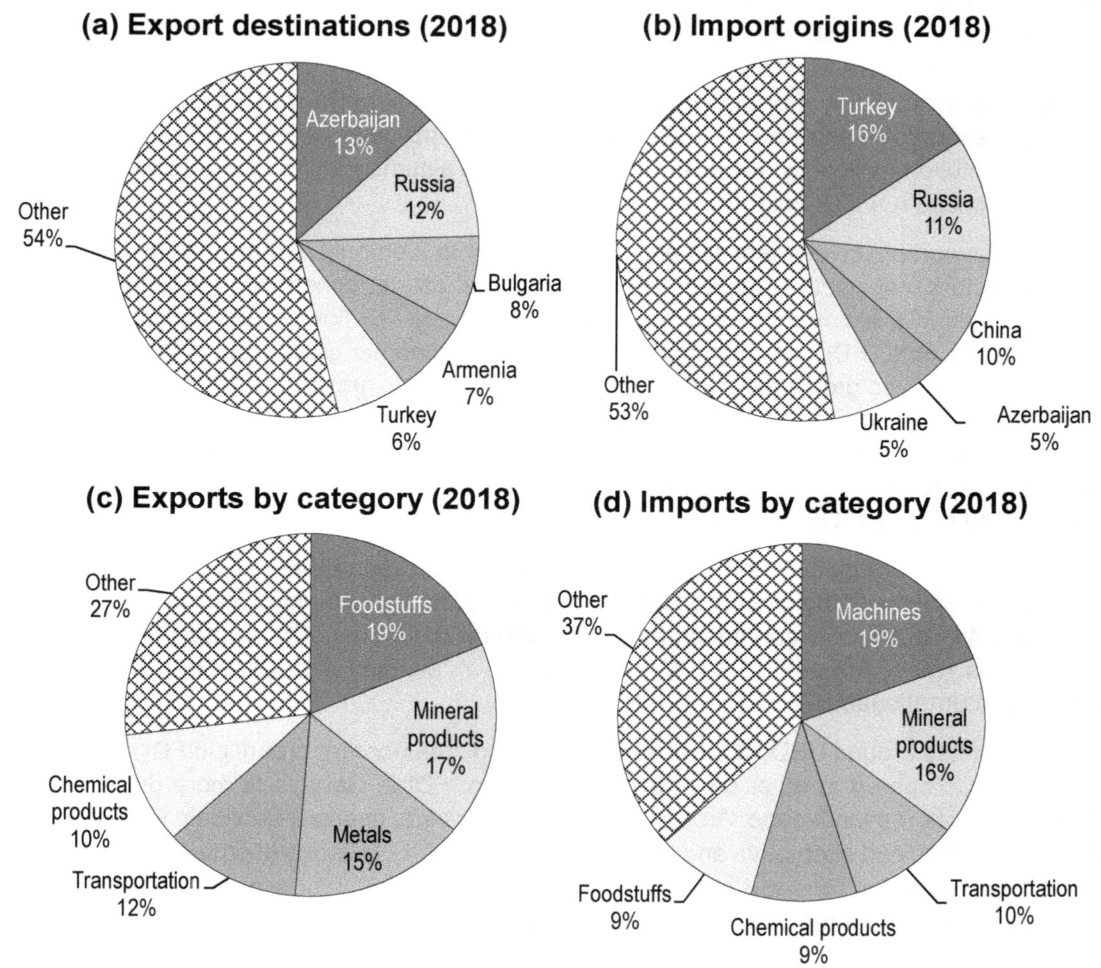

Source: Observatory of Economic Complexity (2019[9]), *Georgia: Exports, Imports and Trade Partners*, Observatory of Economic Complexity, https://oec.world/en/profile/country/geo

Investment climate

Georgia has the most favourable investment climate among EaP countries, and one of the most permissive in the world, making it an attractive destination for investment. Significant structural reforms have been carried out to simplify business procedures, construction permits, cut red tape, simplify licencing and permitting regimes, as well as to improve tax and customs procedures. Such reforms have not only led to an approximation to EU legislation, but also to a significant improvement in the World Bank Doing Business

Indicators. In 2020, Georgia was ranked 7th worldwide, up from 115th in 2005, ranking higher than the United Kingdom and Norway (World Bank, 2020[10]).

The legal basis for regulating domestic and foreign investments is provided by two laws, namely the "Law of Georgia on Promotion and Guarantees of Investment Activity" and the "Law on State Support of Investments" (Government of Georgia, 2006[11]). An investment promotion agency, the Georgian National Investment Agency, has also been established in 2002 to facilitate the investment process by assisting investors in obtaining the required licences and permits, as well as to represent investors at other governmental agencies during licencing and permitting procedures (Grant Thornton, 2018[12]). Georgia's investment promotion agency, Invest in Georgia, was merged with Enterprise Georgia, an agency designed to encourage domestic economic development, in 2017. Invest in Georgia was put in place to promote and support potential FDI projects in the country in the area of energy (particularly renewable energy), hospitality and real estate, manufacturing, logistics hubs, agriculture and food processing and business process outsourcing. Compared to other EaP investment promotion agencies, however, it has limited human resources dedicated to investment promotion activities, although it is in the process of expanding its institutional capacity. Invest in Georgia provides a number of investment facilitation, retention and aftercare services (OECD, 2020[13]).

Despite such a favourable investment climate, productivity improvements and export growth have lagged. Non-tradable sectors, especially transport infrastructure, real estate, construction and financial services, have received most FDI, although there has also been increasing FDI flows to the tourism and renewable energy sectors. To date, FDI has contributed to domestic economic growth but with limited impact on advanced job creation and productivity. To benefit more fully from its growing ability to attract FDI, Georgia should seek to address gaps in connectivity and infrastructure service provision across the country as well as improve skills in the domestic workforce. Georgia continues to build on its remarkable progress on improving its legal framework, notably ongoing reforms of the judiciary to strengthen its independence, accountability and capacity (OECD, 2020[14]).

Georgia has moved more quickly and effectively to root out corruption than other EaP countries, which contributes to perceptions of the country as a safer destination for investments. Transparency International ranked Georgia 44th out of 198 countries in the 2019 edition of its annual Corruption Perceptions Index, ahead of Belarus (66th), Armenia (77th), Moldova (120th), Azerbaijan and Ukraine (both tied for 126th) (Transparency International, 2019[15]).

Georgia has attracted around USD 16.9 billion of announced cross-border greenfield FDI projects between 2003 and 2017. Compared to other countries in the region, FDI in Georgia is more diversified, with no sector that dominates the landscape. Around 19% of FDI goes into financial services, followed by coal, oil and natural gas (12%), and alternative and renewable energy (11%). In terms of other infrastructure-related investments, transportation received around 7% of total greenfield FDI, or around USD 1.2 billion, while building and construction materials received around USD 500 million (Figure 4.2).

Figure 4.2. Greenfield FDI in Georgia by economic activity, 2003-2017

Cumulative greenfield FDI capital between January 2003 and September 2017 in USD million

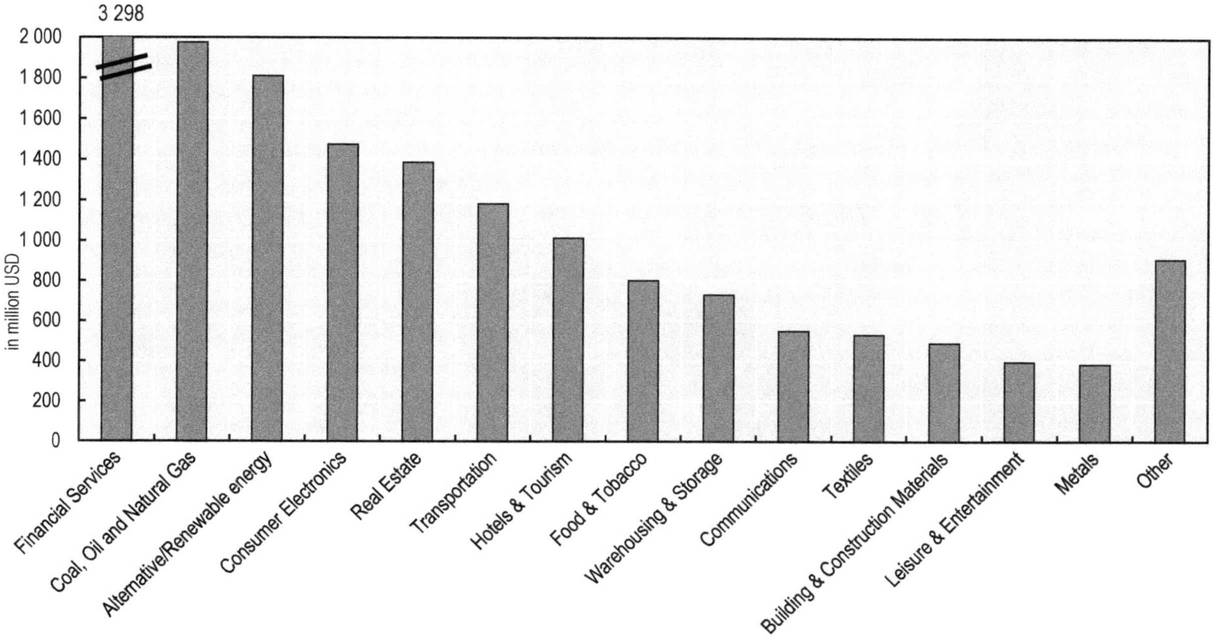

Note: Other includes ceramics and glass, business service, aerospace, business machines and equipment, chemicals, consumer products, rubber, software and IT services, industrial machinery, equipment and tools, automotive components, automotive OEM, pharmaceuticals, healthcare, electronic components, and plastics.
Source: OECD based on fDi Markets (2019[16]), *fDi Markets: the in-depth crossborder investment monitor (database)*, fDi Markets, https://www.fdimarkets.com/

The European Union is an important source of FDI in Georgia. Collectively it invested a total of USD 5.9 billion between 2006 and 2019, which amounts to over 30% of total net FDI in Georgia over that period. The Netherlands, which contributed over 12% of total FDI, and, to a lesser extent, the Czech Republic (4%), Luxembourg (4%), Germany (2%) and Austria (1.4%) have been Georgia's most important EU investors. Other important sources of FDI in Georgia include its neighbours Azerbaijan (14%) and Turkey (9%) and major international financial hubs like the United Kingdom (11%), the United States (6%) and the United Arab Emirates (6%) (Figure 4.3). Although they account for large shares of FDI in other former Soviet Union countries, China and Russia contribute a relatively small share of Georgia's FDI (3% each).

Figure 4.3. FDI in Georgia by source country, 2006-2019

In million USD

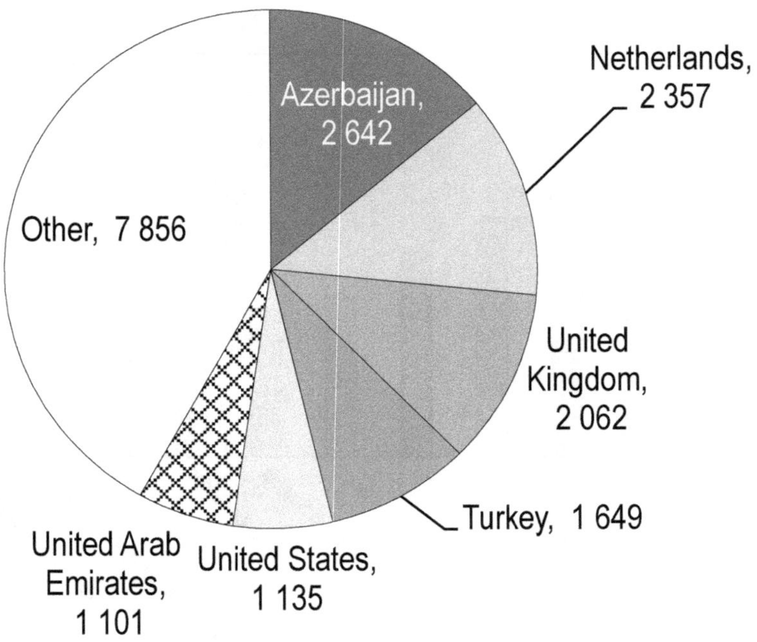

Source: National Statistics Office of Georgia (2021[17]), *Foreign Direct Investments by Countries*, National Statistics Office of Gerogia, https://www.geostat.ge/en/modules/categories/191/foreign-direct-investments

Georgia's public debt was equal to 41.2% of GDP in 2019 and, due to the COVID19 pandemic and associated spending, jumped to 62.8% of GDP in 2020. Proactive monitoring of fiscal risks and a planned fiscal consolidation starting in 2021 are expected to keep safeguard Georgia's debt sustainability (IMF, 2020[18]).

Climate change

Georgia has a relatively low rate of greenhouse gas (GHG) emissions, only being responsible for 0.03% of total global emissions in 2012. Georgia's per capita emissions were a mere 3.8 tCO_2e in 2012, much lower than its 1990 levels of 8.0 tCO_2e, and are among the lowest among EaP countries (only Armenia and Moldova have lower per capita emissions in the present study). They only amount to about a third of the OECD average (12.9 tCO_2e per capita in 2012) (World Bank, 2021[1]).

In the years following the breakup of the Soviet Union, Georgia's annual GHG emissions plummeted to less than a quarter of their pre-independence levels, from 45 606 $ktCO_2e$ in 1990 to 10 1084 $ktCO_2e$ in 2001. While the country's economic situation initially followed a similar trend in the early 1990s, Georgia's GDP has since recovered to levels close to its Soviet-era peak while GHG emissions have increased only slightly over the past decade (see Figure 3.4). As a result, the GHG intensity of Georgia's economy (GHG emissions per unit of GDP) fell by more than half, from 2.7 $kgCO_2e$ per USD (constant 2010 dollars) in 1990 to 1.1 $kgCO_2e$ per USD by 2007 before increasing gradually to 1.2 $kgCO_2e$ by 2015. Compared to Central Asia where emissions intensities range from twice to almost four times higher, the Georgian economy is not particularly emissions intensive, but it still emits more than three times as much GHG per unit of GDP as the OECD average (0.35 $kgCO_2e$ per USD in 2012) (Ministry of Environmental Protection and Agriculture of Georgia, 2019[19]).

Georgia has prepared an updated version of its Nationally Determined Contribution (NDC), which is awaiting final adoption. The proposed updated NDC ratchets up the ambition of the country's mitigation targets, from an unconditional commitment to reduce emissions by 2030 from 15% below the business-as-usual scenario (original NDC) to 30% below 1990 levels (updated NDC). Conditional on international support, Georgia aims to reduce emissions by 50-57% compared to 1990 levels by 2030 (compared to 25% below business-as-usual levels in the original NDC). The government has also developed *Climate Strategy 2030* and the *Climate Action Plan 2021-2023*, both of which are pending final adoption.

Figure 4.4. GHG emissions and GDP of Georgia, 1990-2019

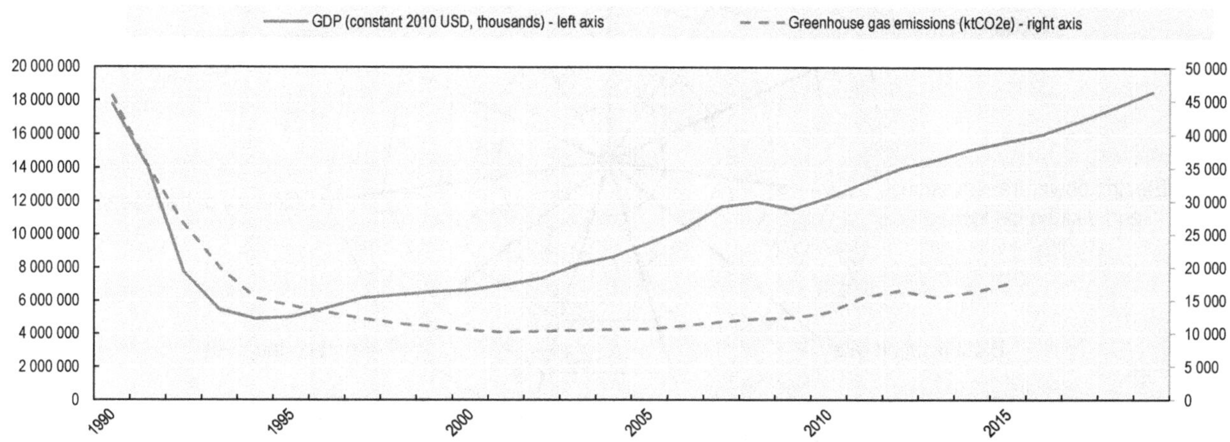

Source: GDP data from World Bank (2021[1]), *World Development Indicators (database)*, World Bank, https://datacatalog.worldbank.org/dataset/world-development-indicators; GHG data from Ministry of Environmental Protection and Agriculture of Georgia (2019[19]), *Georgia's Second Biennial Update Report*, https://unfccc.int/documents/196359

Energy (including fuel combustion for transport) accounts for the majority of Georgia's GHG emissions, at 61.8% in 2015. This share has shrunk compared to 1990 when the energy sector was responsible for 80.5% of emissions. Industrial processes (11.7%), agriculture (18.6%) and waste (7.9%) were responsible for the rest of Georgia's emissions in 2015 (Ministry of Environmental Protection and Agriculture of Georgia, 2019[19]).

Current trends of climate change impacts, such as increasing temperatures, eroding soils and intensifying droughts, floods and hail, are expected to reduce yields in major agricultural regions, such as the eastern region of Kakheti. The incidence of destructive natural disasters such as landslides and mudflows has increased considerably. There were fewer than 10 000 landslide events in Georgia in 1972, but this number has increased to over 50 000 in 2013 (Government of Georgia, 2015[20]).

Georgia's infrastructure needs and current plans

Georgia's existing infrastructure varies in quality, with relatively high-quality electricity infrastructure and lower-quality transport and water infrastructure (Figure 4.5). The World Bank (2018[21]) identified improving connectivity to foreign markets through both hard infrastructure (e.g. transport links) and soft infrastructure (e.g. institutions) as a priority to boost Georgia's productivity. It also highlighted the importance of preserving Georgia's unique environment, which it calls "one of its greatest economic assets". Georgia's low rank in the Logistics Performance Index (119th out of 167 countries) reflects the shortcomings of Georgia's transportation infrastructure. Although international connectivity has improved in recent years, domestic connectivity remains a barrier to integration into global value chains (World Bank, 2018[21]).

Figure 4.5. Quality of infrastructure in Georgia

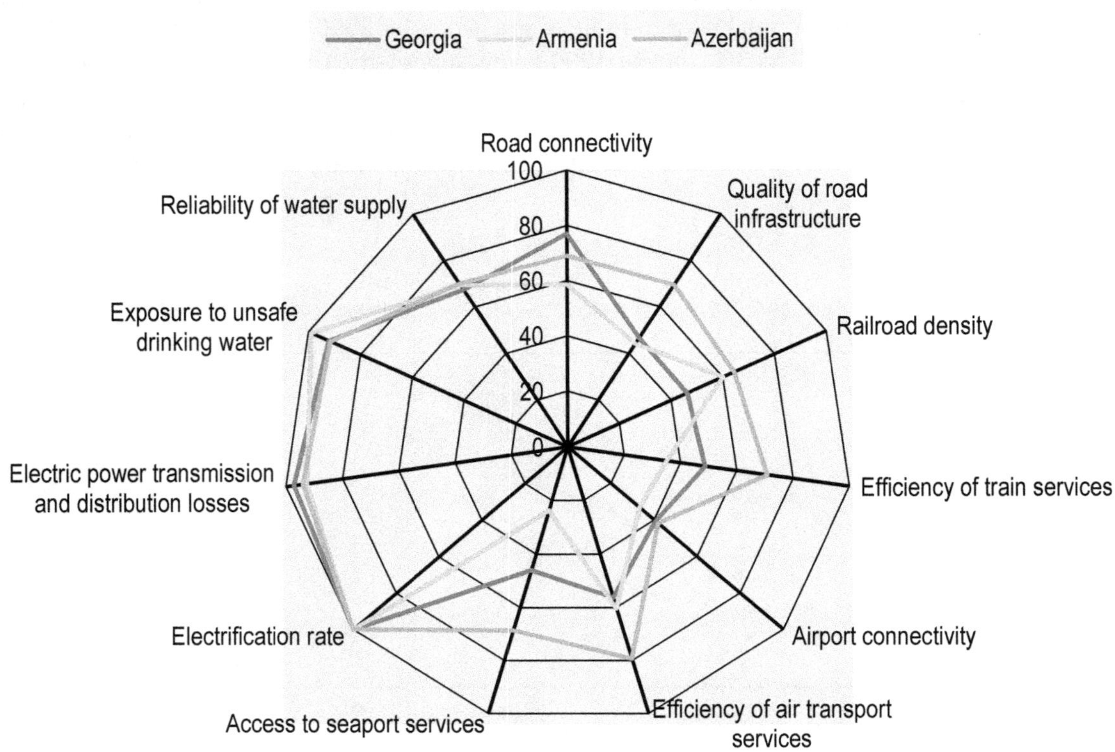

Source: World Economic Forum (2019[22]), *The Global Competitiveness Report 2019*, World Economic Forum, http://www3.weforum.org/docs/WEF_TheGlobalCompetitivenessReport2019.pdf

The OECD's database tracks 171 major infrastructure projects planned or under construction in Georgia, with a cumulative value of USD 23.1 billion. By value, energy projects account for just over half of the investments (50.4%, USD 11.6 billion), and transport projects make up the second largest share (43.9%, USD 10.1 billion) (Figure 4.6). By comparison, water projects (5.0%, USD 1.1 billion) and industry projects (0.5%, USD 155 million) represent much smaller shares of total investment in Georgia's infrastructure.

Figure 4.6. Investment projects in Georgia, by sector

Planned and under construction, in USD million

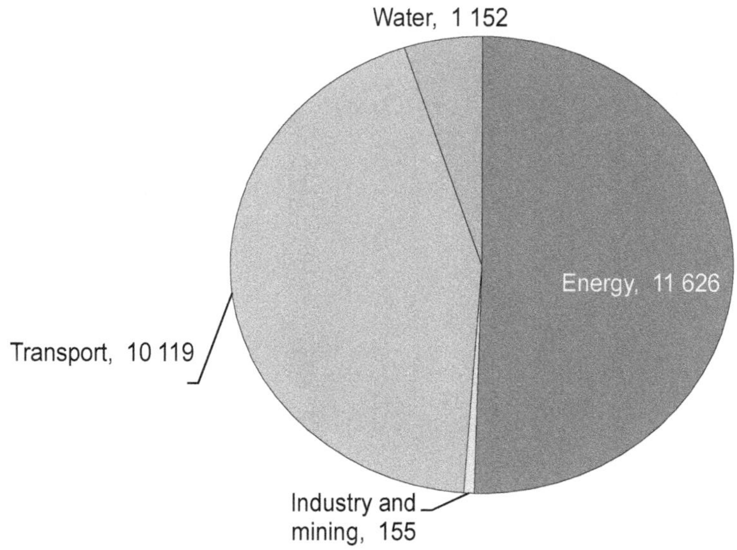

Source: OECD analysis based on accessed databases as of June 2020.

Transport

Recognising its transport infrastructure's shortcoming, Georgia has increased investment in overland transport infrastructure measured in per capita terms. On average, it invested USD 103 per capita annually between 2006 and 2018, while neighbouring Armenia invested only USD 29 (2008-2016), Russia invested USD 97 (2006-2018) and Turkey invested USD 95 (2006-2017). Transport investment spending remains slightly lower than in Azerbaijan (USD 105 on average between 2006 and 2018) (ITF, 2019[23]). The modal share of investments between road and rail has fluctuated somewhat cyclically (Figure 4.7), but the road sector has received the larger share of investment in most years (except 2007, 2011 and 2012).

Figure 4.7. Inland transport infrastructure investment in Georgia (2006-2018)

Modal share (%) of total inland transport infrastructure investment (left axis) and total inland transport infrastructure investment in current USD per capita (right axis)

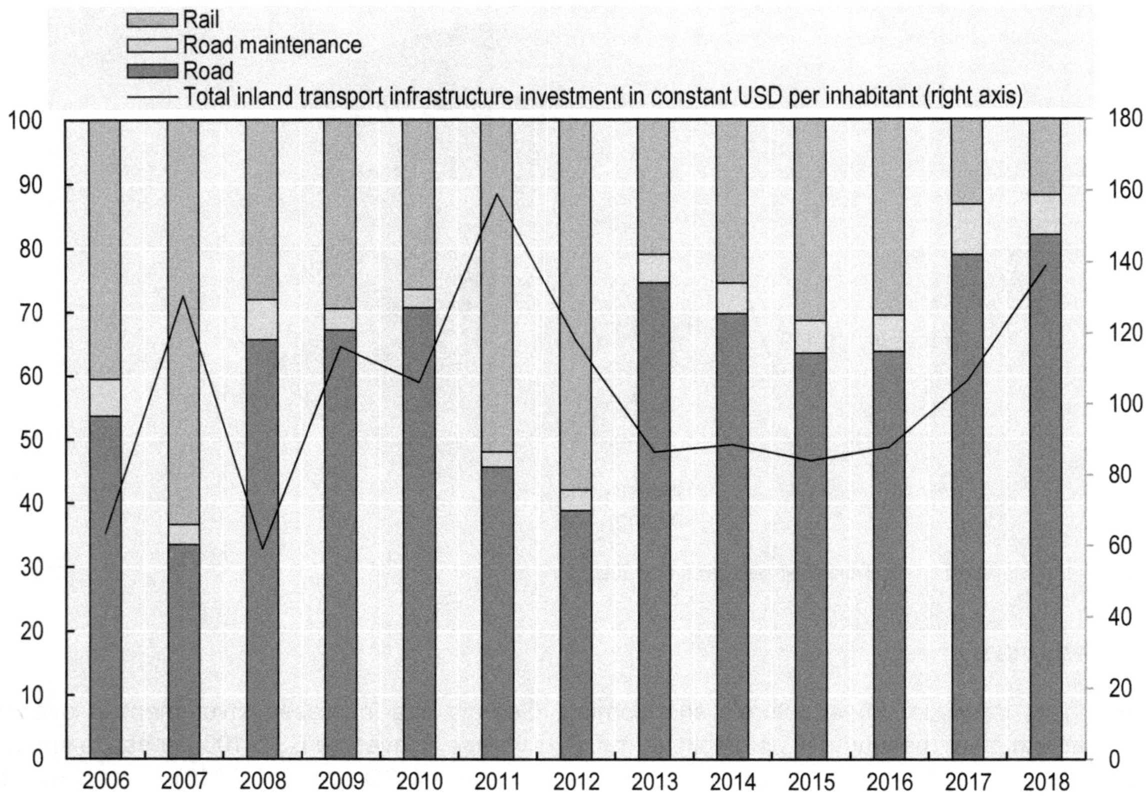

Source: ITF (2019[23]), *Transport performance indicators*, International Transport Forum, https://doi.org/10.1787/trsprt-data-en

Georgia's inland transport modal split for freight has shifted towards road over time. In 2005, 91% of the country's freight, measured in tonne-kilometres, moved by rail, but by 2019 rail's share had dropped to 75% (2.9 billion tkm) while road's had risen to 18% (0.7 billion tkm) (National Statistics Office of Georgia, 2020[24]). For passengers, the modal shares are reversed: 93% of passenger transport (6.9 billion pkm) occurred by road, compared to only 7% (0.5 billion pkm) by rail (UNECE, 2018[25]). This trend is misaligned with the country's goals to decarbonise the transport sector, which would require a shift of passenger and goods transport from road to rail and, therefore, increased investment in rail and multi-modal transport systems (e.g. bike and ride, park and ride). The importance of this modal shift to Georgia's mitigation efforts is expressed in the draft *Climate Change Strategy 2030* and *Climate Change Action Plan 2021-2023*, which are currently awaiting adoption.

The Government of Georgia has made the maintenance of existing road systems a high priority on its agenda, as evidenced by the share of maintenance in total inland infrastructure investments (regularly over 5%). This priority stems in part from the EU Association Agreement and Georgia's efforts to approximate relevant EU directives on social, technical and safety conditions.

Georgia's rail company, Georgian Railways owns rail infrastructure and operates all cargo and passenger service in the country. Georgian Railways is in the process of separating its ownership and operation roles to improve transparency and efficiency, and aims to have done so by 2022 (Benmaamar, Keou and Saslavsky, 2015[26]). The Georgian Partnership Fund (a state-owned investment fund that owns several strategically important companies in the transport and energy sectors) is the company's only shareholder (Georgian Railway, n.d.[27]).Georgia has international rail links to Armenia, Azerbaijan and Turkey. Although a railway line has historically existed between Georgia and the Russian Federation, it passes through the breakaway region of Abkhazia, and due to the frozen conflict, train service has been suspended. 47% of the rail freight by volume passing through Georgia only transits through the country, while imports (25%), exports (10%) and local freight account for the rest (18%) (UNESCAP, 2018[28]).

A key component of Georgia's international rail, road and seaport network is the east-west Trans-Caucasus Transit Corridor, which passes through Azerbaijan and Georgia connecting the Caspian Sea (at the port of Alat near Baku) and the Black Sea (at the existing ports of Poti and Batumi and, potentially, a new deep-water port at Anaklia). In the rail sector, Georgian Railways has improvements to underperforming sections of the corridor priorities for infrastructure development through the Georgian Railways Modernisation Project and the Tbilisi Bypass Project. The construction of both projects, already about 70% completed, has been delayed due to operational constraints. In the road sector, the East-West Highway project is well under way and expected to reach completion by 2023 (World Bank, 2020[29]).

Two other important international corridors cross through Georgia: one running east-west between the capital Tbilisi to Turkey via the Autonomous Republic of Adjara (where Georgia's second-largest city Batumi is located) and another north-south corridor from the Russian Federation through Georgia to Armenia. Due to the frozen conflicts in Abkhazia and South Ossetia, the only open border crossing between Georgia and the Russian Federation is at Larsi, just north of Stepantsminda on the S3 highway (the "Georgian Military Road"). While international road links are relatively good, secondary and local roads need upgrading to improve domestic connectivity (World Bank, 2018[21]).

Georgia has several ports along the Black Sea coast, but its international maritime connections are weak. According to the Liner Shipping Connectivity Index, which rates a country's integration into global liner shipping networks on a scale from 0 to 100 (equal to China's connectivity in 2004), Georgia received a score of just 6 in 2020. By comparison, the Russian Federation and Ukraine had scores of 36 and 29 respectively (UNCTAD, 2021[30]).

Given its strategic position between the Black and Caspian Seas and near large markets such as Turkey, Iran, Europe and Russia, Georgia partakes in several international connectivity initiatives. Georgia is a key component of the EU initiative TRACECA (Transport Corridor Europe-Caucasus-Asia), with two key ports on the Black Sea (Poti and Batumi) and well-established rail and road links to the Caspian Sea via Azerbaijan (TRACECA, 2018[31]). CAREC Corridor 2 also passes through Georgia, linking Caspian Sea ports via Azerbaijan and Georgia to Turkey and the Black Sea (ADB, 2017[32]). Other initiatives include the Middle Corridor Trans-Caspian International Transport Route (along with Azerbaijan and Kazakhstan) and the South-West Transport Corridor (along with Azerbaijan and Iran).

Georgia's transport infrastructure projects planned and under construction amount to around USD 10.1 billion, and consist primarily of roads (65.8% or around USD 6.6 billion) and port projects (24.7%, USD 2.5 billion) (Figure 4.8). Investments in railways (8.7% or USD 2.1 billion) and intermodal projects are comparatively smaller (0.8%, or USD 83 million).

Figure 4.8. Transport projects in Georgia, by sub-sector

Planned and under construcrion in USD million

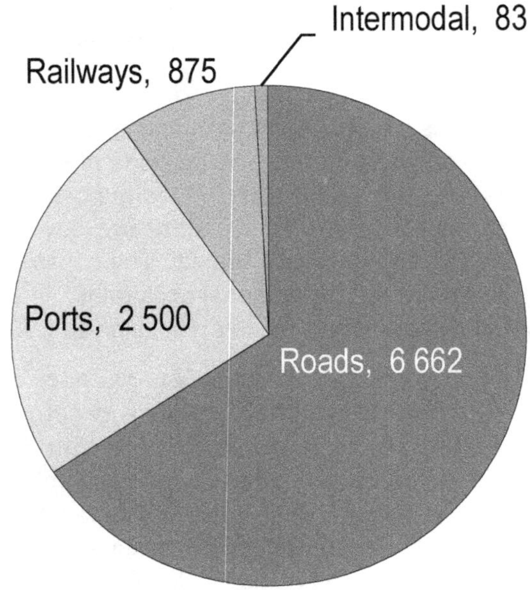

Source: OECD analysis based on accessed databases as of June 2020.

Most of these projects are linked to the country's three main transportation and logistics corridors and aim to improve Georgia's connectivity with neighbouring countries (Table 4.2Table 4.2. Hotspot projects in the transport sector in Georgia). This includes sections of the East-West Highway currently under construction and improvements to the North-South Corridor in the planning stages. These projects, which will improve connectivity and access to global markets as well as increase revenue from freight transit, are considered essential for Georgia's further integration into the global economy. The project is also aligned with the EU Association Agreement and will play a crucial role in reducing poverty and vulnerability in rural and remote areas by connecting people with services, and jobs, export markets and other opportunities (IBRD, IFC and MIGA, 2018[33]). Such projects aimed at developing multi-corridors at the sub-regional level are in line with the government's objective to make the economy a transit hub for the Caucasus and Euro-Asian road transport, thereby stimulating Europe-Asia trade links.

A single large-scale project, the Anaklia Deep Sea Port, accounts for the entirety of Georgia's port investments tracked in the OECD's database. The project aims to construct a new port capable of handling berth container ships with capacity of 10 000 TEU to complement Georgia's two existing Black Sea ports, Batumi and Poti, which are only equipped to handle much smaller capacity vessels (1 700 TEU). The contract to develop the project was initially awarded to the Anaklia Development Consortium, and Phase I was scheduled for completion by 2020. However, due to delays and conflicts between the consortium and the government, the contract was cancelled in 2020, and the government is now seeking new investors to implement the project (Lomsadze, 2020[34])

Table 4.2. Hotspot projects in the transport sector in Georgia

(a) Under construction					
Name	Sub-sector	Description	Project value (USD million)	Funding source	Type of investment
East-West Highway (E60 Tbilisi-Senaki-Leselidze): Section Chumateleti - Argveta	Roads	Construction of 60 km of road on the East-West highway. The project is of regional significance as it is the main corridor for transit through Georgia. A feasibility study was completed in 2014 and the implementation is planned for 2017-2020.	820	Ministry of Regional Development and Infrastructure of Georgia with financial support from multi-donors (unspecified)	Brownfield
Marabda-Kartsakhi Railway (Construction and Rehabilitation)	Railways	First railway bridge to be constructed in Georgia after the collapse of the Soviet Union. Kartsakhi will be connected to Turkey by the tunnel with 4.4 km length.	775	State Oil Fund of Azerbaijan (SOFAZ).	Greenfield; Brownfield
East-West Highway (Khevi-Ubisa Section) Improvement Project	Roads	Construction of a 12 km road network between Khevi and Ubisa along the East-West Highway. The result is improved efficiency and safety of road transport along the East-West highway.	570	ADB; JICA; World Bank; EIB	Brownfield
(b) Planned					
Name	Sub-sector	Description	Project value (USD million)	Funding source	Type of investment
Anaklia Deep Sea Port	Port	Development of a port in Anaklia, on the Black Sea coast. The construction will be conducted in different phases, each time increasing the annual capacity, potentially up to 100 million tonnes once the port reaches the highest capacity. The port has	2 500	Ministry of Economy and Sustainable Development of Georgia	Greenfield
North-South Corridor (Kvesheti-Kobi) Road Project	Roads	The project aims to improve connectivity and safety along the North-South Corridor between on the mountainous road segment between Kvesheti and Kobi. It consists of 23 km of climate-resilient two-lane highways and an additional 5- km of all-weather access roads.	559	ADB	Brownfield
Tbilisi Bypass	Roads	Construction of a 55 km stretch of four lane-roads. The project is part of Georgia's master plan for transport. The project was originally planned for implementation between 2018-2020 but has been delayed.	350	ADB	Brownfield

Note: Refer to the Reader's guide for the present report's definition of 'hotspot' and other information on how the projects above were selected and prioritised. ADB = Asian Development Bank; EIB = European Investment Bank; JICA = Japan International Cooperation Agency.
Source: OECD database as of June 2020.

Energy

The overall quality of Georgia's energy infrastructure is good, matching or surpassing the performance of wealthier neighbours such as Azerbaijan and the Russian Federation. Georgia's transmission and distribution systems are relatively efficient, leading to losses of only 7.3% of electricity output in 2017 compared to 9.7% in the Russian Federation and 9.7% in Azerbaijan (IEA, 2019[35]). Although Georgia has limited domestic oil and gas reserves, several important pipelines pass through Georgia between oil-rich

Azerbaijan and Turkey, including the Baku-Tbilisi-Ceyhan (BTC) and Baku-Tbilisi-Erzurum (BTE) oil pipelines and the South Caucasus pipeline, linking to the Trans-Anatolian Natural Gas Pipeline (TANAP) on the border with Turkey (Emerging Markets Forum, 2019[36]).

Georgia's electricity generation relies primarily on hydroelectric dams, which produce 75% of the country's power (Figure 4.9). Installed hydroelectric generation capacity, however, represents only a fraction of the country's hydroelectric potential: Only 22% is currently exploited in terms of capacity, and only 17% in terms of production (Ministry of Economy and Sustainable Development of Georgia, 2019[37]). Natural gas accounts for most of Georgia's remaining power generation and is particularly important in the winter when the country's hydroelectric dams have reduced output. The country's largest hydroelectric power plant, Enguri, which generates a third of all electricity in Georgia, straddles the border of Abkhazia, one of Georgia's breakaway regions (IEA, 2020[38]). Although an informal agreement between Georgia and Abkhazia initially split output (40% to Abkhazia, 60% to the rest of Georgia), Abkhazian consumption has increased considerably and, in the winter months, now surpasses Enguri's output. Abkhazia does not pay for its consumption, and the situation is a risk to Georgia's energy security and a drain on its budget (World Experience for Georgia, 2017[39]).

Figure 4.9. Electricity generation by source

GWh, 2018

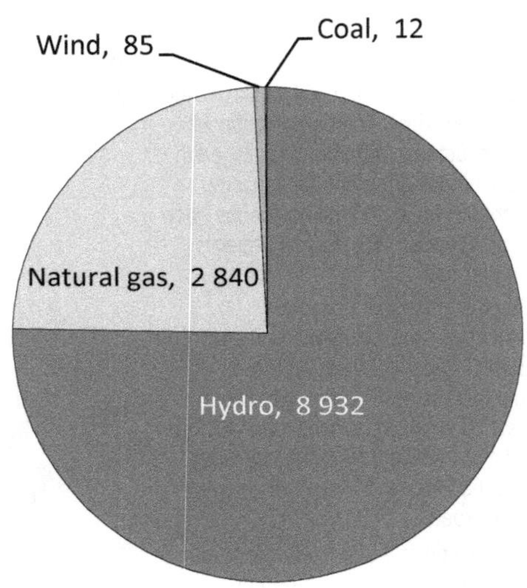

Source: IEA (2020[40]), *Electricity Information 2019*, International Energy Agency, https://www.iea.org/reports/electricity-information-2019

Compared to hydrocarbon-rich Azerbaijan or the Russian Federation, Georgia's energy security situation is more precarious. Its domestic energy production covers only one third of demand, and its limited oil and natural gas production covers only a small fraction of consumption. It is a net importer of coal (0.18 Mtoe in 2017), oil products (1.5 Mt in 2017), natural gas (1.95 Mtoe in 2017) and, in most years, electricity (IEA, 2019[41]). Despite Georgia's limited oil and natural gas reserves, the government set targets to increase annual oil and natural gas production to 3 million tonnes and 2 billion m³ respectively by 2020 (UNECE, 2016[42]). According to the most recent available statistics, annual production in Georgia is far below these targets (35 thousand tonnes of oil production and 9.6 million m³ of natural gas production in 2019) (National Statistics Office of Georgia, 2019[43]).

Since joining the EU's Energy Community in 2017, Georgia has made considerable progress on implementing the necessary legislation across various policy areas. Implementation is particularly advanced on statistics (95%) and, to a lesser extent, environment (53%), electricity (52%), energy efficiency (44%), climate (43%) and renewable energy (33%), while implementation is in the beginning stages on oil (20%), gas (13%) and infrastructure (3%). Georgia's grid is not currently connected to any other Contracting Party of the Energy Community nor to any EU Member State (Energy Community, 2020[8]).

Further development of hydroelectricity remains a priority for Georgia, as indicated in its draft Long-Term Low-Emission Development Strategy (LT-LEDS), which aims to increase the share of power generation from hydro in domestic electricity consumption to at least 85% and install 150 MW of wind power generation by 2030 (United States Agency for International Development, 2017[44]). Georgia has considerable potential for non-hydroelectric renewable electricity generation, and the diversification of electricity sources is also a priority of the government. The *Ten-Year Network Development Plan of Georgia for 2020-2030* seeks to add an additional 1 330 MW of wind power capacity to the Georgian power system by 2030, and the country's nationalised SDG indicators set a target of 30% for the share of Georgia's energy mix derived from renewables (hydro, geothermal, solar, biofuel and waste). Georgia's geothermal potential, for example, is estimated at 3 terawatt hours (TWh) per year. Compared to other renewable energy sources (e.g. hydro, solar, wind), geothermal power generation does not suffer from the same level of seasonal variability and unpredictable output, which could strengthen Georgia's national energy security. Although Georgia has begun using geothermal water for heating and certain agricultural and industrial applications, it does not currently have any geothermal electricity generation capacity. Georgia also has considerable solar energy potential, but major seasonal variations make them less reliable for improving energy security (UNECE, 2016[42]).

Georgia's energy infrastructure projects planned and under construction amount to around USD 11.6 billion. Electricity generation projects account for by far the largest share (USD 10.4 billion, 89%), followed by power transmission and distribution (USD 701 million, 6%) and upstream oil and gas (USD 550 million, 5%). Georgia's power generation projects are in line with the government's plans to increase the capacity of hydropower projects for electricity generation, and increasing momentum for the development of non-hydro renewable energy sources. Over 91% of electricity generation projects by value and 90% by capacity are in hydropower, while wind power plants (5.5% by value and 5% by capacity) and solar photovoltaic projects (1.6% by value, 0.4% by capacity) account for much smaller shares of the total electricity generation projects (Figure 4.10). Natural-gas fired thermal power plants make up 1.5% of power generation projects by value and 4% by capacity. In 2016, the government aimed to further attract investments in the energy sector of over USD 1.1 billion and develop at least 500 MW of installed capacity by 2020 (Government of Georgia, 2016[45]). The government reached this goal, installing 519 MW of new generation capacity between 2016 (3 727 MW) and 2020 (4 246 MW) (Georgian State Electrosystem, 2016[46]; 2020[47]).

Figure 4.10. Electricity generation projects in Georgia, by source

Planned and under construction in MW

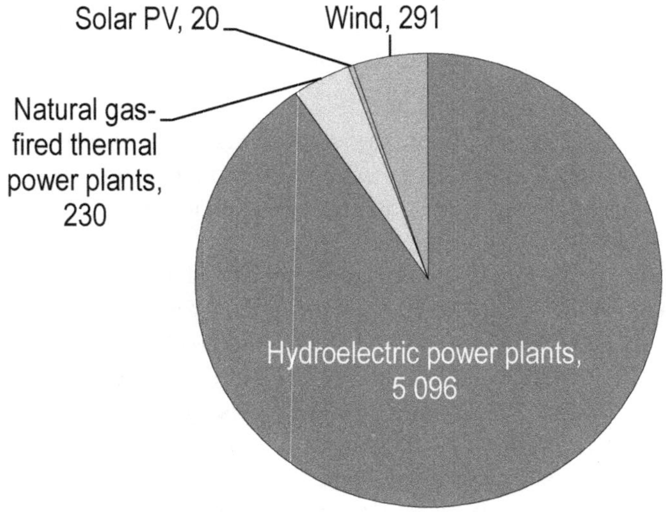

Source: OECD analysis based on accessed databases as of June 2020.

Reliance on hydroelectric power is not without its drawbacks. The electricity generation potential of hydroelectric power plants is vulnerable to the effects of climate change as glaciers melt and precipitation patterns change. Moreover, hydroelectric power plants have a large, direct impact on the environments in which they are built; this is also true of small hydro plants, the cumulative effects of which can be considerable.

Most of Georgia's energy projects are in hydropower, in line with its goal to further develop its hydropower potential (Table 4.3). Such high-impact projects have been mainly undertaken by the private sector, but development partners such as the EBRD and the ADB have also supported such investments. Significant projects under construction include the Tskhenistskali cascade of hydropower projects and the Nenskra HPP. Controversy has marred the latter project since its inception in 2012, notably due to conflicts with the Svan people living in the project area of Upper Svaneti who have protested the project's environmental impacts and flaws in the project consultation process. After several delays, preparatory construction works began on the project in late 2020 (Georgia Today, 2020[48]). There has been growing public opposition to hydroelectric development in Georgia, including against the planned Khudoni HPP, also located in the Upper Svaneti region, and Namakhvani HPP projects, in part due to unsatisfactory Environmental Impact Assessment (EIA) procedures (Civil.Ge, 2020[49]).

Currently, more than 100 hydropower projects at various stages of the planning, approval and construction process with a cumulative capacity of 3 545 MW are listed as prospective additions to the Georgian power system (Georgian State Electrosystem, 2020[47]). Many of these are small hydro projects[3], which if properly designed and operated can contribute to the country's renewable power capacity with a smaller environmental impact compared to large-scale hydroelectric dam projects.

Table 4.3. Hotspot projects in the energy sector in Georgia

(a) Under construction

Name	Sub-sector	Description	Project value (USD million)	New capacity (MW)	Funding source	Type of investment
Nenskra Hydropower Plant	Hydropower	The Nenskra Hydropower plant has a planned capacity of 280 MW and is located in the mountainous Svaneti Region. The project is Georgia's most advanced hydropower installation in the Upper Svaneti region.	1 100	280	AIIB; ADB; EBRD; EIB; KDB; Private sector	Greenfield
Tskhenitskali cascade of hydropower plants	Hydropower	Two hydropower plants on the Tskhenistskali River. The plants have an installed capacity of 312 MW and an expected annual energy generation of 1 192 GWh. The annual output of these plants comprises 9.4% of the entire electricity consumption of Georgia.	534	312	Georgian Co-Investment Fund	Greenfield
Oni Cascade Hydropower Project	Hydropower	Two new hydropower plants on the Rioni River in north-western Georgia, with an installed capacity of 177.2 MW and the plants expected annual energy generation in total is 788.6 GWh.	330	177	Georgian Co-Investment Fund and Peri ltd.	Greenfield

(b) Planned

Name	Sub-sector	Description	Project value (USD million)	New capacity (MW)	Funding source	Type of investment
Khudoni HPP	Hydropower	Power plant on the Enguri River with a capacity of over 702 MW. It is expected that the plant will allow two other existing dams, the Enguri HPP and Vardnili HPP to generate additional energy needed during the rest of the year. The project will account for over 16% of Georgia's hydropower generation. Its construction stopped in 1989 due to the collapse of the Soviet Union and protests over environmental concerns. The project is highly controversial as it is expected that it will displace around 2 000 people (of the 12 000 who live in Upper Svaneti), while a village with 800 inhabitants will be fully resettled.	1 200	702	Not specified	Brownfield
Namakhvani HPP	Hydropower	Two HPPs (333 MW and 100 MW) along the Rioni River scheduled for completion by 2024 near Kutaisi, the second-largest city in Georgia.	730	433	Government of Georgia, Clean Energy Group, ENKA	Greenfield

Note: Refer to the Reader's guide for the present report's definition of 'hotspot' and other information on how the projects above were selected and prioritised. EBRD = European Bank for Reconstruction and Development; EIB = European Investment Bank.
Source: OEC database as of June 2020.

Industry, mining and water

Mining and quarrying make up a small but growing part of Georgia's industrial output. In 2010, Georgia's mining sector produced GEL 255 million worth of output (5% of total industrial output), primarily in metal ores, but by 2019 output had more than tripled to GEL 881 million (7% of total industrial output). The manufacturing sector makes up the majority of the country's industrial output (GEL 10.3 billion, 78%). Foodstuffs and beverages are the two largest components of Georgia's industrial output, accounting for 12% of all output from the manufacturing sector. The generation of electricity (12.5%) and water supply, sewerage and waste management (2.8%) make up the remainder of Georgia's industrial output (Figure 4.11).

Figure 4.11. Industrial output by NACE* subsector

2019, in million GEL

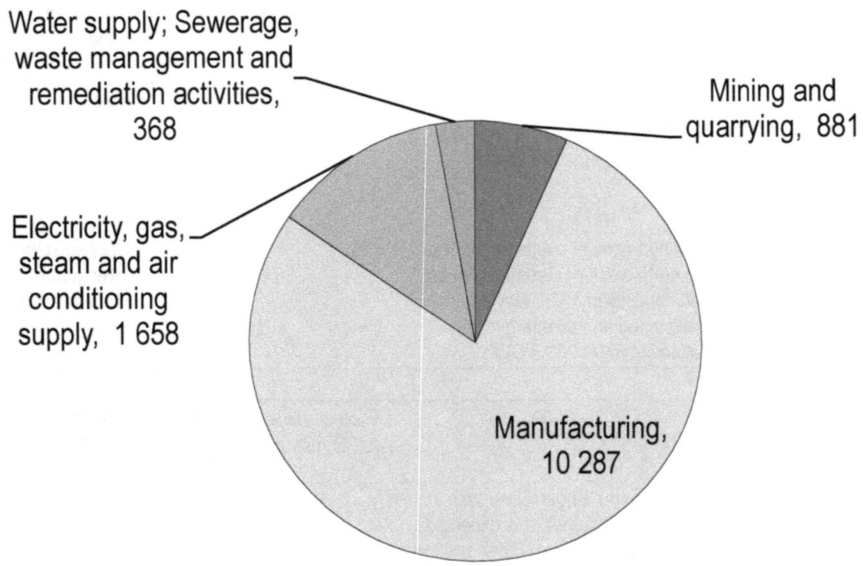

Note: GEL = Georgian lari; * NACE = Nomenclature statistique des activités économiques dans la Communauté européenne [Statistical Classification of Economic Activities in the European Community]
Source: National Statistics Office of Georgia (2020[50]), "Production value in industry", *Industry*, https://www.geostat.ge/en/modules/categories/77/mretsveloba

Georgia is currently facing significant water resource challenges. In particular, there are concerns that, in the long run, Georgia's glaciers will be affected by climate change, leading to significant reductions of water surplus. The country is already experiencing significant variability in precipitation and surface run-off of water, and these are projected to be more severe in the coming years. Glacial runoff is projected to decrease by 40% compared to 2010 levels by 2100, which will severely impact Georgia's energy system and ecosystems (IEA, 2020[38]). Droughts are also expected to put further pressure on water availability. The government developed an urban water supply and sanitation sector development program that planned to invest USD 1.6 billion to ensure water supply and sanitation services to all of its urban residents by 2020 (ADB, n.d.[51]). The pace of development fell short of this ambition: In 2020, 18% of urban residents still had no access to piped water supply (ADB, 2020[52]).

Water projects planned and under construction amount for around USD 1.1 billion and they are mostly focused on water supply and sanitation projects (91%), while only one project worth USD 100 million focuses on irrigation and water management to improve the delivery of irrigation and drainage services in selected areas covered by the project (World Bank, n.d.[53]). Relevant water supply and sanitation projects include an Asian Development Bank-financed program to further upgrade the water and sanitation services in a number of secondary towns and cities, including in Telavi, (ADB, 2020[52]).

Strengths and weaknesses of existing institutional set-up for sustainable infrastructure planning

Strategic planning and links between long-term goals, infrastructure plans and environmental considerations

Georgia is in need of coherent long-term development strategies, having not adopted a single strategy that lays out its vision for economic development beyond 2020. In 2014, Georgia adopted its *Socio-economic Development Strategy*, which aimed to more than double 2013 levels of per capita GDP and boost exports.[4] It did not, however, articulate a clear vision of the infrastructure investments needed to support long-term sustainable growth; it only mentions the important role of transport infrastructure in trade facilitation and the country's goal to improve energy security. In developing a strategic vision for economic development beyond 2020, Georgia should set ambitious, measurable targets with clear ministerial responsibility and define the scope and nature of infrastructure investments that will be required.

Georgia's other adopted strategic documents on economic development, include its *Government Platform 2016-2020* and *Freedom, Rapid Development and Welfare: Government Programme for 2018-2020*, which expand on the country's priorities in the near term, but they do not contain quantitative, time-bound targets nor do they delegate responsibility for progress on government priorities. The most recent programme, *Government Programme 2021-2024: Toward Building a European State*, contains very few quantitative targets on infrastructure development.

Georgia has not yet adopted a long-term strategic document detailing the country's trajectory towards the Paris Agreement's mid-century climate change goals. USAID (2017[44]) has been helping Georgia develop a long-term low-emission development strategy since 2013 and has published a draft with measurable goals to 2030 for key sectors (energy, transport, industry, agriculture, LULUCF), but the government has not formally adopted it. Unlike all long-term low-emission development strategies that parties have communicated to the UNFCCC, Georgia's draft strategy looks only to 2030, not to 2050. Georgia should consider following Ukraine's example, being the first and, to date, only former Soviet Union country to submit a long-term low-emission development strategy with 2050 goals to the UNFCCC (2019[54]). A long-term low emission development strategy to 2050 is under development.

Georgia updated its first NDC, which is pending final adoption. It will be supported by a Climate Strategy and Action Plan, which will act as an implementation tool to achieve its NDC's mitigation and adaptation targets (Ministry of Environmental Protection and Agriculture of Georgia, 2019[55]). Georgia has made considerable progress towards integrating the 2030 Agenda and the SDGs into a national context with the development of its national SDG matrix.

At the local level, 24 municipalities have stepped up to join the Covenant of Mayors, an EU initiative, to commit to reducing GHG emissions by 20-30% by 2020 and 2030. Through the same initiative, several municipalities have also developed Sustainable Energy Action Plans (SEAPs).

Georgia is beginning to move towards a less *ad hoc* system of strategic planning at the sectoral level. The Ten-Year National Development Plans of the Georgian State Electrosystem have acted as unofficial strategies of the country's energy sector development, but Georgia has also elaborated (but not yet adopted) an Energy Strategy 2020-2030. The government has also approved several subsectoral action plans, including the National Renewable Energy Action Plan (NREAP) and the National Energy Efficiency Action Plan, as well as laws on energy efficiency and the energy performance of buildings. Although the development of an overarching energy strategy is a promising step, strategic planning could be strengthened through long-term economy-wide action plans that incorporate strategic milestones based on modelling (IEA, 2020[38]).

Other key sectors, like transport and industry, lack strategies to guide infrastructure development. Although Georgia has adopted transport-related strategies such as its *National Road Safety Strategy* (UNECE, 2016[56]) and the *Tbilisi Sustainable Urban Transport Strategy* (Municipal Development Fund of Georgia, 2015[57]), there is still no national transport development strategy with goals relating to transport infrastructure development. Georgia has adopted its *SME Development Strategy 2016-2020* (Ministry of Economy and Sustainable Development of Georgia, 2015[58]), but does not have strategies relating to industry or mining.

Institutional set-up and decision making processes

Georgia ranked 7th globally in 2020 on the World Bank Group's Ease of Doing Business Index, which measures protection of property rights and investors and the quality of business regulations. By comparison, the country ranked 100th in 2006. Georgia's impressive pace of pro-business reforms have made the country a leader in the region in terms of market liberalisation and attracting FDI. Georgia has also made considerable progress on involving the private sector in infrastructure development by elaborating a regulatory framework for public-private partnerships (PPPs), but government bodies responsible for managing infrastructure face major capacity constraints. To analyse risks effectively and develop, screen and implement infrastructure projects, the institutional capacity of government bodies in infrastructure development need to be strengthened (World Bank, 2018[21]).

Georgia has established a high-level Climate Change Council, chaired by the Minister of Environment Protection and Agriculture. The Council is designed to provide policy direction and guidance on climate action, improve cross-ministerial co-ordination and oversee the country's measuring, reporting and verification (MRV) system.

Georgia has improved its legislative framework and implementation of environmental impact assessments (EIAs), bringing its national legislation in line with the UNECE Convention on Environmental Impact Assessment in a Transboundary Context and taking steps to encourage more meaningful public consultation in the decision-making process (UNECE, 2020[59]). However, Georgia has not yet become a party to the Convention nor the Protocol on Strategic Environmental Assessment, and the quality of public consultations is still subject to considerable criticism. Georgia's performance on public consultation is its lowest score among several indicators on the quality of its policy development and co-ordination processes and much lower than its EaP peers, Armenia and Georgia (Figure 4.12). Overall, Georgia underperforms compared to Armenia and Ukraine, except in the area of parliamentary scrutiny of public policy.

Figure 4.12. Policy development and co-ordination indicators

Armenia (2019), Georgia (2018) and Ukraine (2018)

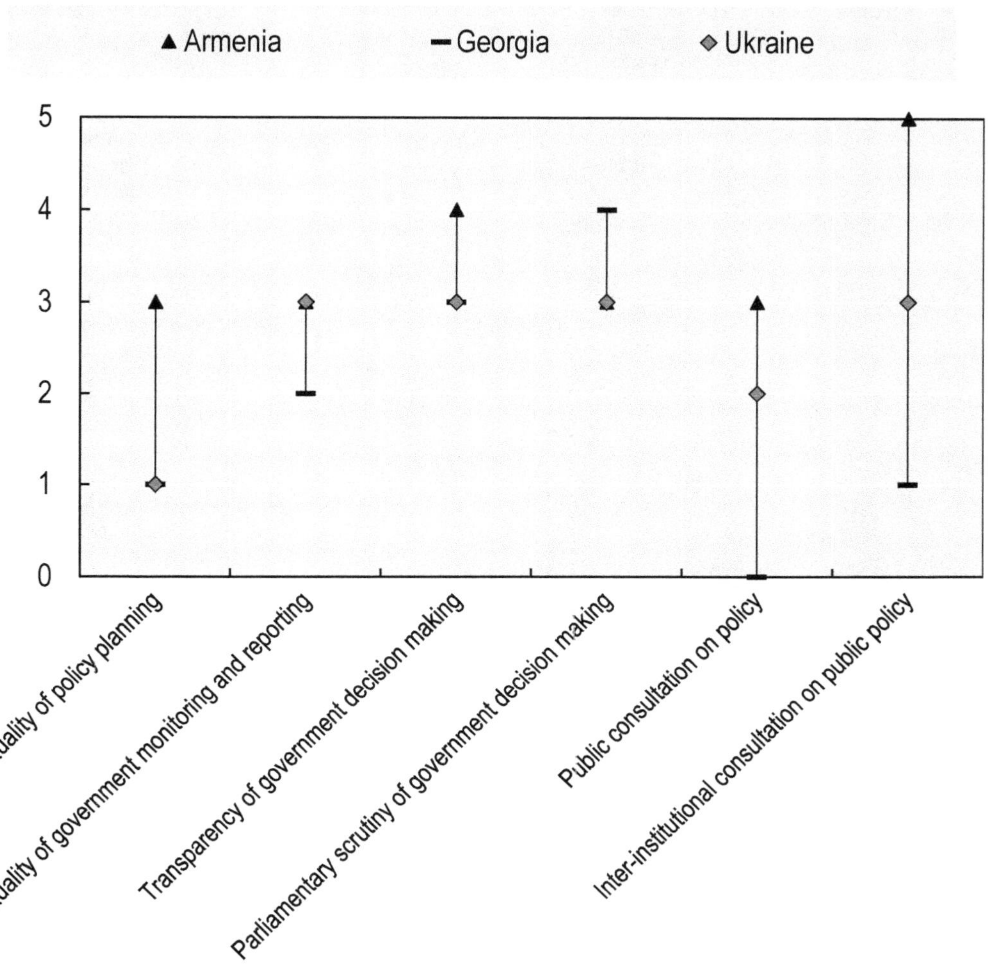

Source: OECD (2019[60]), *The Principles of Public Administration: Baseline Measurement Report: Armenia*, SIGMA, OECD Publishing, Paris, http://www.sigmaweb.org/publications/Baseline-Measurement-Armenia-2019.pdf; OECD (2018[61]), *The Principles of Public Administration: Baseline Measurement Report: Georgia*, SIGMA, OECD Publishing, Paris, http://www.sigmaweb.org/publications/Baseline-Measurement-Report-2018-Georgia.pdf; OECD (2018[62]), *The Principles of Public Administration: Baseline Measurement Report: Ukraine*, SIGMA, OECD Publishing, Paris, http://www.sigmaweb.org/publications/Baseline-Measurement-Report-2018-Ukraine.pdf

Table 4.4. Main strategic documents in force

	Status	Time Horizon	Sectoral Coverage	Main objectives

Updated First Nationally Determined Contribution (NDC)	Submitted in 2017, updated in 2019, awaiting adoption (2021)	2017-2030	Economy-wide	• Unconditional Target: to reduce greenhouse gas emissions by 30% below 1990 levels by 2030
				  ○ Previous Unconditional Target: to reduce emissions by 15% below the business as usual scenario for 2030, this is equal to a reduction in emission intensity per unit of GDP by approximately 34% from 2013-2030.
				• Conditional Target: to reduce emissions by 50-57% below 1990 levels by 2030
				  ○ Previous Conditional Target: to reduce greenhouse gas emissions by 25%, this is equal to a reduction in emission intensity per unit of GDP by approximately 43% from 2013-2030.
				• Main sectors for emission reduction: Energy (transition to renewable energy), Industry (introduction of new technologies), Agriculture/Water (efficient management and policy making)
				Adaptation priorities: introduce innovative irrigation management and water application techniques, implement coastal zone protection technologies, implement list of strategic documents/policies

Socio-Economic Development Strategy – "Georgia 2020"	Adopted in 2014	2014-2020	Governance, Energy, Transport, Water, Industry	• Minimise state interference in the private sector, state intervention only where private sector is inefficient • Develop transport infrastructure to boost trade, specifically exports • Improve irrigation and drainage infrastructure • Ensure a stable and accessible energy supply in the future, reducing dependency on external energy sources Develop ecosystem services by improving management (e.g. sustainable management in the forestry sector)
Freedom, Rapid Development and Prosperity: Government Platform 2016-2020	Adopted in 2016	2016-2020	Governance, Energy, Transport, Water, Industry	• Improve monitoring of government processes and increase public engagement • Improve energy security, in turn reduce energy imports • Further strengthen the private sector (e.g. develop tax incentives) • Develop human capital, with higher education targeted towards the needs of the economy Develop road networks and public transit, helping develop tourism

	Status	Time Horizon	Sectoral Coverage	Main objectives
Freedom, Rapid Development and Welfare: Government Programme for 2018-2020	Adopted in 2018	2018-2020	Governance, Energy, Transport, Water, Industry	• Economic development based on principles of a free market economy • Aim to maintain the ratio of public debt to GDP at a stable level • Fully engage in international economic processes and attract FDI • Utilize local energy resources and diversify energy supply sources • Develop multi-modal transport and create logistics centres which are in line with international standards • Introduce modern technology and innovation to industrial production methods Long-term aim to fully integrate Georgia into the EU
SME Development Strategy 2016-2020	Adopted in 2015	2016-2020	Governance, industry	• Enhance competitiveness of SMEs in both domestic and international markets • Improve the skills of SMEs and develop a modern entrepreneurial culture • Ensure the improvement of the technological ability of SMEs • Aim to increase SMEs output by 10% annually by 2020 • Increase the number of employees in SMEs by 15% Increase the productivity of SMEs by 7%
National Biodiversity Strategy and Action Plan of Georgia 2014-2020	First adopted in 2005	2014-2020	Governance, Energy, Transport, Water, Industry	• Aim to inform at least 50% of the population about the importance of biodiversity • Ensure that the sustainable use of ecosystem services is incorporated into national legislation Actively introduce environmental policies in line with climatic change
National Security Concept of Georgia	Adopted in 2018	No defined timeframe	Governance	• Promote the development of a free, democratic society and strengthen the rule of law • Increase transparency at all levels of government • Ensure environmental security nationally and sub-nationally • Improve relations with the Russian Federation Develop economic cooperation and trade with the United States
Rural Development Strategy of Georgia 2017-2020 and Rural Development Strategy Action Plan 2017-2020	Adopted in 2017	2017-2020	Agriculture, Tourism, Environment	• Modernise agricultural activities and diversify rural economies Improve rural infrastructure and waste management systems
"Produce in Georgia"	Adopted in 2014	No defined timeframe	Industry	• Aim to inject USD 27 million into production industries Promote the development of the industrial sector (e.g. building materials, car building, textiles, electric accessories)

Table 4.5. Other relevant documents

	Statis	Time Horizon	Sectoral Coverage
Regional Development Strategy of Georgia for 2010-2017	Adopted in 2010	2010-2017	Multi-sector
Action Plan for the Implementation of DCFTA for 2014-2017	Adopted in 2014	2014-2017	Multi-sector
National Environmental Action Programme of Georgia for 2017-2021	Adopted in 2017	2017-2021	Multi-sector
Agriculture and Rural Development Strategy 2021-2027	Adopted in 2021	2021-2027	Agriculture
National Strategy and Action Plan on Environmental Education for Sustainable Development 2012-2014	Adopted in 2012-2014	2012-2014	Multi-sector
Long-Term Low-Emission Development Strategy (LT-LEDS)	Drafted in 2013, Not adopted	2013-2030	Multi-sector
National Green Economy Strategy 2021-2030	Not adopted	2021-2030	Multi-sector

References

ADB (2020), *Proposed Loans Georgia: Sustainable Water Supply and Sanitation Sector Development Program*, Asian Development Bank, Manila. [52]

ADB (2017), *The CAREC Corridors - Linking the Russian Federation with South Asia and the Middle East*, https://www.adb.org/news/infographics/carec-corridors-linking-russian-federation-south-asia-and-middle-east. [32]

ADB (n.d.), *Georgia: Developing an Urban Water Supply and Sanitation Sector Strategy and Regulatory Framework for Georgia*, ADB, Manila, https://www.adb.org/sites/default/files/project-document/60275/43556-012-geo-tcr.pdf. [51]

Benmaamar, M., O. Keou and D. Saslavsky (2015), *Georgia's Transport and Logistics Strategy: Achievements to Date and Areas for Improvements*, World Bank, Washington DC, http://documents.worldbank.org/curated/en/623591468191346382/pdf/96577-REVISED-WP-PUBLIC-Georgia-Box391464B-Final-Jan2015.pdf. [26]

Civil.Ge (2020), *Protests Against Namakhvani HPP Continue Despite Police Dispersal*, Civil.Ge, https://civil.ge/archives/382567 (accessed on 14 February 2021). [49]

Ellyatt, H. (2019), *Russia is still occupying 20% of our country, Georgia's prime minister says*, CNBC, https://www.cnbc.com/2019/01/22/russia-is-still-occupying-20percent-of-our-country-georgias-leader-says.html. [3]

Emerging Markets Forum (2019), *The Impact of the Belt and Road Initiative in Central Asia and the South Caucasus: "'Inside-out" Perspectives of Experts from the Region*, Emerging Markets Forum, Gerzensee, http://www.research.pmcg-i.com/images/banners/The%20Belt%20and%20Road%20Initiative%20in%20the%20South%20Caucasus%20Region.pdf. [36]

Energy Community (2020), *2020 Implementation Report*, https://energy-community.org/news/Energy-Community-News/2020/11/23.html#:~:text=The%20Energy%20Community%20Secretariat's%20Annual,from%2048%25%20to%2053%25. (accessed on 26 November 2019). [8]

European Commission (2019), *Eastern Partnership*, https://ec.europa.eu/neighbourhood-enlargement/neighbourhood/eastern-partnership_en. [6]

European Commission (2017), *EU-Georgia Trade: Deep and Comprehensive Free Trade Area (DCFTA)*, European Commission, http://eeas.europa.eu/delegations/georgia/index_en.htm. [7]

fDi Markets (2019), *fDi Markets: the in-depth crossborder investment monitor (database)*, https://www.fdimarkets.com/. [16]

Georgia Today (2020), *Nenskra HPP: Preparatory Construction Works Are Underway*, Georgia Today, http://georgiatoday.ge/news/20377/Nenskra-HPP%3A-Preparatory-Construction-Works-Are-Underway?fbclid=IwAR2RFajxhdHFpAY0X6DnwsHrzDB53vIVhbxblJDtINAzcUg7vmXfh6y1YQM (accessed on 14 February 2021). [48]

Georgian Railway (n.d.), *About Us*, http://www.railway.ge/en/about-us/. [27]

Georgian State Electrosystem (2020), *Ten Year Network Development Plan of Georgia for 2020-2030*, Transmission System Operator JSC "Georgian State Electrosystem", Tbilisi, http://www.gse.com.ge/sw/static/file/TYNDP_GE-2020-2030_ENG.pdf (accessed on 14 February 2021). [47]

Georgian State Electrosystem (2016), *Ten Year Network Development Plan of Georgia for 2016-2026*, Transmission System Operator JSC "Georgian State Electrosystem", Tbilisi, http://www.gse.com.ge/sw/static/file/TYNDP_GE-2016-2026_ENG.pdf (accessed on 14 February 2021). [46]

Government of Georgia (2016), *Freedom Rapid Development Prosperity: Government Platform 2016-2020*, http://gov.ge/files/41_61087_816118_GoG_Platform_LKF_19_05_2017.pdf. [45]

Government of Georgia (2015), *Georgia's Third National Communication to the UNFCCC*, https://unfccc.int/resource/docs/natc/geonc3.pdf. [20]

Government of Georgia (2006), *Law of Georgia on Promotion and Guarantees of Investment Activity*, http://www.matsne.gov.ge. [11]

Grant Thornton (2018), *Doing business in Georgia 2018: Commercial guide for investors*, https://www.grantthornton.ge/globalassets/1.-member-firms/bronze/georgia/doing-business-in-georgia_2018.pdf. [12]

IBRD, IFC and MIGA (2018), *Country Partnership Framework for Georgia for the period FY19-FY22*, IBRD, IFC, MIGA, http://documents.worldbank.org/curated/en/588751525364587100/pdf/WBG-Georgia-CPF-FINAL-4-25-04302018.pdf. [33]

IEA (2020), *Electricity Information 2019*, https://www.iea.org/reports/electricity-information-2019 (accessed on 10 August 2020). [40]

IEA (2020), *Georgia 2020 Energy Policy Review*, OECD Publishing, Paris, https://dx.doi.org/10.1787/9efd2ee9-en. [38]

IEA (2019), *World Energy Balances 2019*, International Energy Agency, Paris, https://doi.org/10.1787/3a876031-en (accessed on 10 August 2020). [41]

IEA (2019), *World Energy Statistics 2019*, International Energy Agency, Paris, https://doi.org/10.1787/2e828dea-en. [35]

IMF (2021), *World Economic Outlook: October 2020*, https://www.imf.org/external/datamapper/NGDP_RPCH@WEO/OEMDC/ADVEC/WEOWORLD. [2]

IMF (2020), *Georgia : Seventh Review Under the Extended Fund Facility Arrangement and Request for Modification of Performance Criteria-Press Release; Staff Report; and Statement by the Executive Director for Georgia*, International Monetary Fund (IMF), Washington, D.C., https://www.imf.org/en/Publications/CR/Issues/2020/12/18/Georgia-Seventh-Review-Under-the-Extended-Fund-Facility-Arrangement-and-Request-for-49973 (accessed on 12 February 2021). [18]

ITF (2019), *Transport Performance Indicators*, https://www.oecd-ilibrary.org/transport/data/itf-transport-statistics/transport-performance-indicators_2122fa17-en. [23]

Lomsadze, G. (2020), “Georgia cancels contract for Black Sea megaport”, *Eurasianet*, https://eurasianet.org/georgia-cancels-contract-for-black-sea-megaport (accessed on 13 February 2021). [34]

Ministry of Economy and Sustainable Development of Georgia (2019), *National Renewable Energy Action Plan (NREAP)*, Ministry of Economy and Sustainable Development of Georgia, Tbilisi, http://www.moesd.gov.ge/uploads/files/2017/energy/samoqmedo_gegma/nreap_v_3_eng_21022020.pdf (accessed on 13 February 2021). [37]

Ministry of Economy and Sustainable Development of Georgia (2015), *SME Development Strategy of Georgia 2016-2020*, http://www.economy.ge/uploads/files/2017/ek__politika/eng_sme_development_strategy.pdf. [58]

Ministry of Environmental Protection and Agriculture of Georgia (2019), *Georgia’s Second Biennial Update Report*, Ministry of Environmental Protection and Agriculture of Georgia, Tblisi, https://unfccc.int/documents/196359 (accessed on 17 October 2019). [19]

Ministry of Environmental Protection and Agriculture of Georgia (2019), *Georgia’s Updated Nationally Determined Contribution*. [55]

Municipal Development Fund of Georgia (2015), *Tbilisi Sustainable Urban Transport Strategy*, http://mdf.org.ge/storage/assets/file/documents%202016/murtazi/Strategic%20Paper%20Report%20PDF%20Geo(18_03_2016)/Strategic%20Paper%20Report%20final%20ENG.pdf. [57]

National Statistics Office of Georgia (2021), *Foreign Direct Investments by Countries*, https://www.geostat.ge/en/modules/categories/191/foreign-direct-investments. [17]

National Statistics Office of Georgia (2020), *Production value in industry*, Industry, https://www.geostat.ge/en/modules/categories/77/mretsveloba (accessed on 14 February 2021). [50]

National Statistics Office of Georgia (2020), *Statistical Yearbook of Georgia 2020*, National Statistics Office of Georgia, Tbilisi, https://www.geostat.ge/media/35685/Yearbook_2020.pdf (accessed on 12 February 2021). [24]

National Statistics Office of Georgia (2019), *Energy Balance of Georgia, 2019*, National Statistics Office of Georgia, Tbilisi, https://www.geostat.ge/en/modules/categories/681/energy-balance-of-georgia-2019 (accessed on 13 February 2021). [43]

Observatory of Economic Complexity (2019), *Georgia: Exports, Imports, and Trade Partners*, https://oec.world/en/profile/country/geo (accessed on 20 August 2020). [9]

OECD (2021), *COVID-19 and greening the economies of Eastern Europe, the Caucasus and Central Asia*, http://www.oecd.org/coronavirus/policy-responses/covid-19-and-greening-the-economies-of-eastern-europe-the-caucasus-and-central-asia-40f4d34f/ (accessed on 10 March 2021). [5]

OECD (2020), *Investment Promotion in Eurasia: A Mapping of Investment Promotion Agencies*, OECD Publishing, Paris, http://www.oecd.org/eurasia/competitiveness-programme/Investment-Promotion-in-Eurasia-A-Mapping-of-Investment-Promotion-Agencies-ENG.pdf (accessed on 11 February 2021). [13]

OECD (2020), *OECD Investment Policy Reviews: Georgia*, OECD Investment Policy Reviews, OECD Publishing, Paris, https://dx.doi.org/10.1787/0d33d7b7-en. [14]

OECD (2019), *Baseline Measurement Report: The Principles of Public Administration: Armenia*, OECD Publishing, Paris, http://www.sigmaweb.org/publications/Baseline-Measurement-Armenia-2019.pdf (accessed on 12 August 2020). [60]

OECD (2018), *The Principles of Public Administration Policy Development and Co-ordination: Baseline Measurement Report: Georgia*, OECD Publishing, Paris, http://www.sigmaweb.org/publications/Baseline-Measurement-Report-2018-Georgia.pdf (accessed on 13 August 2020). [61]

OECD (2018), *The Principles of Public Administration: Baseline Measurement Report: Ukraine*, OECD Publishing, Paris, http://www.sigmaweb.org/publications/Baseline-Measurement-Report-2018-Ukraine.pdf (accessed on 13 August 2020). [62]

Roser, M. et al. (2021), *Coronavirus Pandemic (COVID-19)*, OurWorldInData.Org, https://ourworldindata.org/coronavirus (accessed on 9 September 2020). [4]

TRACECA (2018), *Georgia: General Overview of the Transport Sector*, http://www.traceca-org.org/en/countries/georgia/general-overview-of-the-transport-sector/. [31]

Transparency International (2019), *CPI 2019: Eastern Europe & Central Asia*, https://www.transparency.org/en/news/cpi-2019-eastern-europe-central-asia (accessed on 20 July 2020). [15]

UNCTAD (2021), *Handbook of Statistics: Maritime Transport Indicators*, https://stats.unctad.org/handbook/MaritimeTransport/Indicators.html. [30]

UNECE (2020), *Report of the Meeting of the Parties to the Convention on its eighth session and of the Meeting of the Parties to the Convention serving as the Meeting of the Parties to the Protocol on its fourth session*, United Nations Economic Commission for Europe (UNECE), Vilnius, https://unece.org/sites/default/files/2021-02/ECE.MP_.EIA_.30-ECE.MP_.EIA_.SEA_.13_Advance%20copy.pdf (accessed on 14 February 2021). [59]

UNECE (2018), *2018 Transport Statistics Infocards*, UNECE, http://www.unece.org/trans/main/wp6/infocards.html. [25]

UNECE (2016), *Georgia Environmental Performance Reviews: Third Review*, UNECE, Geneva, https://www.unece.org/fileadmin/DAM/env/epr/epr_studies/ECE_CEP_177.pdf. [42]

UNECE (2016), *Georgia's National Road Safety Strategy*, UNECE, https://www.unece.org/fileadmin/DAM/trans/doc/2018/UNDA/Georgia_s_National_Road_Safety_Strategy_2016.pdf. [56]

UNESCAP (2018), *Capacity Building Workshop on Facilitation of International Railway Transport*, https://www.unescap.org/sites/default/files/Country_Georgia_Railways.pdf. [28]

UNFCCC (2019), *Communication of long-term strategies*, https://unfccc.int/process/the-paris-agreement/long-term-strategies. [54]

United States Agency for International Development (2017), *Enhancing Capacity for Low Emission Development Strategies (EC-LEDS) Clean Energy Program: Georgia's Low Emission Development Strategy (LEDS)*, USAID, Washington DC, https://www.decisionwaregroup.com/assets/wi-172_2017-09-14-georgia-s-low-emission-develdevelopment-strategy_eng.pdf. [44]

World Bank (2021), *World Development Indicators (database)*, https://datacatalog.worldbank.org/dataset/world-development-indicators. [1]

World Bank (2020), *Doing Business 2020*, World Bank Group, Washington, DC, http://dx.doi.org/10.1596/978-1-4648-1440-2. [10]

World Bank (2020), *Improving Freight Transit and Logistics Performance of the Trans-Caucasus Transit Corridor: Strategy and Action Plan*, World Bank Group, Washington, D.C., https://openknowledge.worldbank.org/bitstream/handle/10986/33554/Improving-Freight-Transit-and-Logistics-Performance-of-the-Trans-Caucasus-Transit-Corridor-Strategy-and-Action-Plan.pdf?sequence=1&isAllowed=y (accessed on 13 February 2021). [29]

World Bank (2018), *Georgia from Reformer to Performer*, World Bank, Washington DC, http://documents.worldbank.org/curated/en/496731525097717444/pdf/GEO-SCD-04-24-04272018.pdf. [21]

World Bank (n.d.), *Irrigation and Land Market Development Project*, http://projects.worldbank.org/P133828/?lang=en&tab=overview. [53]

World Economic Forum (2019), *The Global Competitiveness Report 2019*, World Economic Forum, Geneva, http://www3.weforum.org/docs/WEF_TheGlobalCompetitivenessReport2019.pdf (accessed on 23 July 2020). [22]

World Experience for Georgia (2017), *Enguri HPP and Energy Supply to Abkhazia-Energy and National Security Challenge*, https://eadaily.com/ru/news/2017/10/26/energopotreblenie-abhazii-rastet-ezhegodno-na-9-prognoziruyutsya-. [39]

Notes

[1] The EU Eastern Partnership (EaP) is a joint initiative for strengthening the relationships between the European Union, its member states and six countries (hereafter the EaP countries): Armenia, Azerbaijan, Belarus, Georgia, Moldova and Ukraine.

[2] Confirmed case and death figures are underestimates of actual case and death numbers. Methodology and testing rates vary widely, and international comparisons are necessarily flawed.

[3] The definition of small-scale hydro varies widely from country to country, ranging from less than 50 MW (Canada, China) to less than 1.5 MW (Sweden). In Georgia, the government defines small hydro as power plants with a generation capacity between 1 MW and 13 MW; smaller plants are mini (100 kW-1 MW) and micro (up to 100 kW).

[4] This first goal was not achieved, although in terms of purchasing power parity significant progress was made: USD 15.6 thousand in 2019 compared to USD 10.6 thousand in 2013. As for the second goal, exports have increased slightly over the relevant period: USD 3.4 billion in 2013 and USD 3.8 billion in 2018.

5. Moldova's sustainable infrastructure investments

This chapter describes sustainable infrastructure planning in Moldova and presents current trends in investment in large-scale infrastructure projects. It compares Moldova's infrastructure plans in the energy, transport, industry and water sectors against its international commitments under the Paris Agreement on climate change and the Sustainable Development Goals (SDGs). The chapter also explores Moldova's strategic documents for long-term economic development, sectoral development and the environment, including those related to climate change mitigation and adaptation. It identifies misalignments between stated goals and observed investment flows and provides recommendations to improve strategic planning for sustainable infrastructure.

State of play: economy, investment and climate change in Moldova

Economy and trade

Table 5.1. Key indicators on Moldova's economy

Population (2019)	2 657 637
Urbanisation rate (2019)	42.7%
Annual population growth (2019)	-1.8%
Surface area	33 850 km[2]
GDP (USD, current price, 2019)	11 955 million
GDP per capita (USD, current price, 2019)	4 499
Real GDP growth (year-on-year change, 2019, 2020)	3.6%, -4.5%
Inflation (average consumer price, y-o-y change, 2020)	7.5%
Exports of goods and services (% of GDP, 2019)	30.5%
Imports of goods and services (% of GDP, 2019)	55.2%
FDI, net inflows (% of GDP, 2019)	5.0%
General government net lending/borrowing (% of GDP, 2019, 2020)	-1.5%, -5.5%
Unemployment (% of total labour force, 2019)	5.5%
Remittances (% of GDP, 2019)	16.0%
Transparency, accountability and corruption in the public sector rating (1= most corrupt, 6 = least corrupt, 2018)	2.5

Source: World Bank (2021[1]), *World Development Indicators (database)*, World Bank, https://datacatalog.worldbank.org/dataset/world-development-indicators; IMF (2020[2]), *World Economic Outlook: October 2020*, International Monetary Fund https://www.imf.org/external/datamapper/GGXCNL_NGDP@WEO/OEMDC/ADVEC/WEOWORLD

Economy and demographics

Moldova is a landlocked, lower-middle income country in Eastern Europe between Romania and Ukraine. Its population, among the smallest in Eastern Europe, has declined since its peak of 3 million in 1992 to 2.7 million in 2019. Moldova's demographic decline is linked to waves of emigration following independence, initially to Russia and, more recently, also to the European Union. Unlike all other former Soviet republics, except the Baltic states, Moldova did not join the Soviet Union until 1940, with most of its territory previously belonging to the Kingdom of Romania. As such, according to Romanian law, many Moldovans are eligible to apply for citizenship. Between 2002 and 2018 over half a million Moldovans received Romanian citizenship, and demand continues to grow (Point.md, 2018[3]). According to a recent study, Moldova's population may decrease to just over 2 million by 2035 due to a low fertility rates and consistently high net emigration (UNFPA Moldova, 2016[4]).

Immediately following independence from the Soviet Union in 1991, Moldova's GDP plummeted. Transnistria, a highly industrialised region in the east of the country that accounted for 40% of Soviet-era Moldova's economic output, effectively broke away from Moldovan political and economic control in 1992. Transnistria's *de facto* secession compounded with the economic impacts of the Soviet Union's dissolution severely impacted the Moldovan economy throughout the early 1990s, but then growth resumed, particularly after 1999 (Bertelsmann Stiftung, 2018[5]). With the exception of the 2008-2009 Global Financial Crisis and a major contraction in 2014-2015, Moldova's GDP has consistently increased since 1999, growing from USD 4.1 billion in constant 2010 USD to USD 9.9 billion by 2019. GDP per capita has increased substantially in Moldova but is still among the lowest in the countries of the EU Eastern Partnership (EaP),[1] higher only than Ukraine's.

Personal remittances remain an important source of funds for Moldovan households, but the total volume has decreased in recent years. Between 2003 and 2014 they were equal to over 20% of Moldova's GDP, reaching a peak of 34.9% of GDP in 2006. In 2019 they accounted for 16% of GDP, higher than in any other Eastern Partnership country (Georgia, 12.7%; Armenia, 11.2%; Ukraine 10.4%; Azerbaijan, 2.7%; Belarus 2.3%) (World Bank, 2021[1]).

Like neighbouring Ukraine, Moldova is a service-oriented economy with a comparatively large agricultural sector. In 2019, services accounted for 54.3% of Moldova's GDP, almost identical to Ukraine's figure of 54.4%, while agriculture accounts for 9.9%, second only to Armenia (12%) among the Eastern Partner countries. Industry (including construction) and manufacturing make up 22.8% and 10.9% of Moldova's GDP respectively (World Bank, 2021[1]).

As of February 2021, Moldova had the third highest number of confirmed COVID-19 cases per capita among EaP countries after Georgia and Armenia. Since the beginning of the pandemic, Moldova has diagnosed about 40.5 cases per thousand inhabitants compared to 56.5 in Armenia, 22.8 in Azerbaijan, 27 in Belarus, 65.4 in Georgia and 29.3 in Ukraine. Moldova's death rate (937 deaths per million inhabitants) has also been relatively high, second only to Armenia (1 049) in the region, much higher than in Azerbaijan (311), Belarus (562) and Ukraine (187) (Roser et al., 2020[6]).[2] Moldova declared a state of emergency and restricted travel throughout the country, including on public transport, and internationally to slow the virus's spread. Schools transitioned to distance learning, public gatherings were limited and non-essential businesses were closed for several months.

Like elsewhere in EaP countries, the economic consequences of the pandemic have been substantial. Moldova's GDP contracted by about 4.5% in 2020, while neighbouring Ukraine's GDP fell by 7.2%. Some economic stimulus measures announced by the Moldovan government, such as the elimination of certain taxes related to natural resource extraction, could have potentially negative consequences on the environment, while others, like state support for greening small and medium enterprises, could help Moldova's transition towards a greener economy (OECD, 2021[7]).

Trade

Moldova has been a member of the World Trade Organisation since 2001. Like Georgia and Ukraine, Moldova signed an Association Agreement with the European Union, which came into force in 2016. However, Moldova has also expressed interest in the Eurasian Economic Union. Although not a member, it has held observer status in the Union since 2017. Observer status does not constrain Moldova to follow any of the bloc's rules nor does it afford Moldova any rights beyond participation in Union's events, but it may signal a move towards closer integration with Russia and the other Eurasian Economic Union member states rather than with the European Union. To date, Moldova is the only country to which the Eurasian Economic Union has granted observer status (Russell, 2017[8]).

The European Union's Eastern Partnership (EaP) is a key initiative for continued cooperation between the EU, its member states and Moldova. It aims to strengthen ties and encourage reform on a number of policy areas, including on governance, connectivity, economic development and environmental protection.

Moldova has been a Contracting Party of the European Union's Energy Community since 2010. The Energy Community's Secretariat supports Moldova's implementation of reforms in the energy sector, including on energy efficiency, renewable energy development and environmental protection, and Moldova has made considerable progress. The Secretariat rates Moldova's overall implementation as 45% complete (Energy Community, 2020[9]).

Moldova does not have complete sovereign control of its eastern border, which complicates its ability to oversee trade flows. A breakaway region, Transnistria or the self-proclaimed Pridnestrovian Moldavian Republic, occupies a narrow strip of land between the Dniester river and Moldova's internationally recognised border with Ukraine. Like other breakaway states in the EaP countries (Abkhazia and South

Ossetia in Georgia and Artsakh/Nagorno-Karabakh in Azerbaijan), no sovereign state recognises the independence of Transnistria. In stark contrast with these other breakaway regions, however, Transnistria has entered into an agreement with Moldova and Ukraine to facilitate movement across both the internationally recognised and self-proclaimed borders. Since the 2005 agreement and with the support of the European Union Border Assistance Mission to Moldova and Ukraine, cross-border trade has been made easier and more secure. Nevertheless, important issues remain unsolved in the areas of abolition of tax and customs regulations favourable to the illegal re-export business, custom and tax collection and enforcement of border and customs control.

Moldova's most important trade partner is Romania, which accounts for 28% of Moldova's exports and 20% of imports (Figure 5.1(a) and (b)). Over half of Moldova's exports go to European Union member states, most notably Romania (28%), Italy (10%), Germany (8%) and Poland (5%). Russia also remains an important export market (7%) as well as Belarus (2.6%), Turkey (3.7%) and neighbouring Ukraine (3.8%). The European Union accounts for about 40% of Moldova's imports; other key import origin countries include Ukraine (12%), Russia (9%) and China (7%).

Moldova's agriculture and food processing sectors produce about a third of Moldova's exports, including key products like sunflower seeds (6% of exports), corn (3.4%), wheat (3%) and wine (4%). Machine parts, especially insulated wire (17% - Moldova's most important export product), textiles and metals (especially iron products – hot-rolled iron bars, 5%; raw iron, 2%) are also important export sectors. Due to limited domestic supply, Moldova imports refined petroleum to cover local demand. Petroleum alone accounts for 10% of Moldova's imports, the vast majority of the 12% from mineral products. Machinery (20%), chemical products (11%, especially packaged medicaments, 3.3%), metals (9%) and textiles (8%) make up the largest shares of Moldova's imports.

Figure 5.1. Trade of Moldova

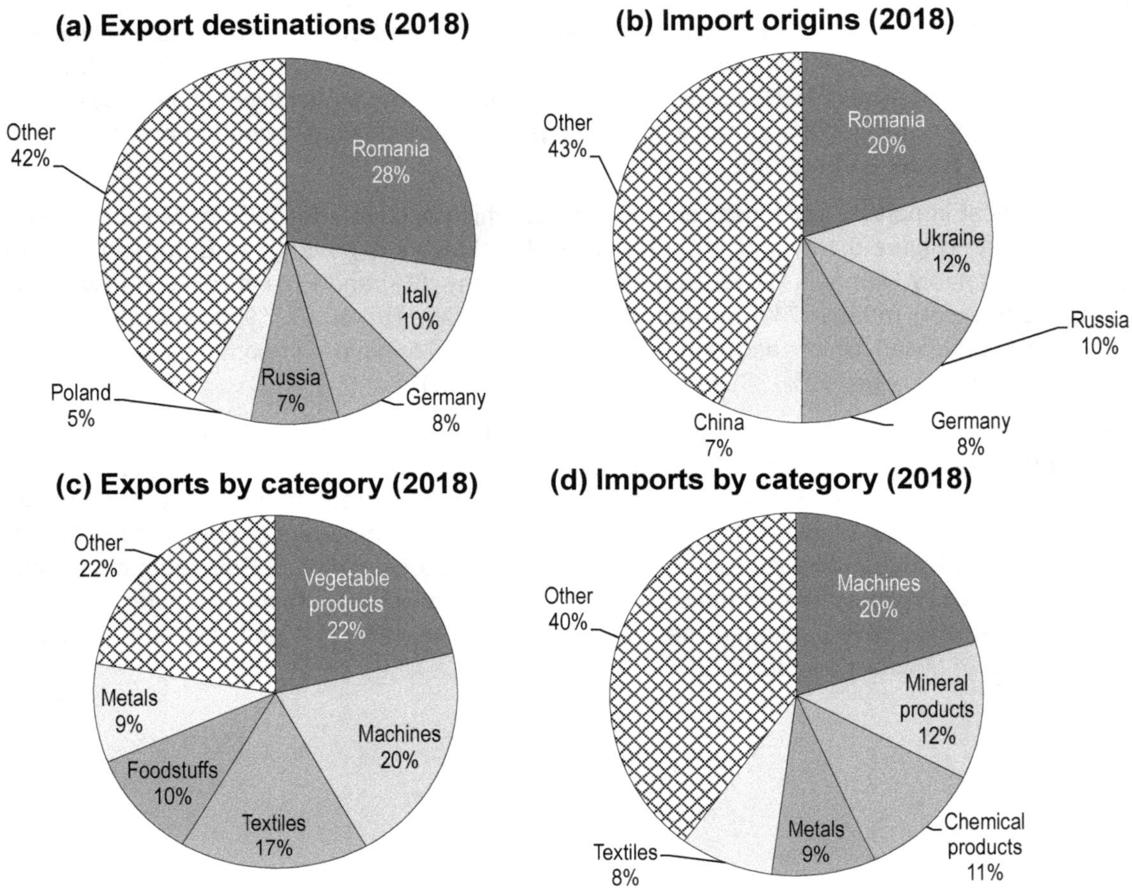

Source: Observatory of Economic Complexity (2019[10]), *Moldova: Exports, Imports and Trade Partners*, Observatory of Economic Complexity, https://oec.world/en/profile/country/mda

Investment climate

Although Moldova has made progress in adopting market principles since independence in 1991, the country's investment climate requires significant reform. Corruption remains deep-rooted and widespread; it poses the greatest barrier to Moldova's efforts to attract foreign investment. Transparency International ranked Moldova 120th out of 198 countries in the 2019 edition of its annual Corruption Perceptions Index, down from 117th in 2018. While Moldova outperforms Azerbaijan and neighbouring Ukraine (tied for 126th place in 2019), institutions in Armenia (77th), Belarus (66th) and Georgia (44th) are perceived as considerably less corrupt (Transparency International, 2019[11]).

The 2014 bank fraud scandal, a large-scale international scheme that resulted in the disappearance of USD 1 billion of largely public money from the Moldovan banking system, dealt a heavy blow to public trust in institutions. However, financial and technical support from the IMF, the World Bank, the EU and some of its member states have begun rebuilding confidence in Moldova's banking sector (Wrobel, 2019[12]).

Commitment to market-oriented reforms and closer cooperation with the European Union has fluctuated in recent years. The 2019 constitutional crisis led to the formation of two successive governments in less than a year, with relations to the European Union on the one hand and Russia on the other as key policy differences.

According to Moldovan law, foreign companies enjoy the same treatment afforded to domestic firms, and its competition laws align with EU practice and legislation. Risks to investors continue to undermine confidence, resulting in low FDI flows. There is, for instance, a track record of state expropriations of both domestic and foreign-owned assets justified as in the interest of public utility (US Department of State, 2019[13]).

Moldova ranks 48th in the World Bank's 2020 Ease of Doing Business report, between its EaP peers Armenia (47th) and Belarus (49th). Although Moldova's regulatory environment is considered more conducive to starting and running a business than that of neighbouring Ukraine (64th), it is significantly more onerous than the systems of Azerbaijan (34th) and Georgia (6th). Construction permits are the weakest point of Moldova's regulatory system, with the country ranking 156th out of 190 countries. On most other indicators, however, Moldova has made consistent progress. For instance, it reduced the time required to open a business (12 days in 2004 compared to 3 days in 2020) and the complexity of the tax system (53 payments requiring over 230 hours on average per year in 2006 compared to 10 payments requiring approximately 180 hours per year in 2020) (World Bank, 2020[14]).

Between 2003 and 2017, Moldova attracted USD 4.2 billion of FDI to greenfield projects. Compared to Armenia, with a GDP only slightly larger than Moldova's, this figure is low: Armenia attracted USD 7.4 billion to greenfield projects over the same period. In Moldova, most greenfield FDI flows concentrated in automotive components (24%) and hydrocarbons (21%) (Figure 5.2). Infrastructure-related investments were much smaller in volume. Alternative/renewable energy sources and the transportation sector attracted only 1% and 4% of FDI inflows respectively.

Figure 5.2. Greenfield FDI in Moldova by economic activity, 2003-2017

Cumulated greenfield FDI capital between January 2003 and September 2017 in USD million

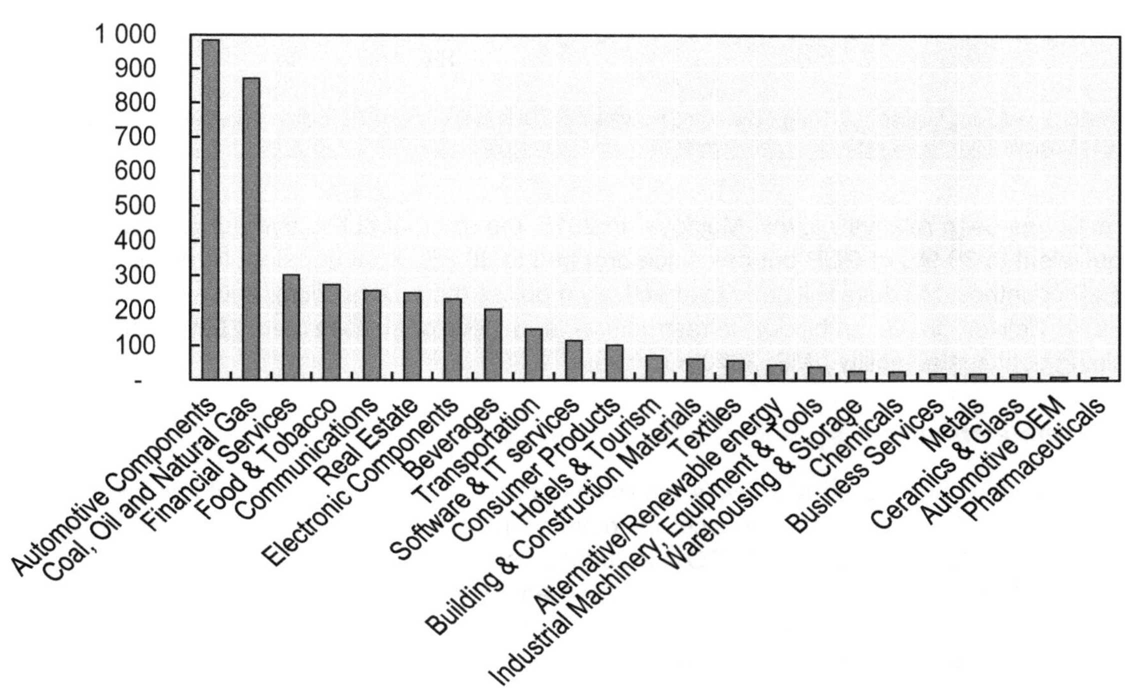

Source: OECD based on fDi Markets (2019[15]), fDi Markets: the in-depth crossborder investment monitor (database), fDi Markets, https://www.fdimarkets.com/

Russia is the most important single-country source of FDI to Moldova, accounting for 28% of inflows in 2015, but the European Union collectively accounts for almost twice Russia's volumes (58%) (Figure 5.3). Within the European Union, the Netherlands (12%), Cyprus (8%), Spain (8%), France (8%) and neighbouring Romania (6%) are the largest investors. The presence of offshore companies in Cyprus and the Netherlands likely inflate these countries' respective shares somewhat (Walter, Luecke and Lupusor, 2017[16]). Beyond the EU and Russia, the United Kingdom (3%) and the United States (2%) provide the most FDI to Moldova.

Figure 5.3. FDI in Moldova by country of origin, 2015

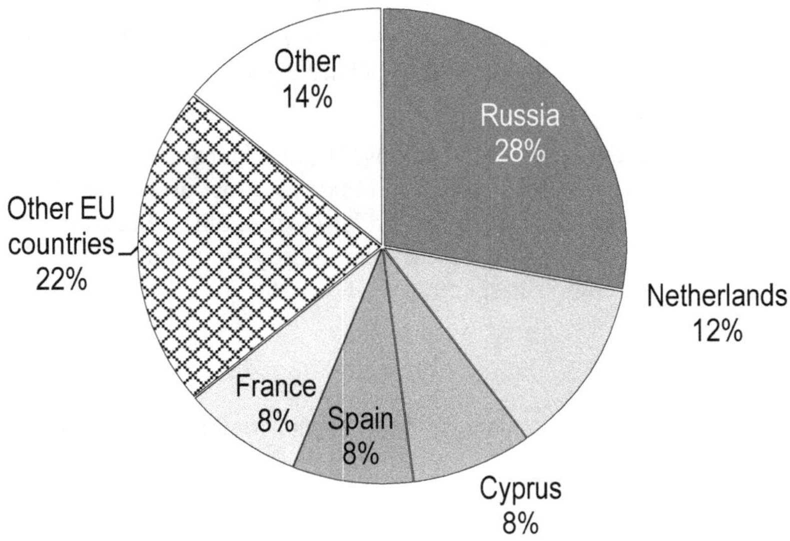

Source: Walter, Luecke and Lupusor (2017[16]), "The economic impact of FDI in Moldova: Results from empirical analysis", German Economic Team (GET) Moldova, https://www.get-moldau.de/wordpress/wp-content/uploads/2018/01/PS_01_2017_en.pdf

Public debt has been relatively low in Moldova. In 2016, the stock of public and publicly guaranteed debt was equivalent to 36.9% of GDP but has since dropped to 30.8%. Although debt levels are lower than in many EaP countries, Moldova will need to effectively mobilise the private sector and external development partners to deliver on its ambitious infrastructure- and development-related 2020 fiscal plans while maintaining debt sustainability (IMF, 2020[17]).

Climate change

Given the country's small size, Moldova's emissions account for only 0.02% of global greenhouse gas (GHG) emissions. Following independence, Moldova's GHG emissions sharply declined throughout the 1990s (from 43 $MtCO_2e$ in 1990 to 11 $MtCO_2e$ in 2000) before plateauing and slightly increasing throughout the 2000s and 2010s to reach 14 $MtCO_2e$ in 2014 and 2015 (Figure 5.4). Despite recent increases, Moldova's annual emissions are still only about a third of their pre-independence levels. Moldova's GDP, by contrast, has experienced two decades of near-constant, often rapid growth, with the notable exception of the 2014 bank fraud scandal and resulting crisis. In 2019 Moldova's economy reached USD 12.0 billion, more than nine times larger than in 2000 when GDP stood at USD 1.3 billion.[3]

As GHG emissions fell and GDP rose, the GHG intensity of Moldova's economy shrank to 1.8 $kgCO_2e$ per USD (in constant 2010 dollars) by 2015 from 10.1 $kgCO_2e$ per USD two decades earlier. However,

Moldova's economy remains significantly more emissions-intensive than the OECD average (0.35 $kgCO_2e$ per USD in 2012). With a shrinking population and reduced GHG emissions, per capita emissions in Moldova have reduced from 10.0 (or 14.6) tCO2e in 1990 to 4.9 tCO2e in 2015 (World Bank, 2021[1]; Climate Change Office of the Republic of Moldova, 2018[18]).[4]

Moldova has submitted an updated version of its Nationally Determined Contribution (NDC) to the UN Framework Convention on Climate Change. The updated NDC increases the ambition of the country's mitigation targets, albeit marginally, from an unconditional commitment to reduce emissions by 2030 from 64-67% of 1990 levels (original NDC) to 70% of 1990 levels (updated NDC). Conditional on international support, Moldova aims to reduce emissions by 88% compared to 1990 levels by 2030 (compared to 78% in the original NDC).

Figure 5.4. GHG emissions and GDP of Moldova, 1990-2019

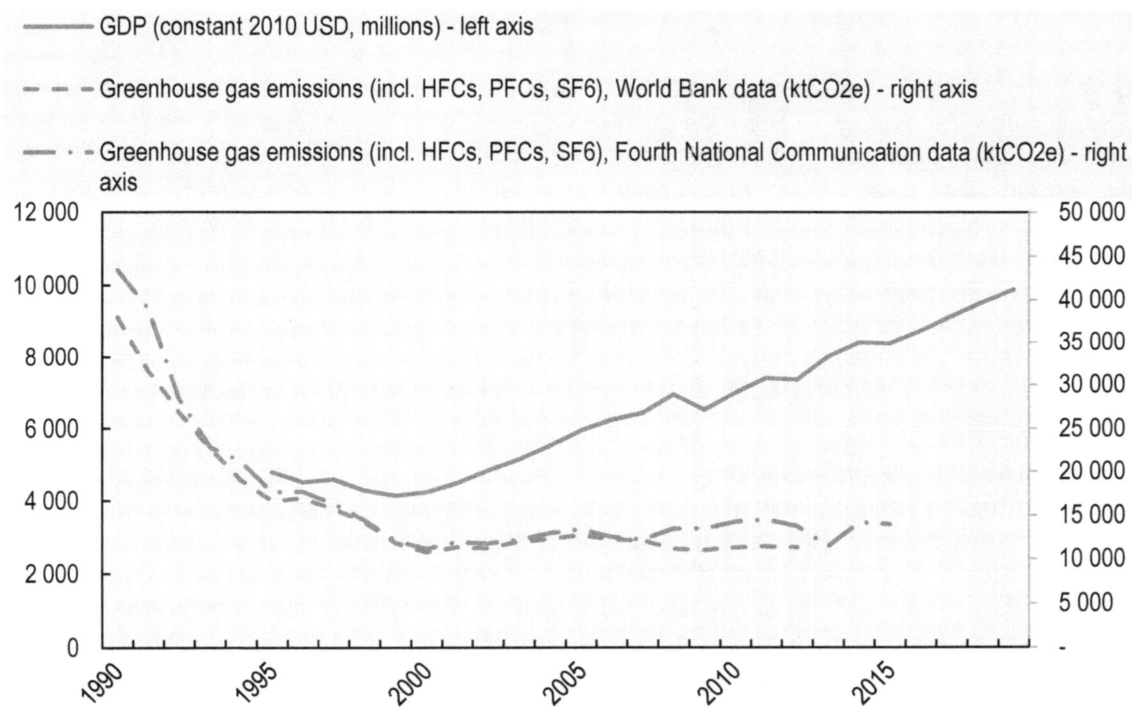

Note: GDP data unavailable prior to 1995

Source: World Bank (2021[1]), World Development Indicators (database), World Bank, https://data.worldbank.org/indicator/EN.ATM.GHGT.ZG; Climate Change Office of the Republic of Moldova (2018[18]), Fourth National Communication of the Republic of Moldova under the United Nations Framework Convention on Climate Change, Climate Change Office, Ministry of Agriculture, Regional Development and Environment, http://www.clima.md/lib.php?l=en&idc=81&

Energy (including fuel combustion from transport) accounts for the largest share of Moldova's GHG emissions (68% in 2015), but the share has declined compared to pre-independence levels (80% in 1990). Waste-related emissions have followed the opposite trajectory, rising from 5% in 1990 to 11% in 2015. The share of Moldova's agriculture-related emissions nearly doubled from 12% in 1990 to 22% in 2000 before falling once more to 15% in 2015. Emissions derived from industrial processes represent a small but rising share of emissions (4% in 1990, 6% in 2015). The absolute values of all categories of GHG emissions remain below their 1990 levels; energy-related emissions decreased the most (9.5 MtCO2e in 2015 compared to 34.6 $MtCO_2e$ in 1990) (Ministry of Environment of the Republic of Armenia, 2020[19]).

The effects of climate change have already become apparent in Moldova. The annual mean temperature rose by 1.0°C on average (1887-2014), with the upwards trend particularly evident following the early 1980s. Precipitation rates have not varied as significantly. Nationally, average precipitation increased slightly (54.7 mm more in 2014 compared to 1887) following trends in the north and centre of the country, while the south recorded a slight decrease in precipitation. According to Moldova's climate change scenarios, average temperature is expected to continue increasing, but precipitation levels could either increase or decrease slightly depending on how GHG concentrations. Despite a longer growing season and milder winter, without adaptation measures the yields of key crops are expected to decrease markedly by 2100. Depending on future GHG concentrations, corn productivity could decrease by 34-67% and winter wheat could decrease by 22-46%,[5] while cultivation of both crops may become impossible in Moldova in the worst-case scenario. Rising temperatures could also exacerbate the risks of forest fires and negatively impact human health (Climate Change Office of the Republic of Moldova, 2018[18]).

Moldova's infrastructure needs and current plans

According to the World Economic Forum's 2019 Competitiveness Index, Moldova's average infrastructure score (66) is below the average in Eurasian countries overall (67.7) but considerably higher than in other lower-middle income countries (60) (World Economic Forum, 2019[20]). According to the World Bank's Logistics Performance Index, Moldova's infrastructure performance has deteriorated in recent years: Moldova fell from 85th in 2014's global ranking to 100th in 2016 and 141st in 2018 (World Bank, 2019[21]). However, while the overall quality of Moldova's infrastructure is relatively low, its indicators are broadly in line with its two neighbouring countries, Romania and Ukraine (Figure 5.5). With the exception of its access to seaport services, where landlocked Moldova faces a distinct disadvantage, and airport connectivity, Moldova's transport infrastructure indicators closely follow Romania's and Ukraine's. On measures of the efficiency of its electricity grid and water supply systems, however, Moldova consistently underperforms compared to its neighbours.

A key infrastructure challenge in Moldova is the disparity between rural and urban areas. Access to adequate infrastructure services such as clean piped water, transportation services, electricity and district heating differs widely between cities and rural regions. For instance, only about 10% of rural residents in Moldova have access to modern heating[6] compared to nearly 80% in urban areas. The disparity is a particularly acute problem in Moldova, the least urbanised country in the Eastern Partnership, since such a large share of its population (57% in 2019) lives in rural areas. Given the concentration of poorer households in rural areas, improving infrastructure service provision outside urban areas is an essential step in meeting Moldova's poverty reduction goals (World Bank, 2016[22]). One of the Moldovan government's main priorities as laid out in the *National Development Strategy "Moldova 2030"* is extending access to physical infrastructure assets to underserviced populations.

Figure 5.5. Quality of infrastructure in Moldova

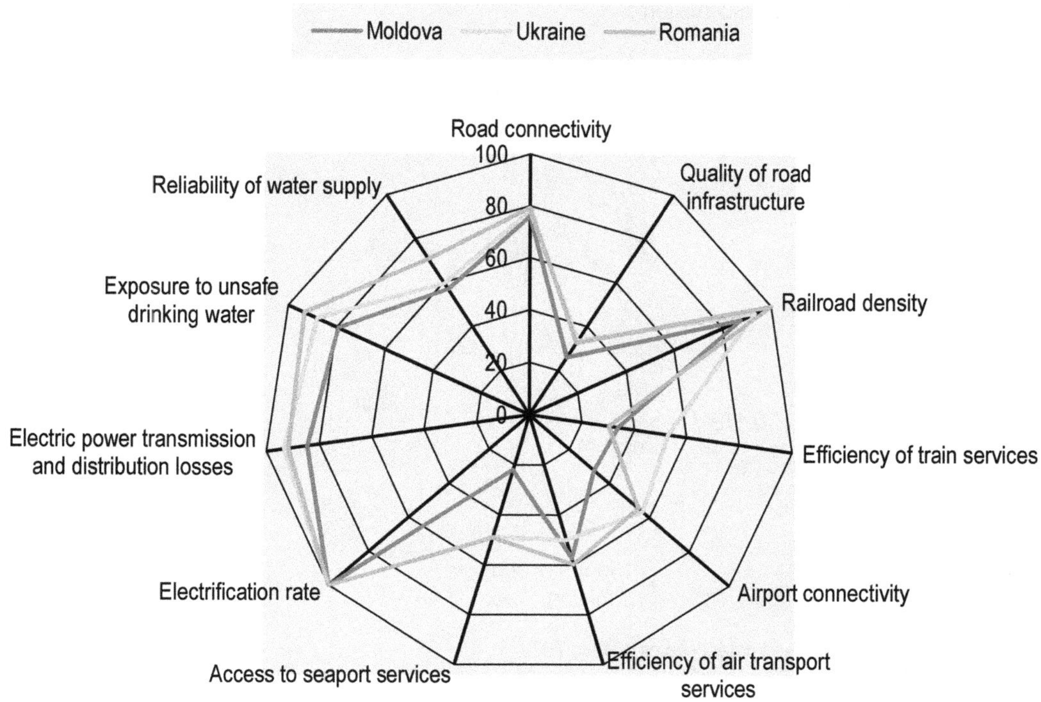

Source: World Economic Forum (2019[20]), *The Global Competitiveness Report 2019*, World Economic Forum, http://www3.weforum.org/docs/WEF_TheGlobalCompetitivenessReport2019.pdf

The OECD's database tracks 20 major infrastructure projects planned or under construction in Moldova, with a cumulative value of USD 2.4 billion. By value, transport projects account for over half of the investments (53%, USD 1.3 billion), and energy projects, particularly in electricity transmission and distribution, make up the second largest share (41%, USD 1.0 billion) (Figure 5.6). By comparison, industry and mining projects (1.7%, USD 40 million) and water projects (4.2%, USD 102 million) represent much smaller shares of total investment in Moldova's infrastructure.

Figure 5.6. Investment projects in Moldova, by sector

Planned and under construction, in USD million

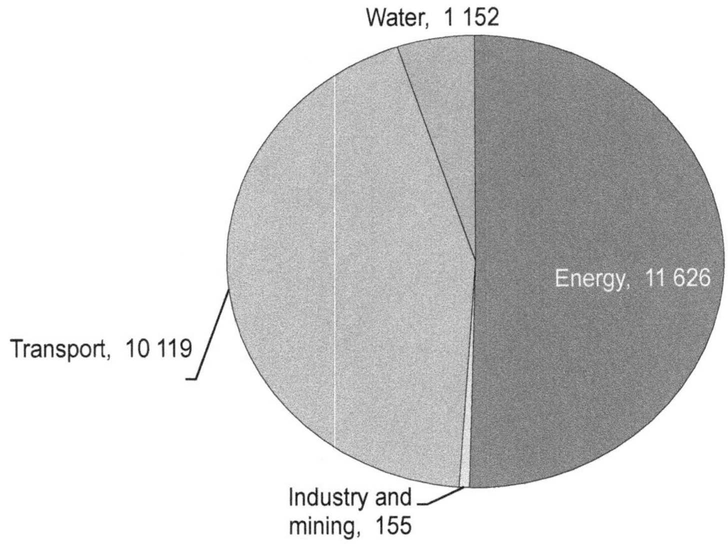

Source: OECD analysis based on accessed databases as of June 2020.

Transport

For a country of its size, Moldova has a relatively extensive network of transport infrastructure, but the Soviet-era stock of assets has suffered from underinvestment and insufficient maintenance leading to suboptimal service delivery, particularly in rural areas. Firms in Moldova identify access to transport and logistics infrastructure services as an obstacle to growth and job creation. Increased investments have resulted in a marked improvement in the quality of Moldova's roads, less than 50% of which were classified as 'poor' or 'very poor' in 2015, compared to over 90% in 2006 (World Bank, 2016[22]).

As with other infrastructure services in Moldova, the quality of transport services differs considerably between urban and rural areas. Poor transport connectivity, especially in rural localities removed from interurban transport corridors, constrains Moldova's continued development, reduces the economic opportunities of rural Moldovans and hinders trade. In response, Moldova's *Transport and Logistics Strategy 2013-2022* has set an objective of developing and rehabilitating the national road network, including secondary roads, to ensure year-round access for all settlements to the country's primary highways.

In terms of public transport, major cities like Chisinau and Balti enjoy public transport services, but only about half of small town have any kind of publicly funded transport services and such services are completely absent in rural areas (World Bank, 2016[22]). Even in Moldova's larger population centres, recent OECD analysis demonstrates that several barriers exist in national and municipal policy frameworks that hinder the development and 'greening' of transport infrastructure and services (OECD, 2019[23]).

Inadequate transport infrastructure quality combined with regulatory barriers increase the costs of trade in Moldova. According to the OECD's Trade Facilitation Indicators, poor border agency co-operation – both external and internal – and documentation are weak points in facilitating cross-border trade (OECD, 2020[24]).

Underinvestment in transport infrastructure is a major factor in the deterioration of Moldova's transport network. Between 2000 and 2018, Moldova spent 0.57% of its GDP on total inland transport infrastructure annually on average, considerably less than other countries in the Eastern Partnership: Armenia, 1.0% (2008-2016); Azerbaijan, 2.0% (2000-2018), Belarus, 2.8% (2005-2018) and Georgia, 2.7% (2002-2018) (ITF, 2019[25]).In broad terms, investments in Moldova have shifted away from rail over the past decade, focusing mostly on road and road maintenance (Figure 5.7).While increased investment in road and road maintenance could improve connectivity, including in rural areas, continued underinvestment in Moldova's existing rail network risks hastening its fall into disrepair.

The modal shift away from rail towards road is evident in the transport of goods and passengers in Moldova. While rail assured 73% of the turnover of goods (measured in tonnes-kilometers, tkm) in 1995 compared to 27% for road, these proportions had reversed by 2019: 86% road vs 14% rail. In absolute terms, rail turnover reduced by 70% from 3.1 billion tkm to 0.9 billion tkm while road increased by 380% from 1.2 billion tkm to 5.6 billion tkm. Rail's modal share of passenger turnover (measured in passenger-kilometres, pkm) has also declined, from 15% in 2006 to 1% in 2020, but unlike for cargo, passenger turnover has shifted towards air travel (from 15% in 2006 to 40% in 2019) rather than road (70% in 2006, 59% in 2019). In absolute terms, rail is the only mode with decreased turnover (down 84% from 471 million pkm to 75 pkm) while all others increased (road by 59%, river by 34% and air by 397%) (National Bureau of Statistics of the Republic of Moldova, 2020[26]). The government has taken steps to counter this shift, supporting regional rail connectivity through the acquisition of new locomotives and the rehabilitation of existing rail infrastructure, relying on part in support from EBRD and EIB (Codreanu, 2019[27]; Ahlemeyer, 2020[28]).

Figure 5.7. Inland transport infrastructure investment in Moldova (2000-2017)

Modal share (%) of total inland infrastructure investment (left axis) and total inland transport infrastructure investment in current USD per capita (right axis)

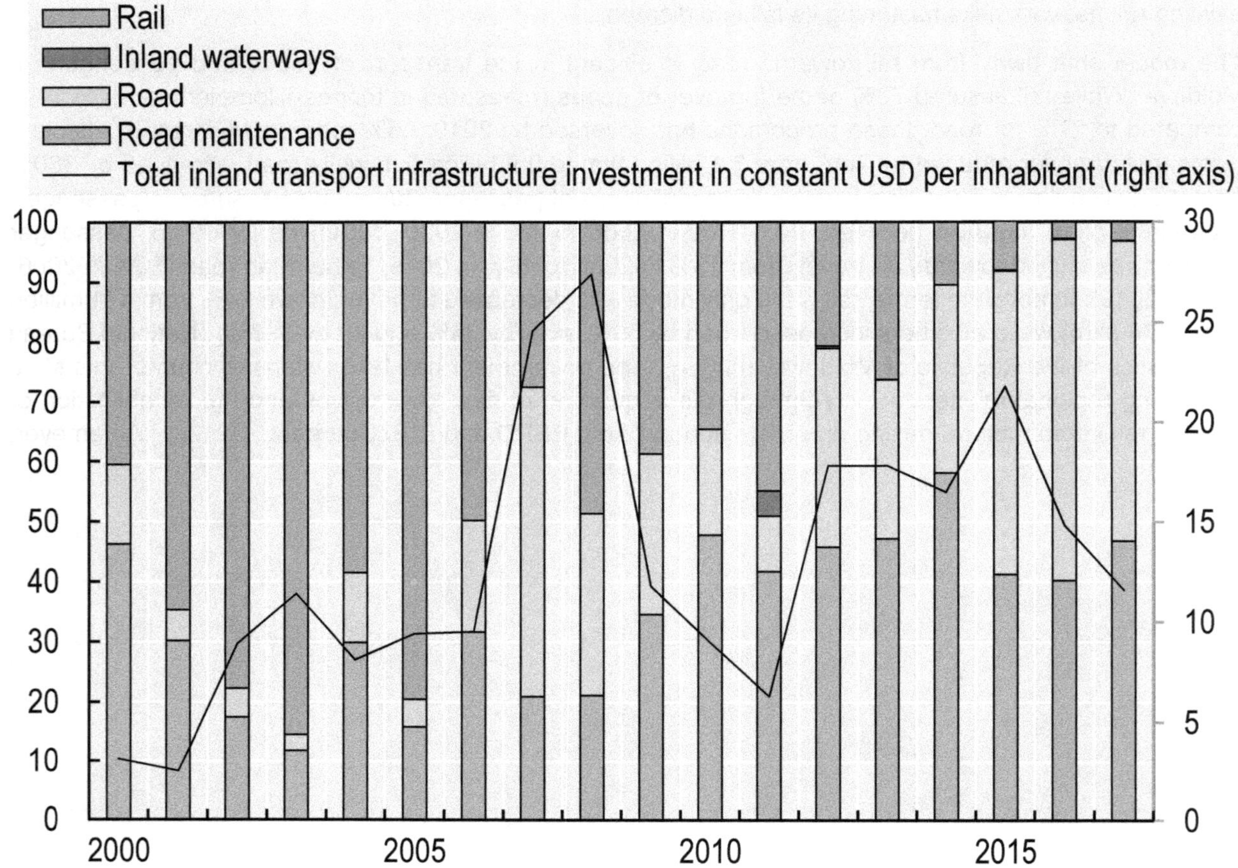

Source: ITF (2019[25]), *Transport performance indicators*, International Transport Forum, https://doi.org/10.1787/trsprt-data-en

Compared to frozen conflicts elsewhere in the Eastern Partnership like Abkhazia and South Ossetia in Georgia and Nagorno-Karabakh/Artsakh in Azerbaijan, the breakaway region of Transnistria is less disruptive to Moldova's international transport connections with Ukraine, particularly following recent developments in border crossing facilitation. Between late 2018 and early 2019, the EU Border Assistance Mission to Moldova and Ukraine (EUBAM) ensured the opening of the Palanca-Maiaky-Udobne Joint Operated Border Crossing Point in southern Moldova for travellers and cargo, bypassing the Transnistrian-controlled portion of the Moldova-Ukraine border. Another EUBAM-supported project resulted in the relaunch of passenger and cargo rail services between Chisinau and Odessa (Ukraine) via Transnistrian territory (EUBAM, 2019[29]).

Transport is the main source of air pollution in Moldova, especially in urban centres, accounting for upwards of 86% of pollutant emissions and, according to some estimates, could be as high as 96%. As road transport use has increased, Moldovan households and companies have relied on imports of foreign used vehicles, many of which enter Moldova with inadequate technical inspections (OECD, 2019[23]). Moldova's government has made tackling this problem a priority in both its environment- and economic development-related strategic documents, such as the *National Development Strategy "Moldova 2030"* (increase share of renewables in transport's final energy use to 10% by 2022) and the *Environmental Strategy for 2014-2023* (approximate environment-related EU Directives, including on fuel standards). Moldova has made considerable progress on transposing transport- and air quality-related EU Directives into national legislation. In 2016, Moldova transposed Directive 1999/32/EC relating to a reduction in the sulphur content of certain liquid fuels. Moldova has also developed legislation that will transpose Directive 2008/50/EC on ambient air quality and cleaner air and Directive 1994/63/EC, which aims to prevent volatile organic compound (VOC) emissions during petrol storage.

Moldova's transport infrastructure projects planned and under construction account for around USD 1.3 billion, primarily in the road sector (79% or USD 1 billion) (Figure 5.8). Rail (19% or USD 241 million) and fluvial port projects (2% or USD 31 million) account for the remainder. All of Moldova's road and rail projects tracked in the OECD's database aim to rehabilitate existing infrastructure.

The hotspot projects identified in the OECD's database of infrastructure projects planned and under construction in Moldova reflect the emphasis placed on road network rehabilitation in the *Transport and Logistics Strategy 2013-2022* (Table 5.2). There is no evidence in the OECD database of projects designed to help Moldova meet some of its transport-related environment objectives, i.e. Moldova 2030's goal to increase the use of renewables in the transport sector.

Figure 5.8. Transport projects in Moldova, by sub-sector

Planned and under construction in USD million

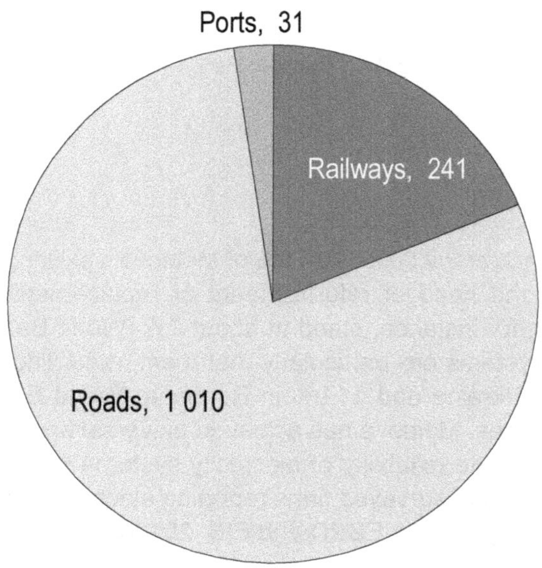

Source: OECD analysis based on accessed databases as of June 2020.

Table 5.2. Hotspot projects in the transport sector in Moldova

Name	Sub-sector	Description	Project value (USD million)	Funding source	Type of investment
(a) Under construction					
Moldova Roads II, III and IV	Road	The project will rehabilitate key national roads with a focus on connections to cross-European corridors.	830	EIB, EBRD	Brownfield
Moldova Rail Infrastructure and Rolling Stock FL	Rail	The project aims to acquire more modern rolling stock for Moldova's rail system, namely diesel locomotives for cargo and passenger transport, and rehabilitate selected stretches of railways	130	EIB	Brownfield
(b) Planned					
Moldova Rail Infrastructure (Bender-Basarabeasca-Etulia-Giurgiulesti)	Rail	The project will rehabilitate 233 km of track along a key railway corridor for trade between Bender (Transnitria-controlled territory) and Giurgiulesti (Moldova's only international fluvial port) via Basarabeasca and Etulia (on the border with Ukraine).	111	EIB	Brownfield
Local Roads Improvement Project	Road	The project aims to rehabilitate and upgrade 300 km of priority local roads to improve rural connectivity.	88	IDA; Government of Moldova	Brownfield

Note: Refer to the Reader's guide for the present report's definition of 'hotspot' and other information on how the projects above were selected and prioritised. EIB = European Investment Bank; EBRD = European Bank for Reconstruction and Development; IDA = International Development Association.
Source: OECD database as of June 2020.

Energy

According to Moldova's *Energy Strategy 2030*, 70-75% of Moldova's existing stock of energy infrastructure assets are in poor condition and need of refurbishment or replacement. The losses incurred by the country's ageing gas pipelines, for instance, stand at about 7% (World Bank, 2016[22]). Moldova's power transmission and distribution systems are particularly inefficient, recording losses of 18.8% of electricity output, compared to 10.3% in Ukraine and 11.9% in Romania (World Economic Forum, 2019[20]). Like other former Soviet Union countries, Moldova has achieved universal access to electricity, but, due to the country's outdated infrastructure, the reliability of electricity systems falls below the regional average in Europe and Central Asia, with 37% of surveyed firms reporting electrical outages in Moldova compared to 33% in the region as a whole (World Bank, EBRD and EIB, 2019[30]).

Moldova is extremely dependent on imports to meet its energy consumption needs. In 2018, Moldova covered only 20% (818 ktoe) of its total primary energy supply through domestic production while relying on net imports to cover the remainder (3 342 ktoe). Moldova exports no gas, coal or electricity, but does export limited quantities of oil products (27 ktoe in 2018) (IEA, 2019[31]) Moldova covers about 90% of its domestic power needs with "imported" electricity from Transnistria (World Bank, 2016[22]), although it has sought to diversify supply with cheaper imports from neighbouring Romania and Ukraine. As a result of the Moldovan government's *de facto* loss of sovereign control over Transnistria, Moldova lost Moldovaskaya GRES, its most important power plant, with an installed capacity of 2 520 MW. Given Transnistria's position between Moldova and, via Ukraine, its main gas supplier Russia, the breakaway state is able to siphon off gas supplies intended for Moldova for which it has neglected to offer any payments to MoldovaGaz, the main Moldovan gas company. Due to this, MoldovaGaz owes a massive debt to Russian SOE Gazprom for gas that never reached territories under the effective control of the Moldovan government (OECD, 2019[23]).

Moldova also relies entirely on imports to meet its domestic demand for coal, which is not used in power generation but an important heating fuel especially for the rural poor, and natural gas, which fuels 94% of domestic power generation (Figure 5.9). Moldova also has limited hydroelectric generation capacity (e.g. a 16-MW run-of-the-river power plant in Costesti), which nearly makes up the remainder of domestic generation (5%). Biofuels account for a further 1%, and other renewables (solar PV, 3 GWh; wind, 23 GWh) jointly account for slightly less than 0.5% of electricity generation in Moldova.

Figure 5.9. Electricity generation by source

GWh, 2018

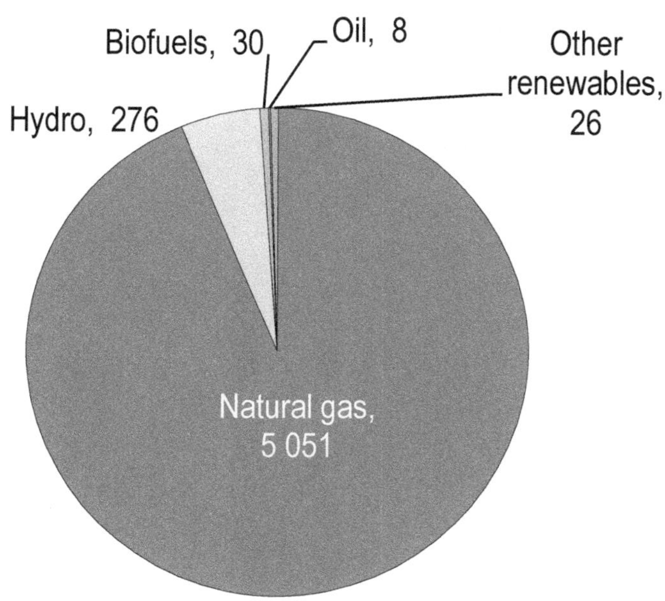

Source: IEA (2021[32]), *Electricity Information 2020*, International Energy Agency, https://www.iea.org/data-and-statistics/

In response to its energy-related challenges, Moldova set out three overarching objectives in its *Energy Strategy 2030*. First, Moldova strives to bolster its energy security and achieve greater independence from imports, notably by building new power generation capacity (to reach 800 MW by 2020). Its second goal, related to the first, is integration into the European energy system, particularly gas supply lines and the European Network of Transmission System Operators for Electricity (ENTSO-E), which the country aims to join by the end of 2020. Lastly, to improve sustainability and diversify energy sources, Moldova aims to develop renewables in its power generation (10% by 2020 – a target repeated in *Moldova 2030*, to be achieved by 2022), total energy consumption (20% by 2020) and fuels (10% biofuels in total fuels by 2020). As a supporting measures for these objectives, Moldova also aims to reduce the energy intensity of its economy (by 10% by 2020) and improve the efficiency of its building stock and transmission and distribution systems.

Moldova adopted a law that transposes EU Directive 2009/28/CE on renewable energy use in 2016. The law establishes a legal framework for the promotion of energy from renewable sources. It sets mandatory national targets for the overall share of energy from renewable sources in gross final consumption of energy and for the share of energy from renewable sources in transport.

Unique among the EaP countries in the present study, Moldova's energy-related infrastructure projects are not concentrated in electricity generation, which only account for 30% of energy projects by value (Figure 5.10). Instead, electric transmission and distribution projects make up the largest share (49%), consisting predominantly of a single large-scale project that aims to connect Chisinau to the existing interchange between Moldova and Romania's electricity networks (Table 5.3) in addition to smaller-scale refurbishments of electricity distribution and transmission lines. These projects, combined with the 12% of energy investments dedicated to a project linking Chisinau to the natural gas interchange on the Moldova-Romania border, are consistent with the second overarching goal of *Moldova Energy Strategy 2030* to integrate Moldova's energy system with Europe's. However, the lack of renewable energy projects and the presence of only a single large-scale project to construct new electricity generation capacity cast doubt on the strategy's other goals by end of 2020 to increase domestic capacity and pivot towards renewable energy.

Figure 5.10. Energy projects in Moldova, by sub-sector

Planned and under construction in USD million

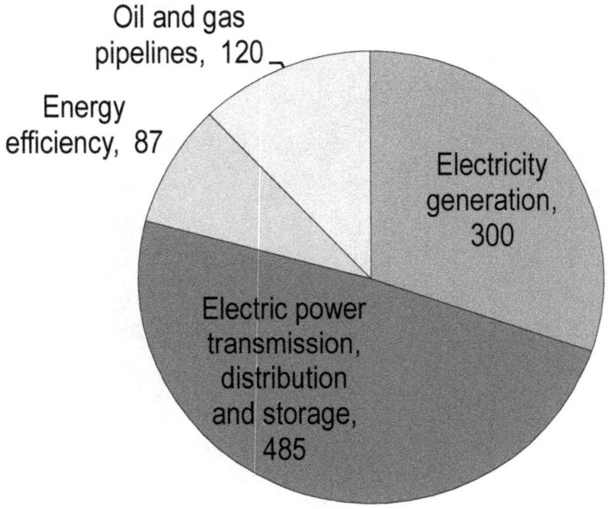

Source: OECD analysis based on accessed databases as of June 2020.

Table 5.3. Hotspot projects in the energy sector in Moldova

Name	Sub-sector	Description	Project value (USD million)	New capacity (MW)	Funding source	Type of investment
	(a) Under construction					
Moldova-Romania Power Interconnector Project	Electricity transmission and distribution	The project will install new power lines and a converter station to connect Chisinau to Isaccea (Romania) via Vulcanesti (southern Moldova).	305	N/A	EBRD, EIB, World Bank, EU	Greenfield
Ungheni-Chisinau Natural Gas Pipeline	Natural gas pipeline	The project will extend the existing line between Iasi (Romania) and Ungheni (Moldova, on the Romanian border) to Chisinau with 120 km of new pipeline.	120	N/A	EBRD, EIB, EU, Romanian government	Greenfield
	(b) Planned					
Name	Sub-sector	Description	Project value (USD million)	New capacity (MW)	Funding source	Type of investment
Burlaceni Combined Cycle Power Plant	Electricity generation (natural gas-fired power plant)	The project aims to construct a condensing power plant in the village of Burlaceni (southern Moldova).	300	500	RWE AG	Greenfield
Moldova Energy Efficiency Project	Energy efficiency	The project retrofits public and residential buildings in various Moldovan cities to improve energy efficiency.	87	N/A	EIB	Brownfield

Note: Refer to the Reader's guide for the present report's definition of 'hotspot' and other information on how the projects above were selected and prioritised. EBRD = European Bank for Reconstruction and Development; EIB = European Investment Bank.
Source: OECD database as of June 2020:

Industry, mining and water

The share of Moldova's GDP derived from industry (excluding the construction sector, which remained broadly stable) decreased from about 20% in 1995-1998 to below 15% by 2009-2014, reflecting a shift in labour and economic output from industry (and agriculture) towards the service sector (World Bank, 2016[22]).

The vast majority (84%) of Moldova's industrial output consists of manufactured goods (Figure 5.11), primarily manufactured food and beverage products. Processed meat products and wine are the country's two most important industrial outputs by value. Unlike most EaP countries, Moldova has only modest mineral deposits and consequently does not have a sizeable mining and quarrying sector, as evidenced by the sector's small share (2%) of industrial output.

Figure 5.11. Industrial output by NACE* subsector

2019, in million MDL

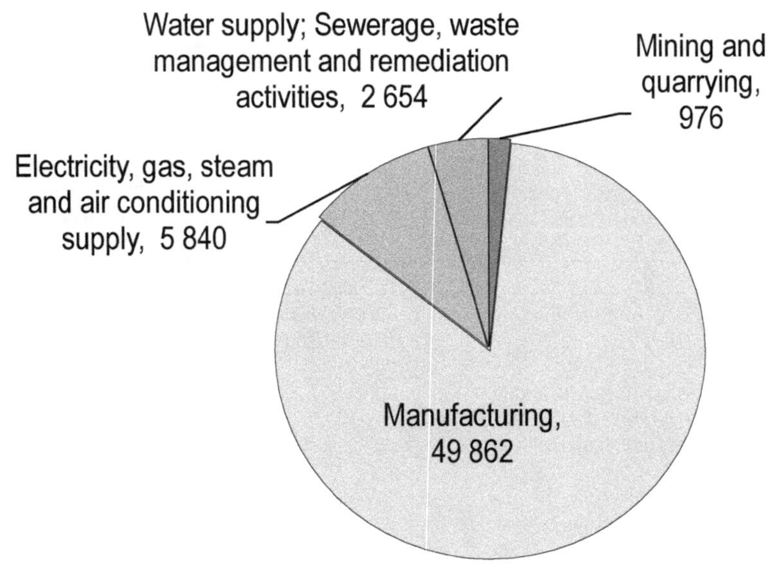

Note: MDL =Moldovan leu; * NACE = Nomenclature statistique des activités économiques dans la Communauté européenne [Statistical Classification of Economic Activities in the European Community]
Source: National Bureau of Statistics of the Republic of Moldova (2020[33]), "Value of manufactured industrial production, by types of activities, 2014-2019", http://statbank.statistica.md/

Moldova's water infrastructure quality is inadequate and underperforms compared to other EaP countries. 22.3% of the population is exposed to unsafe drinking water (compared to 13.7% in Ukraine, the second worst performer in the region on this metric), and its water supply is the least reliable in region, ranking 88th globally (several places below Ukraine, 80th, and the countries of the Caucasus, between 59th and 63rd) (World Economic Forum, 2019[20]).

Moldova's urban-rural disparity of infrastructure service delivery is especially evident in the water supply and sanitation (WSS) sector. 95% of Chisinau's population enjoys access to improved water sources, compared to only 54% of rural residents (only 39% of whom have improved water piped directly to their homes). Only 10% of rural Moldovans have private flush toilets. Moldova's progress on improving service delivery to its population has been slow: It was the only country in Europe that did not achieve its WSS-related Millennium Development Goal of halving the share of its population without access to basic WSS services between 1990 and 2015. Rural water supply often relies on shallow groundwater wells that do not benefit from regular monitoring and fail to meet drinking water quality standards (World Bank, 2016[22]).

Recognising these shortcoming, the government of Moldova has set several water-related targets in its national development planning documents. As part of its overarching goals to widen access to physical infrastructure and communal services and to safeguard the fundamental right to physical health, *Moldova 2030* sets targets to provide 92-99%[7] of the population with safe water supply services (compared to a baseline of 88%) and 81-89% with improved sanitation services (compared to a baseline of 77%). Another target is to construct or refurbish water purification facilitations to working order in all settlements throughout the country with 15 thousand inhabitants or more.

The OECD's database contains only a single industrial project in Moldova, a planned USD 40 million bioethanol plant, contributing to *Energy Strategy 2030*'s goal of reaching 10% biofuels by 2020. In the water sector, although the individual projects are smaller in value, the OECD database tracks

USD 102million worth of water supply and sanitation (WSS) projects (Figure 5.12). These projects focus on developing or refurbishing WSS systems, in line with the targets outlined above, but over half of the investments are focused on urban centres – large and small cities – with only a third explicitly targeting small towns.

Figure 5.12. Industry, mining and water infrastructure projects in Moldova, by sub-sector

Planned and under construction in USD million

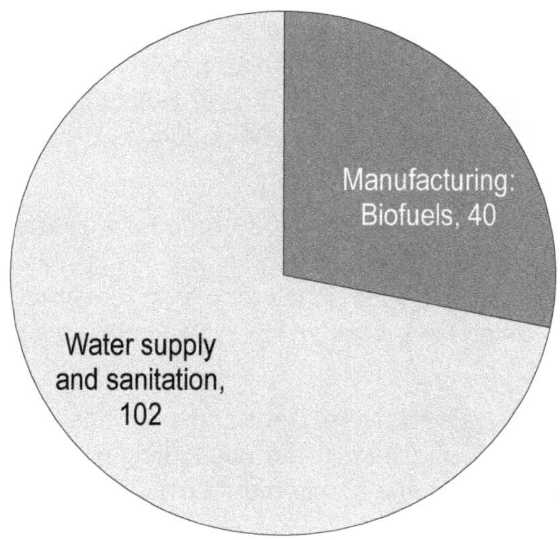

Source: OECD analysis based on accessed databases as of June 2020.

Strengths and weaknesses of existing institutional set-up for sustainable infrastructure planning

Strategic planning and links between long-term goals, infrastructure plans and environmental considerations

Moldova's top-level strategic planning document, the *National Development Strategy "Moldova 2030"*, is the first national development strategy to emphasise the importance of environmental protection. One of its priorities relates directly to the safeguarding of the natural environment.

In *"Moldova 2030"* (approved by the government in June 2020, awaiting adoption by parliament), the government notes unmet objectives in previous strategies (Strategy for Economic Growth and Poverty Reduction 2004-2006, National Development Strategy 2008-2011, National Development Strategy 2012-2020), identifying a fragmented system of independently developed and inadequately coordinated policy documents as a primary cause. OECD analysis of Moldova's public administration system raised similar concerns about incoherent development planning system and the inefficiency caused by contradicting objectives expressed in across several sector- and institution-specific strategies. Both *Moldova 2030* and the OECD's analysis call for standardisation of planning documents and a clearly defined hierarchy of planning documents in which lower-level sectoral and subnational strategies would be subordinate to the overarching development strategy (i.e. *Moldova 2030*) in a cascading structure (OECD, 2015[34]).

In this regard, Moldova could benefit from a clearly defined long-term vision (perhaps, like Kazakhstan's top-level development strategy, to 2050) transcending immediate politically contentious debates. Such long-term planning documents enable countries to look beyond shorter-term political and business cycles to articulate priorities in terms of economic and social development as well as, crucially, the reconciliation of these goals with environmental concerns. *Moldova 2030*'s overarching focus on improving citizens' wellbeing is a promising development in this regard. The government also plans to develop a long-term low-emission development strategy along with a Strategy on National Energy and Climate Plan.

Given *Moldova 2030*'s recent approval, the proposed reforms to the country's strategic planning document system remain unimplemented at present, but traces a pathway to a more coherent system moving forward. Moldova's sectoral development strategies (e.g. *Transport and Logistics Strategy 2013-2022, National Renewable Energy Action Plan of the Republic of Moldova for 2013-2020*, *Energy Strategy 2030* – whose quantitative targets extend to 2020) predate *Moldova 2030*, and their successor documents could offer an opportunity to cement a multi-level system of internally consistent strategic documents. *Moldova 2030* links explicitly to the Sustainable Development Goals, including infrastructure-related goals in the energy, transport and water supply and sanitation (WSS) sectors, and incorporates numerous quantitative environment- and climate-related targets.

Three successive governments between 2018 and 2020 proposed, retracted and re-proposed *Moldova 2030* before it was finally approved by the government in June 2020. Major, unresolved disagreements over, for instance, closer co-operation with (and, in the long term, eventual integration into) the European Union or the Eurasian Economic Union have scuttled attempts to outline a clear, united vision for medium- to long-term development.

Moldova 2030 defines a system of 3-year 'National Development Plans' to map out nearer-term goals and measures. These plans will also be used in the mid-term budgeting processes. Once put into practice, this system should provide a structured way for the government to monitor progress towards longer-term goals.

Moldova has been a party to the UNECE Convention on Environmental Impact Assessment in a Transboundary Context since 1997 and the related Protocol on Strategic Environmental Assessment since 2019. Moldova adopted a law on Environmental Impact Assessment in 2015 and another on Strategy Environmental Assessment in 2017, and has developed and approved a set of guidelines for implementation. Since 2019, one of the main work areas of the EU-funded EU4Environment programme, the successor to the EaP GREEN programme, is supporting reforms and improvements to the environmental assessment processes in Moldova and other EaP countries. The programme is jointly implemented by the OECD, UNECE, UNEP, UNIDO and the World Bank.

Institutional set-up and decision making processes

Moldova's institutional set-up, like in many EaP countries, is characterised by considerable instability. Most notably, in 2017, several ministries were combined, leading to a major restructuring of country's cabinet. The Ministry of Construction and Regional Development absorbed the Ministry of Agriculture and Food Industry as well as the Ministry of Environment to become the Ministry of Agriculture, Regional Development and Environment. Similarly, the Ministry of Economy absorbed the Ministry of Transport and Roads Infrastructure and the Ministry of Informational Technologies and Communications to become the Ministry of Economy and Infrastructure. As a result of the restructuring, the number of cabinet-level ministries in Moldova was reduced from 15 to 9.

Moldova's public administration continues to face challenges, but has been making steady, if uneven, progress since 2009. However, its remaining shortcomings are considerable, and contribute to ineffective and costly service delivery. The country's administration is characterised by numerous fragmented local structures that exacerbate cost overruns, leaving limited fiscal space to invest in infrastructure and much-needed social programmes (World Bank, 2016[22]).

The wide gap in economic opportunities between rural and urban Moldovans stems in part from flaws in the country's institutional set-up. In water supply and sanitation, for instance, the national government retains responsibility for distributing investment funding while service delivery falls to local governments, but national-level institutions in the water sector lack an explicit mandate to extend existing networks to unconnected rural inhabitants. Stronger leadership informed by the realities of Moldova's rural populations is required to make progress on shrinking urban-rural disparities (World Bank, 2016[22]). The leading role in co-ordination, budget alignment and monitoring assigned to the State Chancellery in *Moldova 2030* could present an opportunity to fill the existing institutional gap, especially given the strategy's focus on improving the delivery of and access to infrastructure services.

Co-ordination between state bodies remains a challenge in Moldova for developing coherent policy frameworks and strategic documents. Although co-ordination bodies have been formed (e.g. Inter-Ministerial Working Group on the Promotion of Sustainable Development and Green Economy, Sustainable Development Council under the Prime Minister) and their roles defined, they have not functioned effectively in practice, partially due to political instability (OECD, 2015[34]).

List of relevant strategic documents

Table 5.4. Main strategic documents in force

	Status	Time Horizon	Sectoral Coverage	Main objectives
Updated First Nationally Determined Contribution (NDC)	Submitted in 2017, updated in 2020	2017-30	Economy-wide	• Unconditional target: Reduce net GHG emissions by 70% by 2030 compared to 1990 levels (revised from 2017 submission: 64-67%) • Conditional target: Reduce net GHG emissions by 88% (revised from 2017 submission: 78%) • Main sectors targeted for emission reduction: energy, transport, agriculture, water resources, forestry • Main adaptation tool: capacity building, improved information, integrated disaster risk management, community-level climate change adaptation, technology transfer and uptake
National Development Strategy "Moldova 2030"	Adopted in 2018, retracted in 2019, approved in June 2020 by the government, submitted to parliament	2018-30	Economy-wide	• Widen access to physical infrastructure • Energy: 10% of power generation from renewables by 2022 • Transport: increase use of biofuels (10% of total fuel) • Water: increase share of population with access to clean drinking water and improved sanitation services to 92-99% and 81-89% respectively by 2030
Transport and Logistics Strategy 2013-2022	2013	2013-22	Transport	• Road: integrate road network with European network, ensure year-round access for all settlements to the national road network, rehabilitate all national roads by 2022, attract EUR 120 million per year of external funding for road rehabilitation, improve road quality (45% good, 45% fair and 10% bad by 2022), reduce traffic accidents by 50% by 2020, reduce vehicle operation costs per km

	Status	Time Horizon	Sectoral Coverage	Main objectives
				• Rail: rehabilitate rail lines so cargo and passenger trains can reach a minimum speed of 50 km/h on main railway lines by 2020 • Air: privatise civil aviation sector and liberalise market
Energy Strategy of Moldova 2030	Adopted in 2013		Energy	• Improve energy security, integrate into the European energy system (electricity and gas), improve sustainability • Increase share of renewables in power generation to 10% by 2020 • Increase share of renewables in total energy consumption to 20% by 2020 • Increase share of biofuels in total fuels to 10% by 2020 • Improve energy efficiency and reduce transmission and distribution losses
Environmental Strategy for 2014-2023	Adopted in 2014	2014-23	Economy-wide	• Closer alignment with EU Directives • Reduce GHG emissions by 20% by 2020 compared to 1990 baseline • Reduce air pollution levels to 30% of 1990 levels by 2023

Table 5.5. Other relevant documents

	Status	Time Horizon	Sectoral Coverage
National Renewable Energy Action Plan 2013-2020	Adopted in 2013	2013-20	Energy
Climate Change Adaptation Strategy by 2020 and Action Plan	Adopted in 2014	2014-20	Economy-wide
Low-Emission Development Strategy	Adopted in 2016	2016-30	Economy-wide
Programme on Promotion of Green Economy in the Republic of Moldova for 2018-2020	Adopted in 2018	2018-20	Economy-wide
National Energy Efficiency Programme 2011-2020	Adopted in 2011	2011-20	Energy, construction
Biological Diversity Strategy for the years 2015-2020	Adopted in 2015	2015-20	Ecosystems
National Programme for the Greening of SMEs			
Strategy on Waste Management 2013-2027	Adopted in 2013	2013-27	Waste
Strategy on Water Supply and Sanitation 2014-2028	Adopted in 2014	2014-28	Water

References

Ahlemeyer, V. (2020), *EBRD, EU and EIB modernise rail transport in Moldova*, European Bank for Reconstruction and Development (EBRD), https://www.ebrd.com/news/2020/ebrd-eu-and-eib-modernise-rail-transport-in-moldova.html (accessed on 23 September 2020). [28]

Bertelsmann Stiftung (2018), *Moldova: BTI 2018 Country Report*, Bertelsmann Stiftung, Berlin, https://www.bertelsmann-stiftung.de/fileadmin/files/Projekte/Strategien_fuer_die_EU_Nachbarschaft/BTI_2018_Moldova.pdf (accessed on 11 September 2020). [5]

Climate Change Office of the Republic of Moldova (2018), *Fourth National Communication of the Republic of Moldova under the United Nations Framework Convention on Climate Change*, Climate Change Office, Regional Development and Environment of the Republic of Moldova, http://www.clima.md/lib.php?l=en&idc=81& (accessed on 10 September 2020). [18]

Codreanu, V. (2019), *Regional Rail Connectivity [PowerPoint Presentation]*, Ministry of Economy and Infrastructure of the Republic of Moldova. [27]

Energy Community (2020), *2020 Implementation Report*, https://energy-community.org/news/Energy-Community-News/2020/11/23.html (accessed on 26 November 2019). [9]

EUBAM (2019), *Annual Report: 1 December 2018 - 30 November 2019*, European Union Border Assistance Mission to Moldova and Ukraine (EUBAM), http://eubam.org/wp-content/uploads/2020/03/200327_EUBAM-Annual-Report-2019-EN-final-spreads.pdf (accessed on 15 September 2020). [29]

fDi Markets (2019), *fDi Markets: the in-depth crossborder investment monitor (database)*, https://www.fdimarkets.com/. [15]

IEA (2021), *Electricity Information 2020*, https://www.iea.org/data-and-statistics/ (accessed on 10 August 2020). [32]

IEA (2019), *World Energy Balances 2019*, International Energy Agency, Paris, https://doi.org/10.1787/3a876031-en (accessed on 10 August 2020). [31]

IMF (2020), *Staff Report for the 2020 Article IV Consultation and Sixth Reviews Under the Extended Credit Facility and Extended Fund Facility Arrangements-Press Release; Staff Report; and Statement by the Executive Director for the Republic of Moldova*, International Monetary Fund, Washington, D.C., https://www.imf.org/en/Publications/CR/Issues/2020/03/17/Republic-of-Moldova-Staff-Report-for-the-2020-Article-IV-Consultation-and-Sixth-Reviews-49272 (accessed on 8 September 2020). [17]

IMF (2020), *World Economic Outlook: October 2020*, https://www.imf.org/external/datamapper/GGXCNL_NGDP@WEO/OEMDC/ADVEC/WEOWORLD. [2]

ITF (2019), *Transport Performance Indicators*, https://www.oecd-ilibrary.org/transport/data/itf-transport-statistics/transport-performance-indicators_2122fa17-en. [25]

Ministry of Environment of the Republic of Armenia (2020), *Armenia's Fourth National Communication on Climate Change under the United Nations Framework Convention on Climate Change*, Ministry of Environment of the Republic of Armenia, Yerevan, https://unfccc.int/sites/default/files/resource/NC4_Armenia_.pdf (accessed on 23 July 2020). [19]

National Bureau of Statistics of the Republic of Moldova (2020), *Transport of goods and passengers by Indicators, Means of transport, Years, Unit of measure and Months*, http://statbank.statistica.md/PxWeb/pxweb/en/40%20Statistica%20economica/40%20Statistica%20economica__19%20TRA__TRA030/TRA030100.px/ (accessed on 15 September 2020). [26]

National Bureau of Statistics of the Republic of Moldova (2020), *Value of manufactured industrial production by Economic activities and Years*, http://statbank.statistica.md/PxWeb/pxweb/en/40%20Statistica%20economica/40%20Statistica%20economica__14%20IND__IND020/IND020100.px/ (accessed on 16 September 2020). [33]

Observatory of Economic Complexity (2019), *Moldova: Exports, Imports, and Trade Partners*, https://oec.world/en/profile/country/mda (accessed on 20 August 2020). [10]

OECD (2021), *COVID-19 and greening the economies of Eastern Europe, the Caucasus and Central Asia*, http://www.oecd.org/coronavirus/policy-responses/covid-19-and-greening-the-economies-of-eastern-europe-the-caucasus-and-central-asia-40f4d34f/ (accessed on 10 March 2021). [7]

OECD (2020), *Trade Facilitation Index*, https://www.oecd.org/trade/topics/trade-facilitation/ (accessed on 9 September 2020). [24]

OECD (2019), *Promoting Clean Urban Public Transportation and Green Investment in Moldova*, Green Finance and Investment, OECD Publishing, Paris, https://dx.doi.org/10.1787/31925aae-en. [23]

OECD (2015), *The Principles of Public Administration: Moldova 2015 Baseline Measurement Report*, OECD Publishing, Paris, http://www.sigmaweb.org/publications/Baseline-Measurement-Moldova-2015.pdf (accessed on 16 September 2020). [34]

Point.md (2018), "Более тысячи молдаван ежедневно подают заявки на румынское гражданство [Over a thousand Moldovans apply for Romanian citizenship every day]", *Point.md*, https://point.md/ru/novosti/obschestvo/bolee-tysiachi-moldavan-ezhednevno-podaiut-zaiavki-na-rumynskoe-grazhdanstvo (accessed on 17 August 2020). [3]

Roser, M. et al. (2020), *Coronavirus Pandemic (COVID-19)*, OurWorldInData.Org, https://ourworldindata.org/coronavirus (accessed on 9 September 2020). [6]

Russell, M. (2017), *Eurasian Economic Union: The rocky road to integration*, European Parliamentary Research Service (EPRS), Brussels. [8]

Transparency International (2019), *CPI 2019: Eastern Europe & Central Asia*, https://www.transparency.org/en/news/cpi-2019-eastern-europe-central-asia (accessed on 20 July 2020). [11]

UNFPA Moldova (2016), *Population Situation Analysis in the Republic of Moldova*, UN Population Fund in the Republic of Moldova (UNFPA Moldova), Chisinau, https://moldova.unfpa.org/sites/default/files/pub-pdf/PSA_engleza.pdf (accessed on 17 August 2020). [4]

US Department of State (2019), *2019 Investment Climate Statements: Moldova*, https://www.state.gov/reports/2019-investment-climate-statements/moldova/ (accessed on 20 July 2020). [13]

Walter, W., M. Luecke and A. Lupusor (2017), *The economic impact of FDI in Moldova: Results from an empirical analysis*, German Economic Team (GET) Moldova, Chisinau and Berlin, http://www.get-moldova.de (accessed on 20 August 2020). [16]

World Bank (2021), *World Development Indicators (database)*, https://datacatalog.worldbank.org/dataset/world-development-indicators. [1]

World Bank (2020), *Doing Business 2020*, World Bank Group, Washington, DC, http://dx.doi.org/10.1596/978-1-4648-1440-2. [14]

World Bank (2019), *Country Score Card: Logistics Performance Index*, https://lpi.worldbank.org/international/scorecard/ (accessed on 27 July 2020). [21]

World Bank (2016), *Moldova: Paths to Sustained Prosperity: A Systematic Country Diagnostic*, World Bank, Washington, D.C. [22]

World Bank, EBRD and EIB (2019), *Enterprise Surveys: Moldova Country Profile 2019*, World Bank, the European Bank for Reconstruction and Development (EBRD) and the European Investment Bank (EIB), https://www.enterprisesurveys.org/en/data/exploreeconomies/2019/moldova (accessed on 16 September 2020). [30]

World Economic Forum (2019), *The Global Competitiveness Report 2019*, World Economic Forum, Geneva, http://www3.weforum.org/docs/WEF_TheGlobalCompetitivenessReport2019.pdf (accessed on 23 July 2020). [20]

Wrobel, A. (2019), *Restoring trust in Moldova's banking sector*, Emerging Europe, https://emerging-europe.com/interviews/restoring-trust-in-moldovas-banking-sector/ (accessed on 7 September 2020). [12]

Notes

[1] The EU Eastern Partnership (EaP) is a joint initiative for strengthening the relationships between the European Union, its member states and six countries (hereafter the EaP countries): Armenia, Azerbaijan, Belarus, Georgia, Moldova and Ukraine.

[2] Confirmed case and death figures are underestimates of actual case and death numbers. Methodology and testing rates vary widely, and international comparisons are necessarily flawed.

[3] Data on Moldova's pre-1995 GDP are unavailable

[4] Population estimates in Moldova varying considerably due to the large non-resident population, which means per capita emissions statistics vary in turn. In 1990, World Bank data indicates that the population of Moldova was about 3 million, while the National Bureau of Statistics puts the figure at 4.4 million. The two sources report similar figures for 2015 population, but these numbers are widely perceived as overestimates (UNFPA Moldova, 2016[4]).

[5] The lower figures are based on RCP 2.6 and the upper figures on RCP 4.5.

[6] Here defined as heating with modern fuels, i.e. electricity, gas or central heating.

[7] Depending on the development scenario. *Moldova 2030* sets targets based on three development scenarios.

6. Trends in Ukraine's sustainable infrastructure investments

This chapter describes sustainable infrastructure planning in Ukraine and presents current trends in investment in large-scale infrastructure projects. It compares Ukraine's infrastructure plans in the energy, transport, industry and water sectors against its international commitments under the Paris Agreement on climate change and the Sustainable Development Goals (SDGs). The chapter also explores Ukraine's strategic documents for long-term economic development, sectoral development and the environment, including those related to climate change mitigation and adaptation. It identifies misalignments between stated goals and observed investment flows and provides recommendations to improve strategic planning for sustainable infrastructure.

State of play: economy, investment and climate change in Ukraine

Economy and trade

Table 6.1. Key indicators on Ukraine's economy

Population (2019)	44 385 155
Urbanisation rate (2019)	69.5%
Annual population growth (2018)	-0.5%
Surface area	603 550 km^2
GDP (USD, current price, 2019)	153 781 million
GDP per capita (USD, current price, 2019)	3 659
Real GDP growth (year-on-year change, 2019, 2020)	3.2%, -7.2%
Inflation (average consumer price, y-o-y change, 2020)	7.7%
Exports of goods and services (% of GDP, 2019)	41.2%
Imports of goods and services (% of GDP, 2019)	49.0%
FDI, net inflows (% of GDP, 2019)	2.0%
General government net lending/borrowing (% of GDP, 2019, 2020)	-2%, -8.2%
Unemployment (% of total labour force, 2019)	8.9%
Remittances (% of GDP, 2019)	10.4%
Transparency, accountability and corruption in the public sector rating (1= most corrupt, 6 = least corrupt)	n.d.

Source: World Bank (2021[1]), *World Development Indicators (database)*, World Bank, https://datacatalog.worldbank.org/dataset/world-development-indicators; IMF (2020[2]), *World Economic Outlook: October 2020*, International Monetary Fund https://www.imf.org/external/datamapper/GGXCNL_NGDP@WEO/OEMDC/ADVEC/WEOWORLD

Economy and demographics

Ukraine is a lower-middle income country in Eastern Europe. It lies on the northern shore of the Black Sea and shares borders with Belarus to the north, Russia to the east, Moldova to the southwest and several European Union member states (Hungary, Romania, Poland, Slovak Republic) to the west. It is by far the most populous country in the EU Eastern Partnership (EaP)[1]; its population of just over 44 million is larger than the other five Eastern Partnership countries' populations combined. Since 1993, when Ukraine's population stood at 52 million, the country's population has consistently decreased. Ukraine's demographic decline stems from one of the lowest birth rates in the world (less than 1.5 live births per woman in 2019). Unlike in neighbouring Moldova, net emigration is not the primary driver of Ukraine's decreasing population size. Ukraine actually experienced net immigration between 2010 and 2019, but not enough to compensate for the negative natural population growth rate. If current trends continue, Ukraine's population could be 20% smaller than in 2019 by 2050 (UNDESA, 2019[3]).

Ukraine's GDP has followed a less predictable path. After a decade of decline from its peak prior to the breakup of the Soviet Union (USD 205.8 billion in constant 2010 USD in 1989), the country's GDP reached its low point in 1999 (USD 84.4 billion). From 2000 to 2008, positive growth not only returned but reached unprecedented levels; Ukraine's GDP almost doubled by 2008 (USD 153.7 billion). Ukraine's GDP suffered two major shocks in the following years. First, the global financial crisis in 2008-2009, and then the 2014 Maidan Revolution[2], Russia's temporary occupation of Crimea and the ongoing armed conflict in the eastern Ukrainian territories of Donetsk and Luhansk. These events, combined with other factors linked to the important share of natural resources, energy infrastructure and steelmaking capacities in the temporary occupied regions led to a severe contraction of the Ukrainian economy, and as a result GDP declined by 15% in real terms between 2013 and 2015. A period of recovery followed until 2020 only to be cut short by the COVID-19 pandemic's severe economic impacts on the Ukrainian and global economies. Ukraine is projected to be the Eastern Partnership economy hardest hit by the COVID-19 pandemic, with its GDP shrinking by -7.2% in 2020 (compared to -1.5% in Armenia, -4% in Azerbaijan, -3% in Belarus, -5% in Georgia and -4.5% in Moldova) (IMF, 2020[4]).

As of February 2020, Ukraine had diagnosed 29.3 COVID-19 cases per thousand inhabitants, considerably less than in Armenia (56.5), Georgia (65.4) and neighbouring Moldova (40.5) but more than in Azerbaijan (22.8) and Belarus (27). Ukraine's death rate (562 deaths per million inhabitants) is the fourth highest in the Eastern Partnership after Armenia (1 049), Moldova (937) and Georgia (817). Azerbaijan (311) and neighbouring Belarus (187) have recorded far fewer deaths (Roser et al., 2020[5])[3]. Ukraine declared a state of emergency in March 2020 followed by a countrywide lockdown until May. International and domestic travel were restricted and remote working arrangements were encouraged to slow the virus's spread. Schools, hospitality venues and recreational areas were shut and wearing masks became obligatory in public spaces (OECD, 2020[6]). After initial success in reducing cases, measures were relaxed over the summer until infections began rising rapidly again, leading to a second lockdown (OECD, 2020[7]).

Lockdown measures and the global economic downturn are expected to have a profound impact on Ukraine's economy. In response, the Ukrainian government approved in May 2020 the *Economic Stimulus Programme to Overcome Negative Consequences of Restrictive Measures to Prevent the Occurrence and Spread of Acute Respiratory Disease COVID-19 Caused by SARS-CoV-2 Coronavirus for 2020-2022*. It outlined programmes to support small and medium enterprises and identified the improvement of water supply, sewerage and sanitation as a key priority. However, in some of the government's efforts to revitalise the economy, funds and attention have been redirected from environmental causes. For instance, as part of much wider budget cuts, the budget of the Energy Efficiency Fund was cut by UAH 1.6 billion (OECD, 2021[8]). These cuts helped fund the UAH 64.7 billion (USD 2.4 billion) Fund to Counter COVID-19, which will allocate resources to infrastructure renewal, regional development and support to businesses and citizens (OECD, 2020[7]).

The sectoral split of Ukraine's service-oriented economy is very similar to that of neighbouring Moldova. In 2019, services accounted for 54.4% of Ukraine's GDP (54.3% in Moldova), while agriculture accounted for 9% (9.9% in Moldova), industry (including construction) accounted for 22.6% (22.8% in Moldova) and manufacturing accounted for 10.8% (10.9% in Moldova) (World Bank, 2021[1]).

Trade

Ukraine has been a member of the World Trade Organisation since 2008. Like Georgia and Moldova, Ukraine signed an Association Agreement with the European Union, including a Deep and Comprehensive Free Trade Agreement (DCFTA), which came into force in 2017. The European Union's Eastern Partnership (EaP) is a key initiative for continued cooperation between the EU, its member states and Ukraine. It aims to strengthen ties and encourage reform on a number of policy areas, including on governance, connectivity, economic development and environmental protection.

Previous preparations for an Association Agreement were abandoned in 2013, unleashing a wave of civil unrest that culminated in the 2014 Maidan Revolution. Prior to the revolution, Ukraine's stance on closer ties with the European Union was somewhat more ambiguous. In 2013, the pre-revolution government negotiated and abandoned an Association Agreement with the European Union and, simultaneously, negotiated observer status for Ukraine within the Eurasian Customs Union, a precursor to the Eurasian Economic Union.

Following the revolution, state policy shifted to unambiguous support of closer ties with the European Union. Public opinion has also become less split on the issue: In 2013, 42% of Ukrainians thought the country would join the European Union in the future, while 31% considered integration into the Eurasian Economic Union the more likely option. By 2019, 53% of Ukrainians saw their future in Europe, compared to only 13% that preferred the Eurasian Economic Union. National surveys, however, mask considerable regional differences. Western Ukraine and central Ukraine are staunchly pro-European, with 71% and 60%

of Ukrainians in these regions supporting integration into the EU respectively. Opinions in southern and eastern Ukraine are less unified. EU integration enjoys only 32% support in the south and 34% in the east of Ukraine, while 24% of southerners and 27% of easterners favour joining the Eurasian Economic Union instead. Staying independent of both blocs is the preferred option for 31% of the population in southern Ukraine and 30% in the east (Ilko Kucheriv Democratic Initiatives Charitable Foundation, 2019[9]).

Ukraine has been a Contracting Party of the European Union's Energy Community since 2011. The Energy Community's Secretariat supports Ukraine's implementation of reforms in the energy sector, including on energy efficiency, renewable energy development and environmental protection. Ukraine's progress on transposing legislation and implementing necessary reforms is quite advanced but uneven. The Energy Community Secretariat rates overall implementation of reforms in Ukraine as 61% complete, with gas (84%), statistics (81%), energy efficiency (67%), environment (64%), renewable energy (52%) and climate (51%) as well-advanced areas. However, on other issues, such as infrastructure (8%) and the oil sector (35%), Ukraine's implementation remains at an early stage (Energy Community, 2020[10]).

As a result of armed conflicts beginning in 2014 between Ukraine on the one side and Russia and separatist forces on the other, Ukraine does not have complete sovereign control of its eastern and southern maritime borders. On the Crimean peninsula in the southeast of Ukraine, Russia occupied the Ukrainian territories of the Autonomous Republic of Crimea and Sevastopol in 2014 and, despite international condemnation, has since administered them as *de facto* federal subjects (as a republic and a federal city respectively). In Ukraine's eastern Donetsk and Luhansk *oblast*s (regions) – an area collectively known as the Donbass (or Donbas), two internationally unrecognised breakaway states have been declared and have wrested some *de facto* territorial control from Ukraine's government. The self-proclaimed Donetsk People's Republic and Luhansk People's Republic claim sovereignty over the whole territory of the respective Ukrainian *oblast*s but have only established control over the eastern areas adjacent to the border with Russia. The EU and several OECD countries imposed economic and diplomatic sanctions on Russia because of its temporary occupation of Crimea and involvement in armed conflicts in the breakaway regions in eastern Ukraine. In 2014, the European Council condemned the "inflows of fighters and weapons from the territory of the Russian Federation into Eastern Ukraine as well as the aggression by Russian armed forces on Ukrainian soil" (European Council, 2014[11]). Also in 2014, the OECD postponed all activities related to the accession of Russia to the organisation and signed a memorandum of understanding with Ukraine on strengthening existing cooperation (OECD, 2014[12]; OECD, 2014[13])

The ongoing conflict has had a major impact on the trade relationship between Ukraine and Russia. In 2012, Russia alone accounted for 24% of Ukraine's exports and 31% of imports, making it by far Ukraine's most important trading partner. By 2016, Russia's share of Ukraine's exports and imports had shrunk by about half (11% and 17% respectively), and the downward trend has continued (8% of exports and 15% of imports by 2018) (Observatory of Economic Complexity, 2018[14]). A major component of Ukraine's imports from Russia until 2016 was natural gas. Imported gas, almost exclusively from Russia, supplied the majority of Ukraine's domestic consumption, but Ukraine pivoted towards European suppliers starting in 2012 and, by 2016, almost entirely stopped importing natural gas from Russia altogether (Naftogaz Europe, 2017[15]).

Despite its diminished share of Ukraine's import and export markets, Russia remains one of Ukraine's most important trading partner, particularly as a source of imports (9%), but China has surpassed it as Ukraine's most important trade partner, accounting for 14% of exports and 15% of imports in 2020 (Figure 6.1). The European Union accounts for over 35% of Ukraine's exports and 43% of imports, with Germany (10% of imports, 4% of exports), Poland (7% of exports, 8% of imports), and Italy (4% of exports and exports) as particularly important trading partners. Non-EU, emerging economies, especially Turkey (5%) and India (4%) also account for a considerable share of Ukraine's exports, primarily metal ores and agricultural goods.

In 2020, Ukraine's most important exports 2343 vegetable products (24%), particularly corn and wheat, and metals (19%), predominantly ferrous metals. Although raw materials and low value-added goods account for most of Ukraine's exports, manufacturing – mostly machines and machine parts (9%) – also represents an important export sector. Ukraine mostly imports manufactured goods (machines, 21%; chemical products, 14%; and transportation, 11%) and mineral products, which account for 16%, especially refined petroleum and petroleum gas.

Figure 6.1. Trade of Ukraine

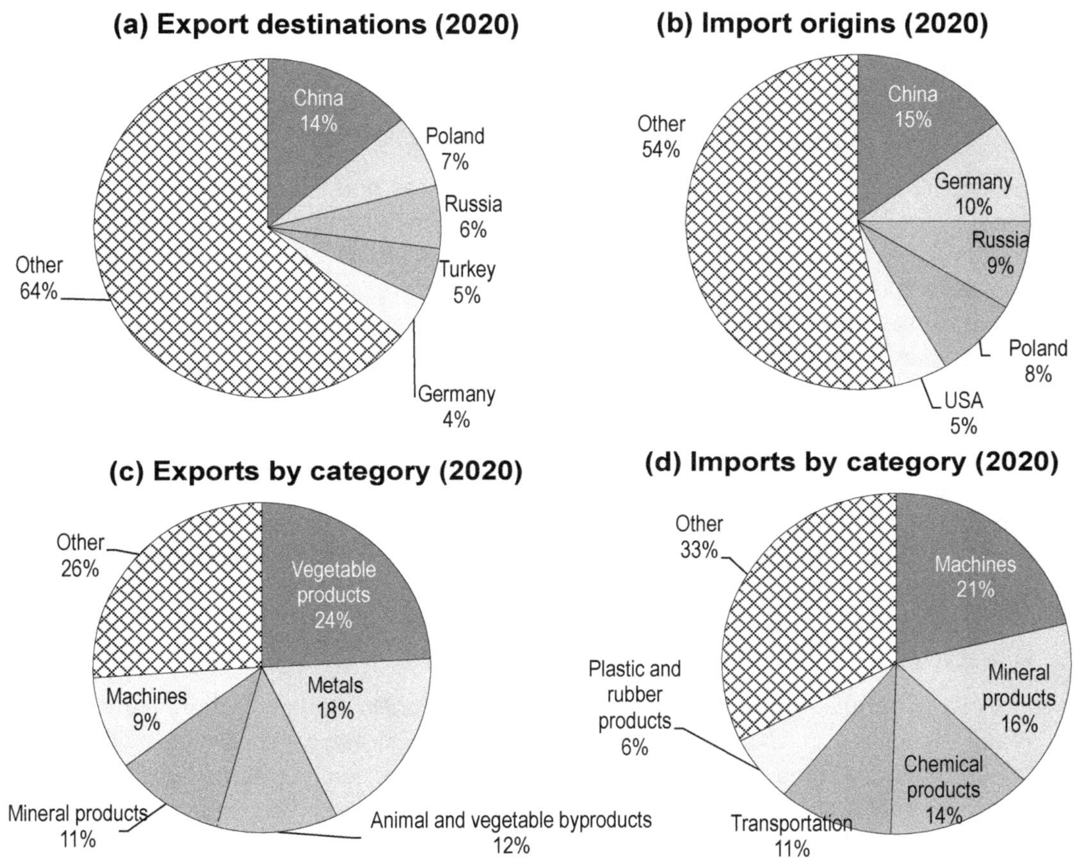

Source: State Statistics Service of Ukraine (2020[16]), Ukraine's foreign trade in goods (January-November 2020), https://ukrstat.org/en/operativ/menu/menu_e/zed.htm

Investment climate

Following the 2014 Maidan revolution, Russian military intervention and the associated economic downturn, Ukraine implemented sweeping reforms to ensure macroeconomic stability, particularly in regulating the country's banking sector and nationalising PrivatBank, the country's largest commercial bank. Ukraine introduced the principle of non-discrimination of foreign investment and enhanced provisions to protect foreign investors' rights (OECD, 2016[17]).

Ukraine has undertaken several institutional reforms to strengthen investment promotion. It established the National Investment Council under the president in 2014; a Business Ombudsman to facilitate conflict resolution between foreign investors and domestic institutions in 2015; and UkraineInvest, an investment promotion agency, in 2016. Unique among EaP investment promotion agencies, UkraineInvest has a dedicated board to supervise its operations. Although Ukraine's board has public sector representatives and independent experts, it lacks representatives from the private sector, academia and civil society. UkraineInvest targets key sectors in its FDI attraction efforts, namely agribusiness, manufacturing, energy, infrastructure and innovation technology. It also targets particular countries in Europe (Denmark, France, Germany, Norway, Sweden) and beyond (Qatar, Saudi Arabia, the United Arab Emirates, USA). While UkraineInvest offers essential services to potential investors (e.g. licence and construction approval, assistance with utilities and legal issues, business matchmaking and cluster programmes, aftercare services), it does not function as an effective one-stop service centre since it does not provide a window to several administrative procedures necessary to start and run a business such as tax registration and work permits (OECD, 2020[18]).

Despite some recent improvements, foreign direct investment (FDI) remains low compared to the size of Ukraine's economy. Net FDI inflows have hovered around 4% of GDP since 2016, broadly in line with trends elsewhere in the Eastern Partnership (with the notable exception of Georgia where net FDI inflows scaled for GDP have been twice to three times as large) (World Bank, 2021[1]).

According to the OECD FDI Restrictiveness Index, which measures barriers to foreign direct investment such as foreign equity limitations and operational restrictions, Ukraine has the most restrictive FDI rules in the Eastern Partnership, a region that, although less open than the OECD average to FDI, is characterised by relatively open economies. In 2019, on a scale from 0 (open) to 1 (closed), Ukraine scored 0.121, which is higher (i.e. more closed) than the regional average for the Eastern Partnership (0.064) and OECD countries (0.085). Unlike in the second and third most restrictive countries in the region, Belarus (0.086) and Azerbaijan (0.077), where restrictions apply primarily to the media sector and, to a lesser degree, business and financial services, Ukraine's restrictiveness applies more broadly, extending to real estate, media, transport and agriculture. In an important step towards loosening restrictions, the moratorium on the sale of agricultural lands was recently lifted (Verkhovna Rada of Ukraine, 2020[19]). Ukraine is the only EaP country with discriminatory screening and approval mechanisms to regulate the entry and operations of foreign investors. On their own, Ukraine's FDI restrictions are unlikely to discourage investors, but the FDI Restrictiveness Index only captures part of the picture. It does not, for instance, measure other components of the investment climate such as the extent of state ownership and how restrictions are implemented in practice (OECD, 2020[18]).

Foreign investors cite poor quality infrastructure, ongoing armed conflict and corruption, particularly in the judiciary, as major obstacles in Ukraine. In its annual Corruption Perceptions index, Transparency International ranked Ukraine 126th out of 198 countries in 2019 edition, tied with Azerbaijan as the two EaP countries perceived as facing the greatest corruption challenges. Although the situation in Ukraine has improved somewhat since before the Ukrainian revolution (144th in 2012), Ukraine is lagging behind other EaP countries in rooting out corruption (Armenia, 77th; Belarus, 66th; Georgia, 44th) (Transparency International, 2019[20]). As part of an effort to eliminate corruption, oligarchic influence on public policy and vested interests, Ukraine established the National Anti-Corruption Bureau, the High Anti-Corruption Court and split the State Financial Service into the State Tax and State Customs Services. These institutions, however, have recently come under increasing pressure and face multiple challenges in carrying out their assigned functions (Verlanov, 2020[21]).

In addition, Ukraine's overall regulatory environment needs considerable reform to facilitate businesses and attract investment. The World Bank's 2020 Ease of Doing Business report ranked Ukraine 64th out of 190 countries overall, lower than its EaP peers Armenia (47th), Azerbaijan (34th), Belarus (49th), Georgia (6th) and Moldova (48th). Ukraine's procedures for getting electricity and resolving insolvency are particularly inefficient and time-consuming; it ranks 128th and 146th worldwide on these metrics respectively. On average, businesses need to pass through 5 procedures requiring 267 days to get electricity, while firms wishing to resolve insolvency can expect to spend 2.9 years and about two-fifths of the estate in question on the various procedures (World Bank, 2020[22]).

That said, in addition to its anti-corruption measures, Ukraine has made some progress in improving other aspects of its investment climate. Ukrainian investment legislation includes the principle of non-discrimination of foreign investment and general provisions on foreign investment protection (OECD, 2016[17]). Ukraine has simplified its tax system, including through a new e-declaration system, reducing the number of payments from 135 per year in 2012 and 28 per year 2013-14 to just 5. Consequently, the time that businesses spent on average in 2012 preparing and filing their taxes halved from 657 hours in 2012 to 328 hours starting in 2018. Progress has been even swifter on simplifying construction permits. Whereas acquiring a permit in 2012 required 21 procedures and took 403 days on average, only 10 procedures and 72.5 days are needed in 2020 (World Bank, 2020[22]).

Between 2003 and 2017, Ukraine attracted USD 38.7 billion of FDI to greenfield projects. Although FDI flows to greenfield projects among EaP countries were greatest in Ukraine over this time period, all of its regional peers except Belarus attracted more greenfield FDI relative to the size of their economies. In Ukraine, most greenfield FDI flows concentrated in real estate (28%), food & tobacco (15%) and financial services (14%) (Figure 6.2). Infrastructure-related investments were also sizeable, with alternative/renewable energy sources and fossil fuels attracting 12% and 10% respectively.

Figure 6.2. Greenfield FDI in Ukraine by economic activity, 2003-2017

Cumulated greenfield FDI capital between January 2003 and September 2017 in USD million

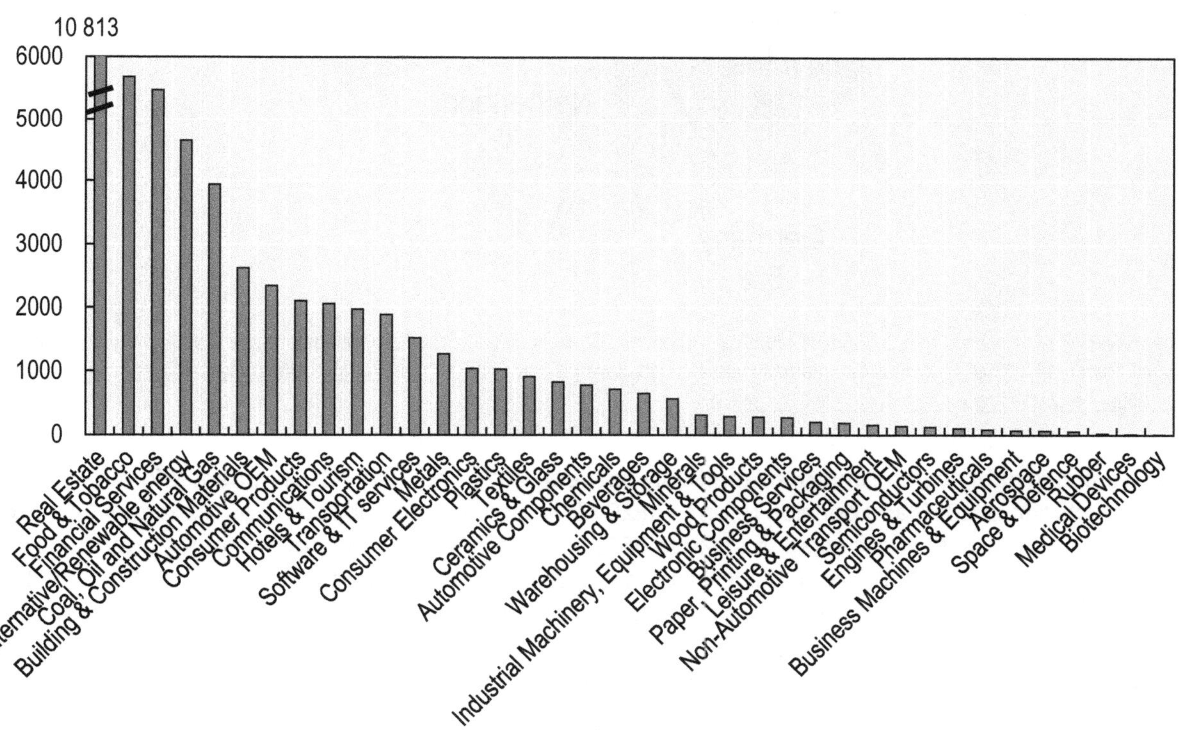

Source: OECD based on fDi Markets (2019[23]), fDi Markets: the in-depth crossborder investment monitor (database), fDi Markets, https://www.fdimarkets.com/

European Union countries account for 74% of Ukraine's FDI inflows (Figure 6.3). According to the National Bank of Ukraine, about two-fifths of Ukraine's FDI in recent years is "round-tripping FDI" (i.e. FDI that is actually domestic in origin but rerouted through a foreign country). The prevalence of this phenomenon likely explains the large shares of countries with particularly favourable tax regimes such as Cyprus (34%), the Netherlands (18%) and Switzerland (6%). Russia plays only a marginal role in Ukraine's FDI inflows, accounting for less than 2% in 2018, although its share used to be considerably larger (8% in 2010). Part of Cyprus's large share, however, may in effect reflect trans-shipping FDI transactions from Russian entities to Ukraine (OECD, 2016[17]).

Figure 6.3. Ukraine's inward FDI stock by country of origin, 2018

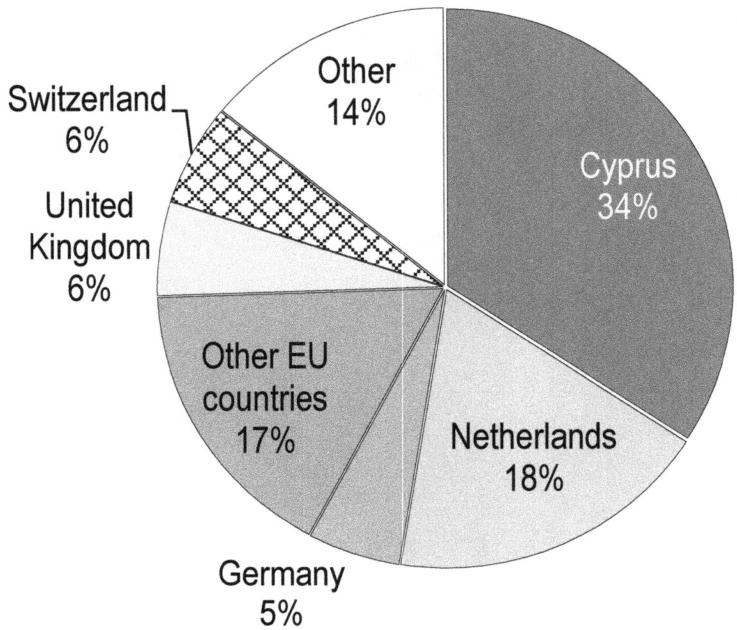

Source: Havlik, P., A. Kochnev and O. Pindyuk (2020[24]), "Economic Challenges and Costs of Reintegrating the Donbas Region in Ukraine", Research Paper 447, Wiener Institut für Internationale Wirtschaftsvergleiche (WIIR), https://wiiw.ac.at/economic-challenges-and-costs-of-reintegrating-the-donbas-region-in-ukraine-dlp-5351.pdf

Ukraine's public debt position improved markedly between 2014 and 2019. Government reforms, including debt restructuring in 2015 and pension reforms in 2017, helped reduce public debt as a share of GDP from 85% to 50%. Public debt is expected to spike to 65% of GDP, reversing the government's previous gains, due to the ongoing COVID-19 crisis, but it will then resume its downward trajectory (61% by 2022, 52% by 2025). Ukraine's public debt will remain manageable provided that the government tightens fiscal policy once economic activity rebounds. Since over 60% of its debt is denominated in foreign currencies, Ukraine's external debt service burden is vulnerable to exchange rate depreciations (IMF, 2020[25]).

Climate change

As the most populous country and largest economy in the Eastern Partnership, Ukraine accounts for most of the region's greenhouse gas (GHG) emissions; its emissions are almost double those of the other five countries combined. As a share of global emissions, Ukraine emits just under 0.8%. Ukraine's GHG emissions declined by two-fifths following the breakup of the Soviet Union from their 1990 peak of 946 $MtCO_2e$ to 564 $MtCO_2e$ in 1995 (Figure 6.4). Following their initial rapid drop, Ukraine's emissions began to decline more gradually, reaching 341 $MtCO_2e$ in 2018 (only a third of Ukraine's GHG emissions in 1990 and 39% lower than in 1995). Ukraine's GDP has charted a less predictable course, particularly over the past two decades. From its pre-independence peak of USD 205.8 billion in constant 2010 USD in 1990, Ukraine's GDP shrank by almost three fifths to 84.4 billion by 1999. Over the past two decades, Ukraine's economy has experienced rapid periods of growth (2000-2008, 2009-2013, 2015-2019) followed by sharp declines linked to mostly external shocks (the Global Financial Crisis in 2008; the Ukrainian revolution and Russian military intervention in 2014; the COVID-19 pandemic in 2020). In real terms, Ukraine's 2019 GDP (USD 135.5 billion) is still 12% lower than its 2008 peak (USD 153.7 billion) prior to the Global Financial Crisis.

Ukraine's GHG reductions have continued both in periods of economic growth and contraction; consequently, Ukraine's economy is considerably less GHG intensive than before independence. While Ukraine emitted 4.6 $kgCO_2e$ per USD (in constant 2010 dollars) in 1990, it generated only 2.6 $kgCO_2e$ for the same economic output in 2018. Despite this improvement, Ukraine's economy remains more GHG-intensive than its EaP peers and significantly more so than the OECD average (0.35 $kgCO_2e$ per USD in 2012). Ukraine's per capita emissions have dropped from 18.4 tCO_2e in 1990 to 7.7 tCO_2e in 2018, the second highest per capita emission rate among EaP countries, after Belarus (9.9 tCO_2e per capita in 2017) (World Bank, 2021[1]).

Figure 6.4. GHG emissions and GDP of Ukraine, 1990-2019

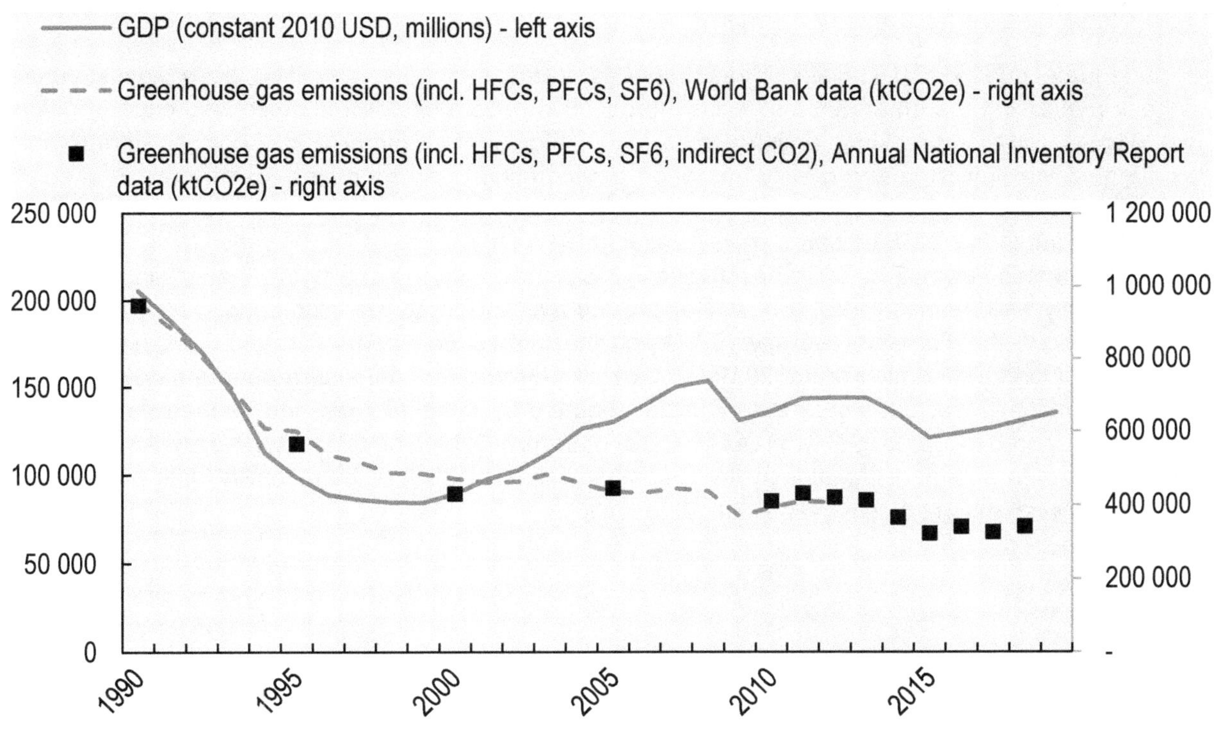

Source: World Bank (2021[1]), World Development Indicators (database), World Bank, https://data.worldbank.org/indicator/EN.ATM.GHGT.ZG; https://mepr.gov.ua/files/docs/Zmina_klimaty/2020/Ukraine_NIR_2020%20draft.pdf; Ministry of Energy and Environmental Protection of Ukraine[4] (2020[26]), Ukraine's Greenhouse Gas Inventory 1990-2018 (draft), https://mepr.gov.ua/files/docs/Zmina_klimaty/2020/Ukraine_NIR_2020%20draft.pdf

Energy (including fuel combustion from transport) accounts for 66% of Ukraine's GHG emissions, slightly less than in 1990 (77%). Energy industries are directly responsible for 45% of energy-related emissions, while fugitive emissions (18%) and transport (15%) account for most of the remainder. The share of GHG emissions generated from industrial processes and products use (IPPU), agriculture and waste increased slightly between 1990 and 2018 (IPPU, 12% to 16%; agriculture, 9% to 13%; waste, 2% to 5%). In absolute terms, the decline in GHG emissions since independence has been steepest in the energy sector; emissions in 2018 are less than a third of their 1990 levels. Emissions from IPPU and agriculture both halved over the past three decades, while waste-related emissions remained about the same (Ministry of Energy and Environmental Protection of Ukraine, 2020[26]).

The effects of climate change are already becoming evident in Ukraine. The average annual temperature in Ukraine increased by about 0.4°C per year between 1970 and 2012 while average precipitation declined slightly. Climate models predict that the average annual temperature could increase by a further 1.5-2°C between 2010 and 2070, while precipitation could decrease slightly in the country's south and increase elsewhere. As a result, the yield of winter wheat, a key crop for export and domestic consumption, could decrease by 6-11% in Ukraine by 2070 (Müller et al., 2016[27]). Rising temperatures as well as increased incidence and intensity of both drought and periods of heightened precipitation could have sweeping impacts across Ukraine's economy. The risk of overflow from tailing ponds and sludge basins could increase, forest fires could intensify and become more common, and the mortality rate of cardiovascular and pulmonary diseases linked to higher temperatures and poor air quality could increase (Ministry of Ecology and Natural Resources of Ukraine, 2013[28]).

Ukraine's infrastructure needs and current plans

The inadequate quality of Ukraine's infrastructure systems has been identified as a key structural bottleneck preventing the emergence of a more productive private sector and diversified exports (World Bank, 2017[29]). Ukraine's rankings on infrastructure indicators in the World Bank's Logistics Performance Index suggest that infrastructure quality has been deteriorating over the past decade, both in absolute terms and compared to other countries. Ukraine ranked 74th globally in 2007 with an average infrastructure score of 2.35, but in the 2018 edition Ukraine placed 119th with a score of 2.22 (World Bank, 2019[30]). In the World Economic Forum's 2019 Competitiveness Index, however, the quality of Ukraine's infrastructure scores relatively well. Its score (70.3) is well above the average for lower-middle income countries (60) and slightly above the Eurasian average (67.7) and most of its EaP peers (Armenia, 69; Georgia, 68; Moldova 66) (World Economic Forum, 2019[31]). Overall, Ukraine's infrastructure performs better than its EaP neighbour, Moldova, but worse than Russia (Figure 6.5). Ukraine's rail and seaport services rate favourably compared to Moldova's, whereas Moldova outranks Ukraine on air transport services. Ukraine's electricity transmission and distribution system is on par with Russia's, but the reliability of its water supply and sanitation systems are closer in line with Moldova's.

Figure 6.5. Quality of infrastructure in Ukraine

Source: World Economic Forum (2019[31]), *The Global Competitiveness Report 2019*, World Economic Forum, http://www3.weforum.org/docs/WEF_TheGlobalCompetitivenessReport2019.pdf

Ukraine's public investment needs are immense. By one estimate, Ukraine needs to invest USD 100 billion over the next ten years. Despite lower labour costs, construction projects cost 22% more in Ukraine than in the European Union on average due to mismanagement of public investment and governance issues, including corruption. Tackling corruption, improving public investment management systems and improving infrastructure service delivery are mutually reinforcing policy objectives required for better private sector productivity and improved wellbeing (World Bank, 2017[29]).

The OECD's database tracks 77 major planned or under construction infrastructure projects in Ukraine with a cumulative value of USD 37.0 billion. By value, transport projects account for the largest share (55%, USD 20.3 billion), followed by the energy sector (40%, USD 15.6 billion) (Figure 6.6). Only a handful of large-scale projects fall under the categories of industry and mining (2 projects worth USD 786 million) and water (4 projects worth USD 494 million). One project combines energy (biomass-fired power generation) and industry (food processing) components.

Figure 6.6. Investment projects in Ukraine, by sector

Planned and under construction, in USD million

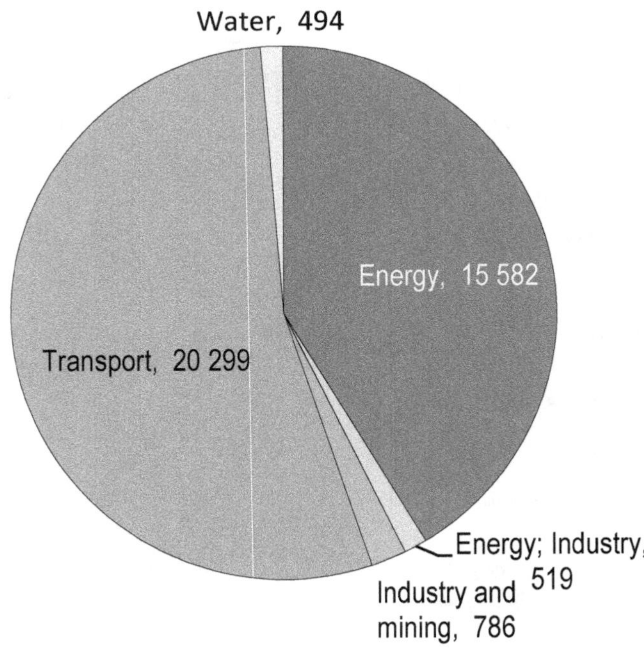

Source: OECD analysis based on accessed databases as of June 2020.

Transport

Ukraine's transport infrastructure network is extensive, consisting of 13 seaports, 163 000 km of roads and 20 950 km of railway, 47.4% of which have been electrified. However, given the country's vast territory and low population density, access to quality service delivery is uneven. For instance, 23% of residents in rural and mountainous areas do not have access to regular bus services (Ministry of Infrastructure of Ukraine, 2017[32]). The road networks of certain regions (Lviv *oblast*, Ternopyl *oblast*) are twice as dense as in Kherson *oblast* or Mykolayiv *oblast* (OECD, 2018[33]).

Several modal shifts are underway in Ukraine's transport sector. The majority of Ukraine's cargo, 182 billion tonnes-kilometres tkm in 2019, still travels by rail, accounting for 54% of total cargo turnover (or 78% excluding pipelines), but turnover has reduced in absolute terms (from 225 billion tkm in 2013) losing some of its modal share to road. Overall, road is the only transport mode to grow in absolute terms and as a share of total cargo turnover increased from 3% to 14% between 2013 and 2019 (or from 6% to 21% excluding pipelines), while cumulative cargo turnover decreased (from 451 billion tkm to 339 billion tkm) and the shares of all other transport modes declined. Transport via pipeline fell by almost half, from 197 billion tkm to 105 tkm, reflecting the shift's in Ukraine's energy supply chains. In passenger transport, rail and road have declined in both absolute and relative terms as passengers have shifted to air travel. While rail and road accounted for 52 billion pkm (54%) and 40 billion pkm (42%) respectively in 2003, passenger turnover reduced to 28 billion pkm (27%) for rail and 34 billion pkm (32%) by 2019. By contrast, air travel has expanded rapidly, from 3.3 billion pkm (3%) in 2003 to 30 billion pkm (28%) in 2019 (State Statistics Service of Ukraine, 2020[34]).

Overall, Ukraine's transport infrastructure is in decline. The national road network has suffered from chronic underinvestment and, due in part to lax enforcement of truck weight limits, premature deterioration.

Approximately half of Ukraine's major national roads fail to satisfy road roughness requirements and nearly two-fifths do not meet strength requirements. Poor road quality contributes to Ukraine's high rate of fatalities from road accidents (almost 14 per year per 100 000 inhabitants compared to 12 in Poland, 9 in Hungary and Slovakia and 4 in the Netherlands). Due to these quality concerns and insufficient capacity to meet traffic growth, traffic across Ukraine is considerably slower than in the European Union, where the average traffic speed is between twice and three times greater (World Bank, 2017[29]).

In 2020, the government embarked on a large-scale infrastructure investment programme amounting to UAH 125 billion (approximately USD 4.4 billion). The programme, dubbed "Big Construction", aimed to construct or rehabilitate 6 500 km of roads as well as several hundred public buildings (e.g. schools, kindergartens, stadiums, hospital emergency wards). It has, however, come under considerable criticism due to the programme's volume during the ongoing COVID-19 pandemic (Talant, 2020[35]). The programme is set to continue in 2021 (President of Ukraine, 2021[36]).

Ukraine's export industries rely heavily on its rail network, which performs better overall than its road system, with over 70% of non-pipeline freight traffic travelling by rail. However, the quality of Ukraine's rail assets and consequently service delivery is deteriorating due to insufficient maintenance and aging assets, particularly rolling stock, 70% of which dates from the 1980s. Ukraine's port infrastructure also needs urgent refurbishment or replacement; over 80% is considered obsolete or in a depreciated state. Over a tenth of berths are not in working condition, and sea ports lack adequate multimodal infrastructure (OECD, 2018[33]).

The cumulative effect of these quality concerns is that transport and logistics costs for exporting grain from Ukrainian farms to Black Sea ports exceed similar service costs in France and Germany by as much as 40% (World Bank, 2017[29]). Regulatory barriers also contribute to higher trade costs. According to the OECD's Trade Facilitation Indicators, poor border agency co-operation – both external and internal – and convoluted procedures are weak points in facilitating cross-border trade, but some progress has been made in recent years on streamlining procedures (OECD, 2020[37]).

To address its transport infrastructure quality concerns, Ukraine's *National Transport Strategy 2030* proposes that annual expenditure on roads should rise to UAH 35-40 billion (40-60% higher than in 2016) and that 90% of transport assets should be renewed by 2030. It sets out improving road safety as a priority and aims to increase the quality of public roads so that 70% meet regulatory requirements by 2030. In terms of connectivity, it aims to bolster rail links between regional centres with a network of higher speed trains (160-200 km/h by 2025; 250-400 km/h by 2030). Decentralisation of planning and maintenance responsibilities and the liberalisation of the transport sector to attract private sector competition and investment are key components of the strategy. It sets an objective to increase the role of non-public ownership structures for rail transport carriers to 25% by 2025 and 40% by 2030 (Ministry of Infrastructure of Ukraine, 2017[32]).

The *National Transport Strategy 2030* also sets a number of environment-related targets. Through increased investments in public transport, alternative fuels (50% of fuel use by 2030) and electric transport (75% of domestic traffic by 2030), Ukraine aims to reduce GHG emissions from mobile sources by 60% compared to 1990 levels.

Ukraine's transport infrastructure projects planned and under construction account for around USD 20.3 billion, mostly concentrated in the road sector (68%) (Figure 6.7). The majority of Ukraine's largest-scale transport projects are also in the road sector, including a new ring road for Kyiv, rehabilitation projects aimed at improving road safety and plans aimed at improving export corridors (Table 6.2). Urban public transport projects in Kyiv, Kharkiv and other major cities (USD 3.1 billion or 15%) and rail projects (USD 1.7 billion or 8%) account for most of the remainder. Other projects include improvements to Kyiv's Boryspil International Airport and the Black Sea ports of Kherson, Odessa, Olvia and Yuzhny. Projects shifting Ukraine's rail sector towards high-speed service and enabling a transition towards electric vehicles in the road sector are notably absent despite the targets set in *National Transport Strategy 2030*.

Figure 6.7. Transport projects in Ukraine, by sub-sector

Planned and under construction in USD million

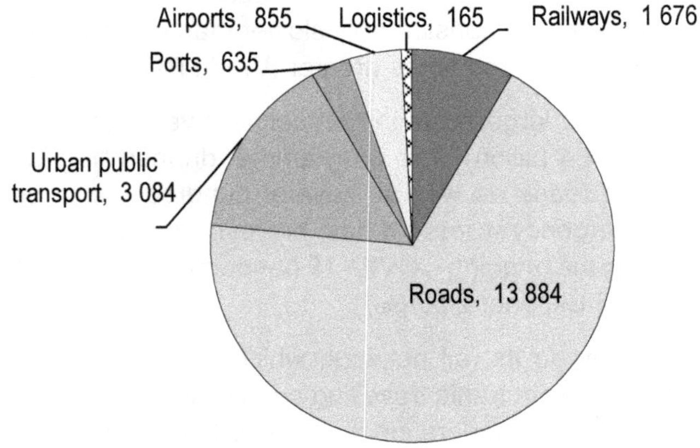

Source: OECD analysis based on accessed databases as of June 2020.

Table 6.2. Hotspot projects in the transport sector in Ukraine

Name	Sub-sector	Description	Project value (USD million)	Funding source	Type of investment
(a) Under construction					
Kyiv Ring Road	Road	The 214-km ring road includes 65 km of existing roads and 149 of new construction linking 3 international and 4 national transport corridors around the city of Kyiv	6 418	Government of Ukraine, City of Kyiv	Greenfield
European Roads Ukraine II and III	Road	The project will rehabilitate stretches of strategically important highway around Kyiv, Lviv and in several other regions of Ukraine.	2 235	EIB	Brownfield
Kyiv Metro Line #4: Podilsko-Vyhurivska	Urban public transport	The project will create a new line to extend Kyiv's metro system to link the northeast and southwest of the city across the Dnieper river and include 16 stations and 20 km of track.	2 000	CRIG, CPCG, City of Kyiv	Greenfield
(b) Planned					
Name	Sub-sector	Description	Project value (USD million)	Funding source	Type of investment
"Go Highway" Project	Road	The project will link four of Ukraine's Black Sea ports to the Baltic Sea in northern Poland. The Ukrainian section consists of 1088 km of highway.	2 400	EU, Government of Ukraine	Greenfield
Boryspil Airport Development	Air	The project will increase the airport's capacity and improve security and passenger comfort.	726	EIB	Brownfield
Second Roads and Safety Improvement Project	Road	The project aims to improve road quality and safety on international highway M03.	562	IBRD, Government of Ukraine	Brownfield

Note: Refer to the Reader's guide for the present report's definition of 'hotspot' and other information on how the projects above were selected and prioritised. CPCG = China Pacific Construction Group; CRIG = China Railway International Group; EIB = European Investment Bank; IBRD = International Bank for Reconstruction and Development.
Source: OECD database as of June 2020.

Energy

Ukraine is the most energy-intensive economy in the Eastern Partnership and second only to Turkmenistan in the former Soviet Union. Its energy use per USD 1 000 of GDP (in USD at purchasing power parity) is 0.25 toe (tonnes of oil equivalent), over twice the global average (0.11 toe) (IEA, 2020[38]).

Ukraine has achieved universal access to electricity and gas for its population, but major concerns about energy supply reliability and security remain. Ukraine has extensive infrastructure in the energy sector, including the third-largest gas storage facilities worldwide, but most of Ukraine's assets date from the Soviet era and have not been sufficiently maintained (EBRD, 2018[39]). These shortcomings are reflected not only in its poor performance on the getting electricity metric of the Doing Business index (128th place worldwide), but also in high loss rates along its gas networks and its electricity transmission and distribution network (over 10% of generated power) (World Bank, 2017[29]; World Economic Forum, 2019[31]).

Ukraine is a net importer of energy. In 2018, Ukraine covered about 65% (60.9 Mtoe) of its total primary energy supply with domestic production thanks to its large nuclear generation capacity (22.1 Mtoe) and domestic production of coal (14.4 Mtoe), natural gas (16.5 Mtoe), biofuels and waste (3.7 Mtoe) and crude oil (2.3 Mtoe). Imports make up the remaining third of Ukraine's energy supply. Ukraine imports almost as much natural gas 8.5 Mtoe), coal (13.8 Mtoe) and crude oil 1.3 Mtoe) as it produces domestically. In terms of oil products, Ukraine's imports (10.2 Mtoe) far exceed its exports (297 ktoe). Ukraine also exports biofuels and waste (542 ktoe) and electricity (524 ktoe) (IEA, 2019[40]).

Major shifts have taken place in Ukraine's natural gas imports, which have historically come from Russia but are now predominantly from European Union member states. Ukraine could, however, become energy self-sufficient over the next decade if its conventional and non-conventional gas reserves, including its extensive shale gas reserves, were exploited (World Bank, 2017[29]). Development of Ukraine's shale gas reserves via hydraulic fracturing ('fracking') has been met with criticism due to major environmental risks, including water supply and air contamination, costly and harmful waste disposal and increased seismic activity (CEE Bankwatch Network and National Ecological Centre of Ukraine, 2015[41]). In the natural gas retail market for household customers, Naftogas's public service obligation (PSO) was cancelled in 2020, leading to increasing competition from other suppliers. An analogous PSO for district heating is scheduled for cancellation in 2021 (Pirani, 2020[42]).

Ukraine generates 53% of its electricity from fifteen nuclear reactors located at four plants across the country, making it the world's 7th largest producer of nuclear energy (Figure 6.8). Energoatom, a large state-owned enterprise, operates all four of Ukraine's nuclear power plants (NPPs), including Zaporizhzhia NPP. Zaporizhzhia NPP, the largest NPP in Europe, consists of six 1000-MW reactors and on its own generates about a fifth of Ukraine's average annual electricity output.

Coal-fired thermal power plants account for a further 31% of Ukraine's power generation. Although historically Ukraine has benefited from large domestic reserves of coal, 89 of the country's 102 state-owned mines and a considerable share of national coal reserves are located in the temporarily occupied territories of Donetsk *oblast* and Luhansk *oblast.* Of the remaining 33 mines, only four of them are profitable (Energy Community Secretariat, 2019[43]). Due in part to the conflict in eastern Ukraine, coal production has dropped by more than half (64.4 million tonnes in 2013 vs 24.2 and 26.3 million tonnes in 2017 and 2018) (State Statistics Service of Ukraine, 2020[44]). Finally, natural gas, both imported and to a much lesser extent domestically produced, generates 6% of Ukraine's electricity, while hydroelectric power plants (7%), wind (1%) and solar PV (1%) account for most of the remainder.

Figure 6.8. Electricity generation by source

GWh, 2018

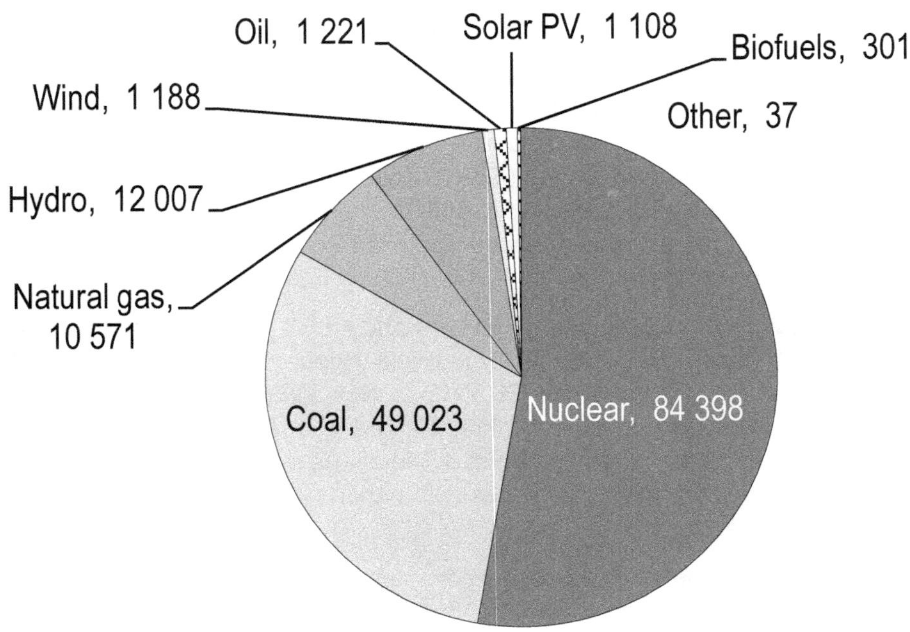

Source: IEA (2021[45]), *Electricity Information 2020*, International Energy Agency, https://www.iea.org/data-and-statistics

Energy independence, in addition to improving reliability and sustainability of energy supply, is one of the six headline strategic objectives in the energy-sector development strategy that Ukraine adopted in 2017, *Energy Strategy of Ukraine for the period to 2035: "Security, energy efficiency, competitiveness"*. The strategy projects that Ukraine's total primary energy supply (TPES) will dip from 90.1 Mtoe in 2015 to 82.3 Mtoe in 2020 before growing to 96 Mtoe by 2035. The initial decline, brought about predominantly from reduced coal use but also less intensive use of oil products, will be counteracted as an increased supply of biomass, biofuels and waste (from 2.1 Mtoe in 2015 to 11 Mtoe by 2035), solar and wind energy (from 0.1 Mtoe to 10 Mtoe) and natural gas (from 26.1 Mtoe to 29 Mtoe) assets come online. The supply of nuclear energy is expected to increase from 23 Mtoe in 2015 to 28 in 2025 before returning to 24 by 2035 as older power plants are decommissioned (Ministry of Energy and Coal Industry of Ukraine, 2017[46]). Addressing its energy security concerns, Ukraine expects to rely on a greater share of renewables in its TPES: from 4% in 2015, Ukraine aims to reach 12% by 2025 and 25% by 2035. The strategy also confronts the country's high energy intensity of GDP, which Ukraine aims to reduce from 0.28 to 0.13 toe per USD 1000 (OECD, 2020[47]).

Compounding quality concerns with Ukraine's physical infrastructure assets, the state-owned enterprises (SOEs) that run much of the country's energy sector operate at low levels of productivity, lack sufficient transparency and benefit from preferential access to resources, preventing new market entrants (World Bank, 2017[29]). The OECD reviewed Ukraine's energy sector SOEs with a particular focus on Naftogas and, based on its analysis, recommended that the government continue pursuing reforms begun in 2014. In line with OECD Guidelines on Corporate Governance of SOEs, this will require particular efforts to strengthen the state-owner's ability to professionally and effectively exercise ownership rights, while continuing to improve corporate governance practices within the company. These reforms can go a long way in potentially shielding the group from undue political interference. Additionally, without addressing risks of corruption and breach of integrity in certain areas of the hydrocarbons sector (including notably in gas distribution and supply as well as in licensing) and in the broader reform environment, the full benefits of improved corporate governance practices cannot be realised (OECD, 2019[48]). Reforms to corporate governance in a few SOEs have already progressed to an advanced stage, but these remain the exception rather than the rule (OECD, 2020[47]).

OECD analysis aimed at providing recommendations for the government's planned revisions of the *Energy Strategy of Ukraine to 2035* concludes that the strategy is broadly consistent with international commitments (e.g. Ukraine's energy objectives as laid out in the Sustainable Development Goals, the EU-Ukraine Association Agreement) but is inconsistent with existing energy policy objectives. For instance, although the strategy includes plans to liquidate underperforming state-owned coal mines by 2025, it does not lay out any measures to phase out Ukraine's coal-fired thermal power plants. Given that, according to the strategy, Ukraine seeks to integrate with the European Network of Transmission System Operators for Electricity (ENTSO-E) and the European power market by 2023, its continued support for aging, unreliable power plants could prevent effective integration (OECD, 2020[47]).

According to the OECD's database of large-scale infrastructure projects planned and under construction, Ukraine's current energy investments are predominantly in new power generation projects (59%), with projects in electric power transmission, distribution and storage (25%) and natural gas pipelines (13%) accounting for much of the remainder (Figure 6.9(a)). In terms of new power generation capacity, a single nuclear power project, the addition of two reactors to the Khmelnitsky NPP, accounts for 45% (Figure 6.9(b)). Construction began on the two reactors, Khmelnitsky-3 and Khmelnitsky-4, in the 1980s, but following the 1986 Chernobyl disaster Ukraine adopted a moratorium on new NPP construction in 1990. Although the moratorium was relatively short lived and was repealed shortly after independence, construction on the two reactors has not yet resumed, despite relatively advanced progress on construction (75% and 28% respectively) (IAEA, 2020[49]). Following renewed interest, the project underwent a feasibility study and has sought and secured financiers (Table 6.3). Renewables are well represented among the power generation projects planned and under construction tracked by the OECD's database, with wind and solar photovoltaic projects accounting for 34% and 8% of new capacity respectively. In addition to nuclear and renewable power generation, Ukraine also plans to add new coal-fired power generation units to the Slavyansk power plant in eastern Ukraine. The proposed expansion of Ukraine's coal-fired generation capacity belies the government's strategic goal of reducing coal's share of the country's TPES in the coming decade. In terms of transmission distribution and storage projects, Ukraine plans to construct a large-scale 1000-MW hydropower pumped storage facility to bolster reliability of supply. The other tracked projects in this sub-sector are refurbishments of existing transmission and distribution infrastructure.

Figure 6.9. Energy projects in Ukraine, by sub-sector (in USD million) and electricity generation projects by source (in MW)

Planned and under construction

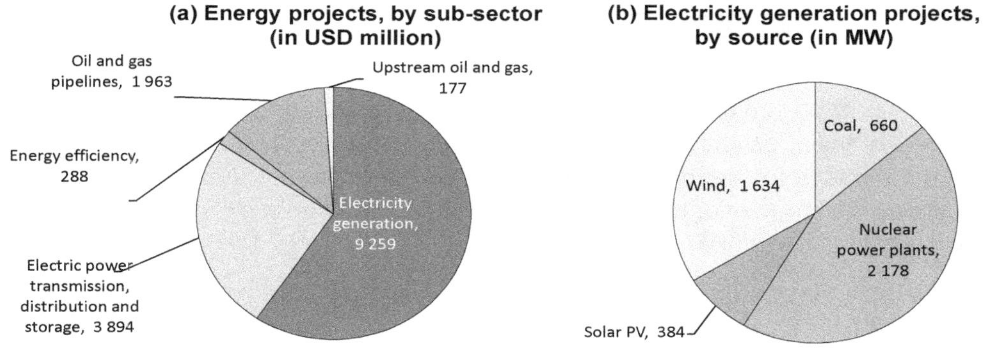

Source: OECD analysis based on accessed databases as of June 2020.

Table 6.3. Hotspot projects in the energy sector in Ukraine

Name	Sub-sector	Description	Project value (USD million)	New capacity (MW)	Funding source	Type of investment
(a) Under construction						
Ukraine Municipal Infrastructure Framework Loan	Electricity transmission and distribution	The project will refurbish and extend the life of critical urban infrastructure, including electricity transmission and distribution systems.	868	N/A	EIB	Brownfield
Slavyansk II	Coal-fired power plant	The project will add two new units (6A and 6B) to the Slavyansk coal-fired power plant in eastern Ukraine.	684	660	Donbasenergo;	Greenfield
Hydro Power Plant Rehabilitation Project	Hydroelectric power plant	This project will modernise seven existing hydroelectric power plants across Ukraine, improving efficiency and reliability.	665	N/A	EBRD	Brownfield
(b) Planned						
Name	Sub-sector	Description	Project value (USD million)	New capacity (MW)	Funding source	Type of investment
Khmelnitsky NPP – Units 3 and 4	Nuclear power plant	The project aims to complete construction of a third and fourth VVER-1000 reactor at the Khmelnitsky NPP.	4 000	2 178	Energoatom; Barclays; Skoda	Brownfield
Kaniv Hydropower Pumped Storage Plant	Pumped storage	The project will construct a pumped storage facility providing 1 000 MW of reserve capacity.	1 395		EIB, World Bank, EBRD, Deutsche Bank	Greenfield
Zophia Wind Project	Wind	The project plans to develop the wind farm in three phases: Zophia I (42.5 MW), Zophia II (300 MW) and Zophia III (450 MW).	1 120	792.5	NBT	Greenfield

Note: Refer to the Reader's guide for the present report's definition of 'hotspot' and other information on how the projects above were selected and prioritised. EBRD = European Bank for Reconstruction and Development; EIB = European Investment Bank; NBT = a Norwegian wind power developer.
Source: OECD database as of June 2020.

Industry, mining and water

Over time, Ukraine's economy has shifted away from industry and towards services. Industry represented 39% of Ukraine's GDP in 1999 but by 2015 it had fallen to 24%, while services' share increased from 47% to 63% over the same period. Historically, coal mining has been a very important industry in Ukraine, particularly in the eastern Donbas region. In recent years, the ongoing armed conflict in eastern Ukraine, where much of the mining and heavy industry sectors are concentrated, has severely impacted these industries and former workers' employment prospects, since their skillsets are often misaligned with the demands of the labour market elsewhere in the country (World Bank, 2017[29]). The Russian occupation of Crimea had a similar impact on iron ore mining in Ukraine, since the country lost *de facto* sovereign control over the Kerch iron ore basin, estimated to account for about 14% of Ukraine's reserves (Vorotnikov, 2015[50]). A long-term strategy for the development of subsoil resources to 2030 was adopted in 2011 (Government of Ukraine, 2011[51]), prior to the Maidan revolution, but its underlying assumptions no longer correspond to Ukraine's situation.

Mining continues to play an important albeit diminished role in Ukraine's industrial output (14%), overshadowed by the much larger manufacturing sector (61%). The manufacture of food products, beverages and tobacco products accounts for about a third of Ukraine's manufacturing sector, almost twice as large by value as the manufacture of basic metals and fabricated metal products, the next largest category (Figure 6.10). Ukraine has made the development of small and medium enterprises (SMEs) a central part of its development goals. They employed 6.6 million people in 2017 and generated 61% of added value. By 2024, Ukraine aims to boost these figures to 9.3 million people and 74% respectively. The government also aims to increase industrial production by 4.5-7% annually between 2020 and 2024, placing particular emphasis on the manufacture of machines (7-10% annual growth between 2020 and 2024) (Government of Ukraine, 2017[52]).

Figure 6.10. Industrial output by NACE* subsector

2019, million UAH

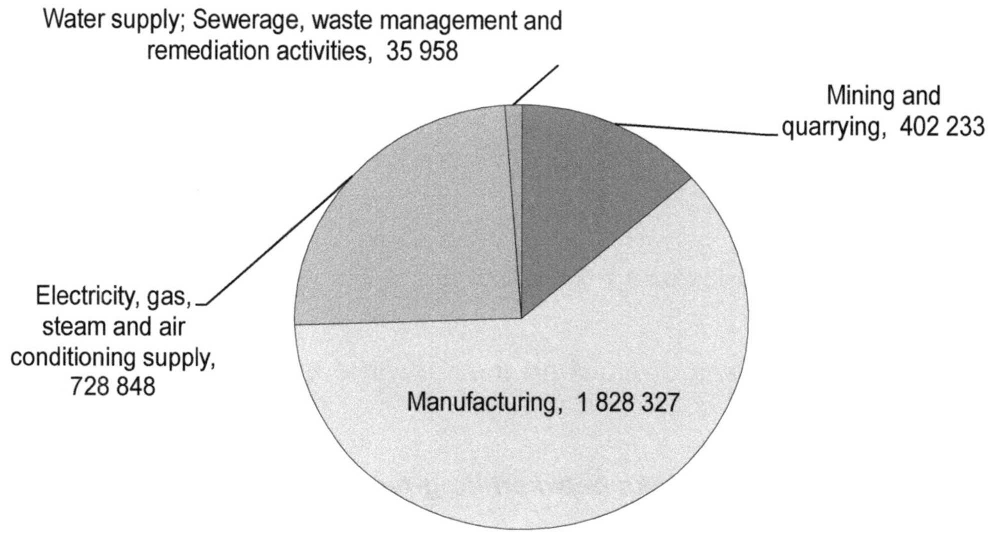

Note: UAH = Ukrainian hryvnya; ** NACE = Nomenclature statistique des activités économiques dans la Communauté européenne [Statistical Classification of Economic Activities in the European Community]
Source: State Statistics Service of Ukraine (2020[44]), Output of industrial products by types, https://ukrstat.org/en/operativ/menu/menu_e/prom.htm

By number, water supply and sanitation (WSS) projects, particularly the rehabilitation and modernisation of existing systems, represent over half of the projects tracked in the OECD infrastructure database in the industry, mining and water sectors, but due to their smaller average value they cumulatively represent 24% of all projects' value (Figure 6.11). All of the WSS projects tracked by the OECD database are in urban settings, which points to a misalignment in Ukraine's WSS-related investments. Access to WSS services differs considerably across Ukraine, particularly between cities and rural areas, where socioeconomic class becomes a determinant of access to adequate WSS. For instance, in urban areas, over 90% of the population across all quintiles from richest to poorest have access to water and sewerage, while in rural areas access ranges from about 45% for the poorest quintile to about 67% for the richest quintile (World Bank, 2017[29]). A single large-scale iron ore mining project and two manufacturing projects – a combined sunflower oil plant and biomass project and the modernisation of an existing steel mill – account for 21% and 55% of investments respectively.

Figure 6.11. Industry, mining and water infrastructure projects in Ukraine, by sub-sector

Planned and under construction in million USD

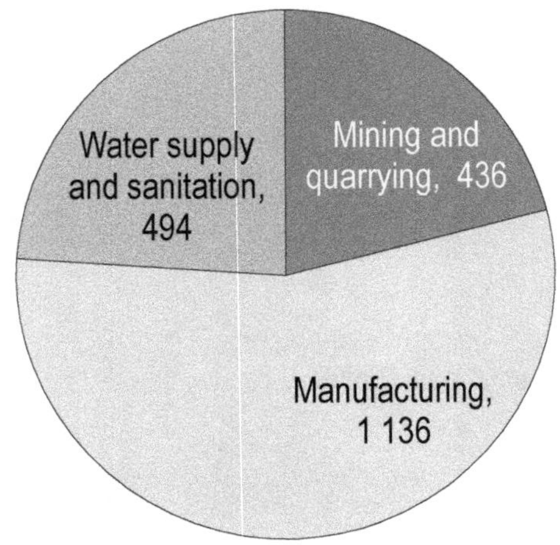

Source: OECD analysis based on accessed databases as of June 2020

Strengths and weaknesses of existing institutional set-up for sustainable infrastructure planning

Strategic planning and links between long-term goals, infrastructure plans and environmental considerations

Ukraine has established a hierarchy of policy planning documents, but some of its most important strategic documents (e.g. the Sustainable Development Strategy 2020, the Medium-Term Government Priority Action Plan until 2020) lack a defined status in the country's legal framework. There are also no requirements or processes for developing sectoral strategies, many of which set the government's objectives referenced throughout the present chapter (i.e. Transport Strategy 2030, Energy Strategy 2035) (OECD, 2018[53]).

According to Ukraine's existing legal framework, the Government Action Plan identifies the priority tasks of an administration over its mandate, which is then broken down into annual Government Priority Action Plans. The current Budget Code requires an annual budget for the upcoming year and an indicative budget for the subsequent two-year period based on the Government Action Plan, but in practice the annual budget has been the main fiscal planning mechanism. Changes are currently underway, however, with the CMU adopting pilot medium-term spending projections, Future Directions of Budget Policy for 2018-2020 (OECD, 2018[53]).

Consequently, Ukraine's infrastructure-related development strategies fall outside of its legal framework for strategic policy planning. To improve the coherence of its strategic planning and the links between long-term, medium-term and near-term plans, Ukraine should consider expanding its legal framework for strategic planning documents to include top-level long-term sustainable development strategies and sectoral strategies.

Ukraine has led the way among EaP countries, becoming the first to adopt a long-term low-emission development strategy to 2050, the *Ukraine 2050 Low Emission Development Strategy*, which sets mid-century GHG emission reduction targets by sector. Ukraine does not, however, have a functional top-level development strategy to follow its Sustainable Development Strategy 2020. Although a draft Sustainable Development Strategy 2030 has been developed, no follow-up to the current 2020 strategy has been formally adopted. Ukraine would benefit from a guiding top-level sustainable development document to 2030 (like neighbouring Moldova) or 2050 (like Kazakhstan) aligned with both the SDGs, its long-term low-emission development strategy and its existing sectoral documents. Such long-term planning documents enable countries to look beyond shorter-term political and business cycles to articulate priorities in terms of economic and social development as well as, crucially, the reconciliation of these goals with environmental concerns.

Ukraine has been a party to the UNECE Convention on Environmental Impact Assessment in a Transboundary Context since 1999 and the related Protocol on Strategic Environmental Assessment since 2015. Ukraine has transposed both agreements into national legislation, but assessment procedures in practice continue to suffer from insufficiencies. Since 2019, one of the main work areas of the EU-funded EU4Environment programme, the successor to the EaP GREEN programme, is supporting reforms and improvements to the environmental assessment processes in Ukraine and other EaP countries. The programme is jointly implemented by the OECD, UNECE, UNEP, UNIDO and the World Bank.

Institutional set-up and decision making processes

Following the 2014 Ukrainian revolution, Ukraine has had five cabinets formed to address different priorities in Ukraine's shifting political landscape. As a result, the number, names and responsibilities of many of Ukraine's infrastructure-related ministry-level institutions have been in flux. In 2019, the Ministry of Economic Development and Trade absorbed the agriculture portfolio to become the Ministry of Economic Development, Trade and Agriculture. Also in 2019, the Ministry of Energy and Coal Mining and the Ministry of Ecology and Natural Resources merged to form the short-lived Ministry of Energy and Environmental Protection (August 2019 – May 2020) before splitting once more. The Ministry of Ecology and Natural Resources retained its earlier name; the Ministry of Energy dropped explicit reference to the coal mining industry in its name while still maintaining coal mining in its portfolio. The Ministry of Infrastructure, responsible for the transport sector, has remained constant throughout these changes, but the 2020 cabinet change led to the creation of a new ministry, the Ministry of Strategic Industries, whose remit will include industrial development. These regular reconfigurations of responsibilities and staff could impede effective policy making and complicate the state's ability to consolidate and implement sustainable policies.

Ukraine's administrative instability and shortcomings in its strategic planning practices jointly lead to incoherent policy directions and implementation. On key policy issues like the state's push towards decentralisation, succeeding administrations have proposed and then retracted various versions of decentralised powers leading to slow and uneven progress towards an uncertain goal. Since there is no overarching plan to guide the prioritisation and sequencing of third-tier activities, such as regional infrastructure development and capacity building for subnational civil servants, stakeholders in the decentralisation process risk acting in an uncoordinated and even contradictory manner (OECD, 2018[33]).

Ukraine's reforms implemented since 2015 have improved its public investment management system somewhat, notably introducing requirements in the country's Budget Code to base the selection of some infrastructure projects on clearly defined criteria and cost-benefit analysis. Further steps towards strengthening public financial management institutions could ultimately improve infrastructure and service delivery by improving the transparency, efficiency and accountability mechanisms in the use of public resources. Ukraine's prioritisation of reforms that help root out corruption and cultivate public trust in government should continue, since reducing corruption will reduce costly financial mismanagement and augment reform efforts across the government (World Bank, 2017[29]).

Ukraine's performance on several indicators of the quality of its policy development and co-ordination processes is middling compared to its regional peers, Armenia and Georgia (Figure 6.12). Ukraine's monitoring and reporting procedures, for instance, are better developed than in Georgia and similar to those used in Armenia, but overall Ukraine lags behind its peers on most metrics. Ukraine has, however, demonstrated relatively strong coordination mechanisms between its centre-of-government institutions for the preparation of its Government Priority Action Plan (OECD, 2018[53]). Such mechanisms should be expanded to the inter-ministerial coordination on other key policy issues, such as infrastructure development and green economy priorities.

Figure 6.12. Policy development and co-ordination indicators

Armenia (2019), Georgia (2018) and Ukraine (2018)

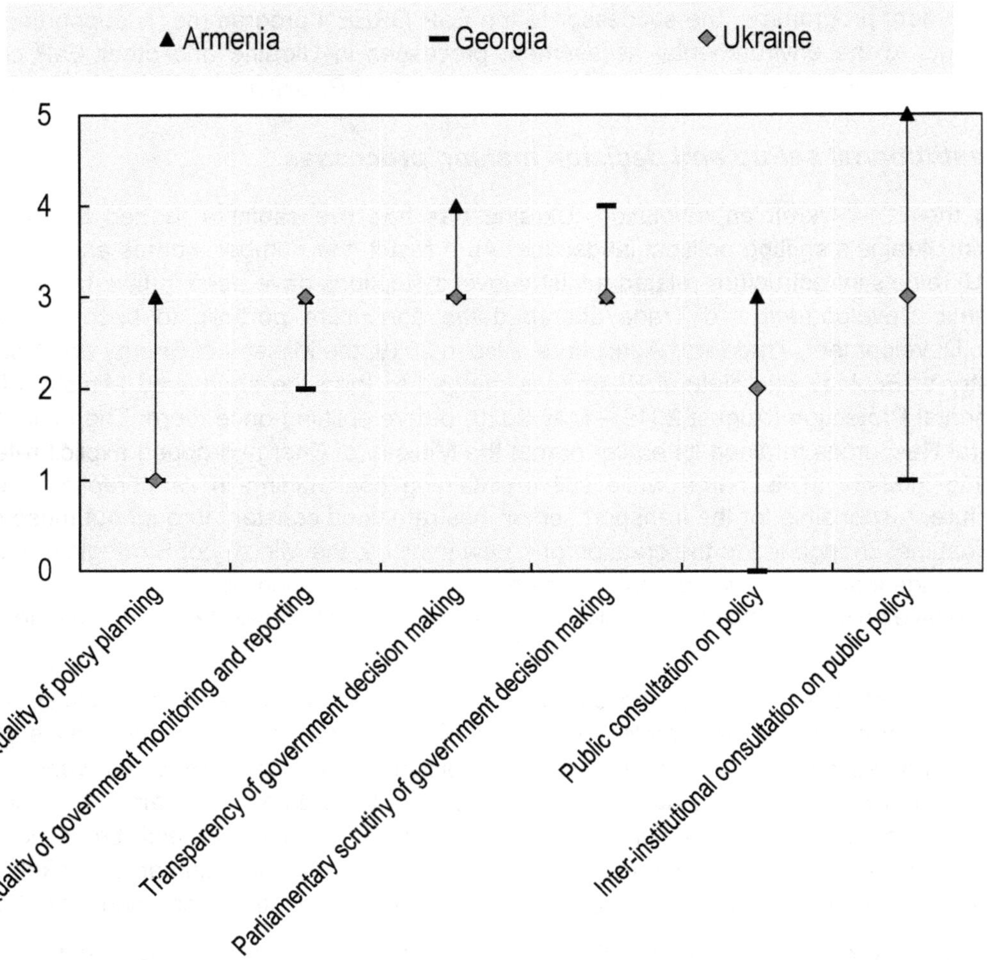

Source: OECD (2019[54]), *The Principles of Public Administration: Baseline Measurement Report: Armenia*, SIGMA, OECD Publishing, Paris, http://www.sigmaweb.org/publications/Baseline-Measurement-Armenia-2019.pdf; OECD (2018[55]), *The Principles of Public Administration: Baseline Measurement Report: Georgia*, SIGMA, OECD Publishing, Paris, http://www.sigmaweb.org/publications/Baseline-Measurement-Report-2018-Georgia.pdf; OECD (2018[53]), *The Principles of Public Administration: Baseline Measurement Report: Ukraine*, SIGMA, OECD Publishing, Paris, http://www.sigmaweb.org/publications/Baseline-Measurement-Report-2018-Ukraine.pdf

List of relevant strategic documents

Table 6.4. Main strategic documents in force

	Status	Time Horizon	Sectoral Coverage	Main objectives
First Nationally Determined Contribution (NDC)	Submitted in 2015	2015-2030	Economy-wide	• Target: Reduce GHG emissions (including land use, land use change and forestry) by at least 40% compared to 1990 levels by 2030 Main sectors for emission reduction: energy, industry, agriculture
Ukraine 2050 Low Emission Development Strategy	Submitted in 2017	2017-2050	Economy-wide	Target: Reduce GHG emissions by 47% ("energy efficiency" scenario), 67% ("renewable energy" scenario) or 66% ("modernisation and innovation" scenario) by 2050
Concept for Implementation of the State Policy on Climate Change up to 2030	Adopted in 2016	2016-2030	Economy-wide	• Strengthen institutional capacity for the development and implementation of the country's climate Reduce GHG emissions, including through rate revisions of the tax on carbon dioxide emissions from fixed sources (introduced in 2011)
Sustainable Development Strategy 'Ukraine 2020'	Adopted in 2015	2015-2020	Economy-wide	• Implement reforms allowing for Ukraine to apply for EU membership by 2020 • Become a top 30 performer in the World Bank's Doing Business rankings Reach top 50 ranking in Transparency International's Corruption Perception Index
National Transport Development Strategy 2030	Adopted in 2017	2017-2030	Transport	• Reduce GHG emissions from mobile sources by 60% (compared to 1990 levels) and total air pollutant emissions from mobile sources by 70% (compared to 2015 levels) • Increase share of electric transport in domestic traffic to 75% by 2030 Increase share of alternative fuels to 50% by 2030
Energy Strategy of Ukraine for the period to 2035: "Security, energy efficiency, competitiveness".	Adopted in 2017	2017-2035	Energy	• Increase the share of renewables in TPES from 4% in 2015 to 12% by 2025 and 25% by 2035 Reduce energy intensity of GDP from 0.28 to 0.13 toe per USD 1000 by 2035
National Renewable Energy Action Plan to 2020	Adopted in 2014	2014-2020	Energy	Increase the share of renewables in energy consumption to 11%
National Energy Efficiency Action Plan to 2020	Adopted in 2015	2015-2020	Energy	Achieve 9% energy savings of average final domestic energy consumption
Programme for the Development of Mineral Resource Base of Ukraine for the Period to the year 2030	Adopted in 2011	2011-2030	Mining	Further develop well-established mining industries (i.e. coal, iron ore) and diversify into other minerals
Concept of the State target programme for the development of airports for the period to 2023	Adopted in 2013	2013-2023	Transport	Modernise major airports in Ukraine (e.g. Kyiv-Boryspil, Odessa, Kyiv-Zhuliany, Kherson, Dnepretrovsk, Zaporizhzhia, Ivano-Frankivsk, Uzhhorod, Chernivtsk)

	Status	Time Horizon	Sectoral Coverage	Main objectives
SME Development Strategy 2016-2020	Adopted in 2015	2016-2020	Governance, industry	• Enhance competitiveness of SMEs in both domestic and international markets • Improve the skills of SMEs and develop a modern entrepreneurial culture • Ensure the improvement of the technological ability of SMEs • Aim to increase SMEs output by 10% annually by 2020 • Increase the number of employees in SMEs by 15% Increase the productivity of SMEs by 7%

Table 6.5. Other relevant documents

	Status	Time Horizon	Sectoral Coverage
Priority Task Action Plan for 2020	Adopted in 2020	2020	Multi-sector
Export Strategy of Ukraine: Roadmap of Strategic Development of Trade	Adopted in 2017	2017-2021	Multi-sector
Strategy for Small and Medium-sized Enterprise Development in Ukraine until 2020	Adopted in 2017	2017-2020	Multi-sector
2030 National Strategy on Waste Management	Adopted in 2017	2017-2030	Waste
Main Foundations (Strategy) of the State Environment Policy through to 2020 / Main Foundations (Strategy) of the State Environment Policy through to 2030	Adopted in 2011, extended in 2019	2011-2020; 2019-2030	Multi-sector
Concept for the State Heat Supply Implementation	Adopted in 2017	Unclear	Heat supply

References

CEE Bankwatch Network and National Ecological Centre of Ukraine (2015), *The dash for gas in Ukraine: Current trends in the production of unconventional reserves*, https://bankwatch.org/wp-content/uploads/2015/02/dash-for-gas-UA.pdf. [41]

EBRD (2018), *Ukraine Diagnostic*, https://www.ebrd.com/documents/strategy-and-policy-coordination/ukraine.pdf?blobnocache=true#:~:text=The%20diagnostics%20are%20shared%20with,during%20the%20country%20strategy%20process.&text=The%20diagnostic%20analyses%20obstacles%20that,able%20to%20gener. [39]

Energy Community (2020), *2020 Implementation Report*, https://energy-community.org/news/Energy-Community-News/2020/11/23.html (accessed on 26 November 2019). [10]

Energy Community Secretariat (2019), *Rocking the Boat: What is Keeping the Energy Community's Coal Sector Afloat?*, https://www.energy-community.org/dam/jcr:23503de3-fccd-48f8-a469-c633e9ac5232/EnC%20Coal%20Study%20Report%20WEB.pdf. [43]

European Council (2014), *Special meeting of the European Council (30 August 2014) - Conclusions*, European Council, Brussels. [11]

fDi Markets (2019), *fDi Markets: the in-depth crossborder investment monitor (database)*, https://www.fdimarkets.com/. [23]

Government of Ukraine (2017), *Strategic Action Plan of the Ministry of Economic Development and Trade of Ukraine for 2017-2024*, https://www.me.gov.ua/Documents/Download?id=c515a819-deb3-4622-a0df-2bc4496ef19b. [52]

Government of Ukraine (2011), *Whole-State Program for Development of Mineral Resource Base of Ukraine for the Period to the year 2030*, http://geoinf.kiev.ua/wp/wp-content/uploads/2016/04/Annex-C-Ukraine-Minerals-Development-Program.pdf. [51]

Havlik, P., A. Kochnev and O. Pindyuk (2020), *Economic Challenges and Costs of Reintigrating the Donbas Region of Ukraine*, Wiener Institut für Internationale Wirtschaftsvergleiche (WIIW), https://wiiw.ac.at/economic-challenges-and-costs-of-reintegrating-the-donbas-region-in-ukraine-dlp-5351.pdf. [24]

IAEA (2020), *Country Nuclear Power Profiles: Ukraine*, International Atomic Energy Agency, https://cnpp.iaea.org/countryprofiles/Ukraine/Ukraine.htm. [49]

IEA (2021), *Electricity Information 2020*, https://www.iea.org/data-and-statistics (accessed on 10 August 2020). [45]

IEA (2020), *Ukraine energy profile*, https://www.iea.org/reports/ukraine-energy-profile (accessed on 10 October 2020). [38]

IEA (2019), *World Energy Balances 2019*, International Energy Agency, Paris, https://doi.org/10.1787/3a876031-en (accessed on 10 August 2020). [40]

Ilko Kucheriv Democratic Initiatives Charitable Foundation (2019), *Європейська інтеграція України: динаміка громадської думки [European integration of Ukraine: changes in public opinion]*, Ilko Kucheriv Democratic Initiatives Charitable Foundation, Kyiv. [9]

IMF (2020), *Ukraine : Request for Stand-by Arrangement-Press Release; Staff Report; and Statement by the Executive Director for Ukraine*, International Monetary Fund, https://www.imf.org/en/Publications/CR/Issues/2020/06/10/Ukraine-Request-for-Stand-by-Arrangement-Press-Release-Staff-Report-and-Statement-by-the-49501. [25]

IMF (2020), *World Economic Outlook (April 2020) - Real GDP growth*, International Monetary Fund, https://www.imf.org/external/datamapper/NGDP_RPCH@WEO/UKR?year=2018 (accessed on 6 October 2020). [4]

IMF (2020), *World Economic Outlook: October 2020*, https://www.imf.org/external/datamapper/GGXCNL_NGDP@WEO/OEMDC/ADVEC/WEOWORLD. [2]

Ministry of Ecology and Natural Resources of Ukraine (2013), *IV Национальное сообщение Украины по вопросам изменения климата [4th National Communication of Ukraine on climate change]*, https://unfccc.int/sites/default/files/resource/U%206nc_v7_final_%5B1%5D.pdf. [28]

Ministry of Energy and Coal Industry of Ukraine (2017), *Енергетична стратегія України на період до 2035 року "Безпека, енергоефективність, конкурентоспроможність" [Energy Strategy of Ukraine for the period to 2035 "Security, energy efficiency and competitiveness"]*, http://extwprlegs1.fao.org/docs/pdf/ukr176363.pdf. [46]

Ministry of Energy and Environmental Protection of Ukraine (2020), *Ukraine's Greenhouse Gas Inventory 1990-2018 (draft)*, https://mepr.gov.ua/files/docs/Zmina_klimaty/2020/Ukraine_NIR_2020%20draft.pdf. [26]

Ministry of Infrastructure of Ukraine (2017), *National Transport Strategy of Ukraine 2030*, https://mtu.gov.ua/files/for_investors/230118/National%20Transport%20Strategy%20of%20Ukraine.pdf. [32]

Müller, D. et al. (2016), *Impact of Climate Change on Wheat Production in Ukraine*, German-Ukrainian Agricultural Policy Dialogue, https://www.apd-ukraine.de/images/APD_APR_05-2016_impact_on_wheat_eng_fin.pdf. [27]

Naftogaz Europe (2017), *Natural Gas Supplies to Ukraine 2008-2016*, https://naftogaz-europe.com/article/en/NaturalGasSuppliestoUkraine (accessed on 10 October 2020). [15]

Observatory of Economic Complexity (2018), *Ukraine: Exports, Imports, and Trade Partners*, https://oec.world/en/profile/country/ukr (accessed on 9 October 2020). [14]

OECD (2021), *COVID-19 and greening the economies of Eastern Europe, the Caucasus and Central Asia*, http://www.oecd.org/coronavirus/policy-responses/covid-19-and-greening-the-economies-of-eastern-europe-the-caucasus-and-central-asia-40f4d34f/ (accessed on 10 March 2021). [8]

OECD (2020), *COVID-19 crisis response in Eastern Partner countries*, OECD, Paris, https://www.oecd.org/coronavirus/policy-responses/covid-19-crisis-response-in-eu-eastern-partner-countries-7759afa3/ (accessed on 9 September 2020). [6]

OECD (2020), *Investment Perspectives in Eastern Partnership Countries*, http://www.oecd.org/investment/Investment-perspectives-in-Eastern-Partner-countries.pdf. [18]

OECD (2020), *Monitoring the Energy Strategy of Ukraine 2035*, https://www.oecd.org/eurasia/competitiveness-programme/eastern-partners/Monitoring-the-energy-strategy-Ukraine-2035-EN-.pdf. [47]

OECD (2020), *The COVID-19 Crisis in Ukraine*, OECD Publishing, Paris, https://www.oecd.org/eurasia/competitiveness-programme/eastern-partners/COVID-19-CRISIS-IN-UKRAINE.pdf (accessed on 22 February 2021). [7]

OECD (2020), *Trade Facilitation Index*, https://www.oecd.org/trade/topics/trade-facilitation/ (accessed on 9 September 2020). [37]

OECD (2019), *Baseline Measurement Report: The Principles of Public Administration: Armenia*, OECD Publishing, Paris, http://www.sigmaweb.org/publications/Baseline-Measurement-Armenia-2019.pdf (accessed on 12 August 2020). [54]

OECD (2019), *State-Owned Enterprise Reform in the Hydrocarbons Sector in Ukraine*, http://www.oecd.org/corporate/SOE-Reform-in-the-Hydrocarbons-Sector-in-Ukraine-ENG.pdf (accessed on 22 February 2021). [48]

OECD (2018), *Maintaining the Momentum of Decentralisation in Ukraine*, OECD Multi-level Governance Studies, OECD Publishing, Paris, https://dx.doi.org/10.1787/9789264301436-en. [33]

OECD (2018), *The Principles of Public Administration Policy Development and Co-ordination: Baseline Measurement Report: Georgia*, OECD Publishing, Paris, http://www.sigmaweb.org/publications/Baseline-Measurement-Report-2018-Georgia.pdf (accessed on 13 August 2020). [55]

OECD (2018), *The Principles of Public Administration: Baseline Measurement Report: Ukraine*, OECD Publishing, Paris, http://www.sigmaweb.org/publications/Baseline-Measurement-Report-2018-Ukraine.pdf (accessed on 13 August 2020). [53]

OECD (2016), *OECD Investment Policy Reviews: Ukraine 2016*, OECD Investment Policy Reviews, OECD Publishing, Paris, https://dx.doi.org/10.1787/9789264257368-en. [17]

OECD (2014), *OECD bolsters relationship with Ukraine*, https://www.oecd.org/newsroom/oecd-bolsters-relationship-with-ukraine.htm (accessed on 22 February 2021). [13]

OECD (2014), *Statement by the OECD regarding the status of the accession process with Russia & co-operation with Ukraine*, https://www.oecd.org/newsroom/statement-by-the-oecd-regarding-the-status-of-the-accession-process-with-russia-and-co-operation-with-ukraine.htm (accessed on 22 February 2021). [12]

Pirani, S. (2020), *The market takes shape: The Ukrainian gas sector to 2030*, Oxford Institute for Energy Studies, https://www.oxfordenergy.org/wpcms/wp-content/uploads/2020/11/Insight-77-The-market-takes-shape-the-Ukrainian-gas-sector-to-2030.pdf (accessed on 22 February 2021). [42]

President of Ukraine (2021), *Президент: Інфраструктура – це ставлення держави до своїх людей [President: Infrastructure is the state's attitude to its people]*, https://www.president.gov.ua/news/prezident-infrastruktura-ce-stavlennya-derzhavi-do-svoyih-ly-66665 (accessed on 22 February 2021). [36]

Roser, M. et al. (2020), *Coronavirus Pandemic (COVID-19)*, OurWorldInData.Org, https://ourworldindata.org/coronavirus (accessed on 9 September 2020). [5]

State Statistics Service of Ukraine (2020), *Economic Statistics / Economic Activity / Transport and communications*, https://ukrstat.org/en/operativ/menu/menu_e/tiz.htm (accessed on 20 October 2020). [34]

State Statistics Service of Ukraine (2020), *Output of basic industrial products*, https://ukrstat.org/en/operativ/operativ2006/pr/prm_ric/prm_ric_e/vov2005_e.htm (accessed on 10 October 2020). [44]

Talant, B. (2020), *Zelensky's 'Big Construction' road repairs project sparks controversy*, Kyiv Post, https://www.kyivpost.com/ukraine-politics/zelenskys-big-construction-road-repairs-project-sparks-controversy.html?cn-reloaded=1 (accessed on 22 February 2021). [35]

Transparency International (2019), *CPI 2019: Eastern Europe & Central Asia*, https://www.transparency.org/en/news/cpi-2019-eastern-europe-central-asia (accessed on 20 July 2020). [20]

Ukrstat (2020), *Ukraine's foreign trade in goods*, State Statistics Service of Ukraine, https://ukrstat.org/en/operativ/operativ2020/zd/ztt/ztt_e/arh_ztt2020_e.html (accessed on 22 February 2021). [16]

UNDESA (2019), *World Population Prospects 2019: Highlights*, United Nations Department of Economic and Social Affairs (UNDESA), Population Division, https://www.un.org/development/desa/pd/sites/www.un.org.development.desa.pd/files/files/documents/2020/Jan/wpp2019_highlights.pdf (accessed on 8 October 2020). [3]

Verkhovna Rada of Ukraine (2020), *Проект Закону про внесення змін до деяких законодавчих актів України щодо обігу земель сільськогосподарського призначення [Draft law on the amendments to certain legislative acts concerning the turnover of agricultural lands]*, https://w1.c1.rada.gov.ua/pls/zweb2/webproc4_1?pf3511=67059 (accessed on 22 February 2021). [19]

Verlanov, S. (2020), "Taming Ukraine's oligarchs", *Atlantic Council*, https://www.atlanticcouncil.org/blogs/ukrainealert/taming-ukraines-oligarchs/ (accessed on 22 February 2021). [21]

Vorotnikov, V. (2015), *Ukraine's Iron Ore Hangs in the Balance*, Engineering and Mining Journal, https://www.e-mj.com/features/ukraine-s-iron-ore-hangs-in-the-balance/. [50]

World Bank (2021), *World Development Indicators (database)*, https://datacatalog.worldbank.org/dataset/world-development-indicators. [1]

World Bank (2020), *Doing Business 2020*, World Bank Group, Washington, DC, http://dx.doi.org/10.1596/978-1-4648-1440-2. [22]

World Bank (2019), *Country Score Card: Logistics Performance Index*, https://lpi.worldbank.org/international/scorecard/ (accessed on 27 July 2020). [30]

World Bank (2017), *Ukraine - Systemic Country Diagnostic: Toward sustainable recovery and shared prosperity*, http://documents.worldbank.org/curated/en/268021494851394908/Ukraine-Systematic-Country-Diagnostic-toward-sustainable-recovery-and-shared-prosperity. [29]

World Economic Forum (2019), *The Global Competitiveness Report 2019*, World Economic Forum, Geneva, http://www3.weforum.org/docs/WEF_TheGlobalCompetitivenessReport2019.pdf (accessed on 23 July 2020). [31]

Notes

[1] The EU Eastern Partnership (EaP) is a joint initiative for strengthening the relationships between the European Union, its member states and six countries (hereafter the EaP countries): Armenia, Azerbaijan, Belarus, Georgia, Moldova and Ukraine.

[2] Also known as the Revolution of Dignity and the Euromaidan Revolution.

[3] Confirmed case and death figures are underestimates of actual case and death numbers. Methodology and testing rates vary widely, and international comparisons are necessarily flawed.

[4] As of May 2020, the Ministry of Environmental Protection and Natural Resources. From August 2019 to May 2020, Ukraine's the independent Ministry of Environmental Protection and Natural Resources was merged with the Ministry of Energy and Coal Mining to create the Ministry of Energy and Environmental Protection.

www.ingramcontent.com/pod-product-compliance
Lightning Source LLC
Chambersburg PA
CBHW061212240926
51846CB00006B/1200
* 9 7 8 9 2 6 4 5 3 2 0 4 5 *